Modern Organizations in Virtual Communities

Jerzy Kisielnicki, Ph.D.
Warsaw University, Poland

IRM Press
Publisher of innovative scholarly and professional
information technology titles in the cyberage

Hershey • London • Melbourne • Singapore • Beijing

Acquisitions Editor:	Mehdi Khosrow-Pour
Managing Editor:	Jan Travers
Assistant Managing Editor:	Amanda Appicello
Copy Editor:	Amanda Appicello
Cover Design:	Tedi Wingard
Printed at:	Integrated Book Technology

Published in the United States of America by
    IRM Press
    1331 E. Chocolate Avenue
    Hershey PA 17033-1117
    Tel: 717-533-8845
    Fax: 717-533-8661
    E-mail: cust@idea-group.com
    Web site: http://www.irm-press.com

and in the United Kingdom by
    IRM Press
    3 Henrietta Street
    Covent Garden
    London WC2E 8LU
    Tel: 44 20 7240 0856
    Fax: 44 20 7379 3313
    Web site: http://www.eurospan.co.uk

Library of Congress Cataloguing-in-Publication Data

Kisielnicki, Jerzy.
   Modern organizations in virtual communities / Jerzy Kisielnicki.
     p. cm.
   Includes bibliographical references and index.
    ISBN 1-931777-16-0 (paper)
     1. Business enterprises--Computer networks. 2. Management information systems. 3.
   Information technology -- Technological innovations. I. Title.

  HD30.37 .K57 2002
  658'.054678--dc21   2002017330

eISBN: 1-931777-36-5

British Cataloguing-in-Publication Data
A Cataloguing-in-Publication record for this book is available from the British Library.

Other New Releases from IRM Press

Modern Organizations in Virtual Communities

Table of Contents

Foreword

The New Millennium is not only a date in the calendar. It is also the time when new possibilities of IT have a revolutionary influence on the world.

The growth of IT creates new phenomena and trends, like:
• creation of information societies, which we can call virtual communities,
• formulation of new rules of functioning of modern organizations,
• new job places and rules for managers and entrepreneurs in modern organizations, and
• new methods and systems to supported decisions in the constantly changing world.

A recent Nobel Prize in Physics is closely connected with the growth of IT. H. Kroemer and J.Kilby from the United States and Z.Alterow from Russia received the Nobel Prize for their contribution to IT. Also, the 2001 Nobel Prize in Physics for E.Cornell, W.Ketterl and C.Wieman, all from the United States for the achievement of Bose-Einstein condensation, will support the development of IT in the future. The 2001 Nobel Prize in Economy for G.Akerlpf, A.Spance and J.Stiglitz, all from the United States, for asymmetric information, is proof of appreciation for scientists who, having worked in this field, created new rules of functioning of modern organizations.

As it is known, the growth of IT, especially the Internet, has a great influence on modern communities. IT offers everyone new techniques of activity. We have to change our approach to business and management. We often use the new terms like; "New economy" or "New face of management."

If we analyze theoretical and practical achievements in business and management we can observe the following steps in the world development of schools of management:
• productivity,
• motivation,
• decisions making.

Presently, we are heading towards management in the conditions of full information. Information has become an economic resource of special significance.

The basic problems of modern organizations are decision making problems in activities where we have limited resources (for example: ground, manpower, capital), and we want to fulfill the needs of society. For solving modern organizations problems, a lot of different computers tools is required. The new approach to management is connecting with knowledge. We can say that contemporary management is the management of information and particularly the management of knowledge. IT allows for carrying activity in cyber-space where the time of information transfer and decision making is very short.

Present problems of society that we can solve with supporting new possibilities are:
- E- business and E- market,
- Virtual organizations.

In my book, *Modern Organization in Virtual Communities*, I would like to show differences between traditional approaches and new approaches to the changes in organization. I would like to discuss the following problems:
- Direct information systems for management, which supports decentralization and democratic style of management in organization;
- Creating fluid and elastic structure of organization;
- Place and role of managers in modern organization;
- Globalizations and connected change of culture style in management; and
- New elements in opportunity or alternative cost for decision making in modern organization.

These are the basic problems. Are they sufficient? The answer can be varied. I think that the list of problems is long and unfortunately, this book will have only mentioned the more important problems.

I would like to mention at the end, what is modern organization? Today, it's modern organization; in the future, it will be the old organization.

Jerzy Kisielnicki
October 2001

Preface

As access to the Internet becomes more widespread, its influence is felt in all areas of society. Consumers shop online; journals publish both paper and electronic versions of their work; courses are taught online and research is easily accessible because of all the information available on the Web. In addition to how the Internet can be used to modify brick and mortar establishments, it has created social and educational dimensions of its own. Virtual communities, social, business and educationally based organizations are brought together exclusively through online technologies. As these virtual communities become more accessible and widely used, academics and practitioners must understand their impact and their role in society in order to fully appreciate the effect these virtual communities are having on all aspects of society. The chapters of this book address the most current research and practice in the field of virtual communities and the technologies that support them. From examining the fundamental definitions of what a virtual community is to exploring the influence they are having on librarians, governmental organizations, universities and individuals, the work contained herein presents a comprehensive look at these communities and the technology and software used to support them. The authors represent a wide variety of perspectives and provide insights from many different cultures and educational and industrial backgrounds.

Chapter 1 entitled, "Knowledge Management Strategies for Virtual Organizations" by Janice Burn and Colin Ash of the Edith Cowan University (Australia) expands upon the concepts of the virtual organizational change model by using the example of information and communication technologies to illustrate three levels of the development mode—virtual work, virtual sourcing and virtual encounters. The chapter explains these modes' relationship to knowledge management, individually, organizationally, and community-wide through the exploration of information technologies.

Chapter 2 entitled, "The Competence-Based View on the Management of Virtual Web Organizations" by Ulrick Franke of Cranfield University (United Kingdom) discusses a competence-based model of virtual Web management organizations. The chapter presents an overview of a set of common sub-competencies underlying the three virtual Web management's main competencies of initiating and maintaining virtual Web platforms and forming dynamic virtual corporations. The model further describes the content of the individual sub-competencies and explains their purpose, their inter-relatedness and their temporal dimensions.

Chapter 3 entitled, "The Virtual Corporation and Trust: Balancing Between Identity and Innovation" by Wendy Jansen, Hans Jäger and Wilchard Steenbakkers of the Royal Netherlands Military Academy (The Netherlands) discusses the unique role of virtual corporations in the knowledge sharing arena. The chapter focuses on the softer aspects of cooperation. The authors indicate that the virtual cooperation must have an identity which is strong enough to inspire trust to achieve innovation through knowledge sharing, but not so strong that it inhibits communal development. The authors discuss ways in which virtual communities can achieve and maintain that identity.

Chapter 4 entitled, "Exploring the Common Ground of Virtual Communities: Working Towards a 'Workable Definition'" by Vanessa Dirksen and Bas Smit of the Universiteit van Amsterdam (The Netherlands) reports on initial propositions, research questions and approach towards finding a workable definition of virtual communities. Through comparative ethnographic research, the authors define virtual communities in terms of their inherent social activity, the interaction between groups of people and information and communication technologies.

Chapter 5 entitled, "Virtual Transactional and Relational Exchanges: The Enabling Effects of Information Technology" by Andrew Gaudes and Mary Brabston of the University of Manitoba (Canada) evaluates the transactional and relational components of virtual organizing and compares them to the transactional and relational exchange-enabling characteristics of various forms of information technology. The findings presented in the chapter suggest that further examination of the link between organizational performance and outcomes would be particularly beneficial.

Chapter 6 entitled, "Requirements Engineering During Virtual Software Development: Towards Balance" by Jo Hanisch of the University of South Australia proposes a framework indicating that project managers need to encourage a balance between formal methods and social aspects in requirements engineering to suit the virtual team members. The chapter first reviews the concept of virtual teams and virtual software development, and then the requirements of the engineering phase of software development are reviewed. The chapter provides a starting point for debate concerning two opposing forces perceived in the IS literature within requirements engineering and virtual software development.

Chapter 7 entitled, "Virtual Organization as a Chance for Enterprise Development" by Jerzy Kisielnicki of Warsaw University (Poland) attempts to substantiate the theory that enterprise has been developed with the development of information technology thanks to the possibilities offered by virtual organization. The survey reported on in the chapter shows a connection between virtual organizations with the problems of unemployment, especially among people with a higher education.

Chapter 8 entitled, "The Development of Trust in Virtual Communities" by Catherine Ridings of Lehigh University and David Gefen of Drexel University (USA) applies an existing scale to measure trust in the context of virtual communities on the Internet and explores factors that build trust in these communities. The results of the study reported in the chapter show that trust is composed of two dimensions: trusting in others' abilities and trust in others' kindness/integrity. The authors also found that trust affects communities participants' desire to provide information on line.

Chapter 9 entitled, "Opportunities for Service-Learning Partnerships in the Information Systems Curriculum" by Jonathan Lazar and Doris Lidtke of Towson University (USA) presents the issues involved in implementing a service-learning paradigm in an information systems curriculum. The chapter presents examples of successful service-learning courses and discusses new possibilities for implementing service learning within courses or as courses.

Chapter 10 entitled, "Information Security for Libraries" by Gregory Newby of the University of North Carolina at Chapel Hill (USA) presents a pragmatic approach to addressing the information security needs of libraries. The author discusses who must be involved in the information security process, namely that active measures must be taken by administrative staff to minimize the risk of damage, theft, subversion or sabotage. The chapter discusses necessary security personnel, privacy policies, public access workstations, and securing the libraries Internet connection.

Chapter 11 entitled, "Faculty of Information Studies Knowledge Repository (FISKR)" by M. Asim Qayyum, Gerry Oxford, Sungin Lee, Laryssa Tyson and Chun Wei Choo presents a prototype of a knowledge repository that is designed to be an electronic repository of online pedagogical resources and is designed and implemented as a Web-based software system. The repository described stores resources or pointers to resources of many different kinds including electronic and printed material, courses, slide presentations, videos and other relevant resources. The repository allows these resources to be retrieved in different forms such as taxonomies or reading lists and allows viewers to view them in a Web browser as simple Web pages.

Chapter 12 entitled, "From Lackey to Leader: The Evolution of the Librarian in the Age of the Internet" by Jennifer Croud, Michael Manning and Janine Schmidt of the University of Queensland (Australia) discusses the evolution of librarians in the age of the Internet, specifically discussing the role of librarians and the University of Queensland Library. The authors discuss the varying roles of librarians as teachers, research partners, and Web page designers.

Chapter 13 entitled, "Library Web Site Assessment" by Ray White of South East Metropolitan College of TAFE and S.P. Maj of Edith Cowan University (Australia) presents a tool used to assess Web pages based on a model used in the e-commerce sector. The chapter discusses the use of this tool to analyze the Web pages of libraries in the Australian Vocational Education and Training sector. The results discussed in the chapter clearly show the strengths and weaknesses of various Web pages. Finally, the authors discuss the problems that arise because of a lack of standard methods and guidelines for authoring Web pages.

Chapter 14 entitled, "The World Wide Web and Law Enforcement" by Richard Halapin of Indiana University of Pennsylvania (USA) looks at how civic and public organizations have not kept up with the rate of growth of Web pages. The chapter describes the roadblocks that have hindered public access to governmental information. The author discusses what needs to be done to make information available to the public, namely governmental organizations must turn data into information and governments need to be willing to release the data they have and legislative barriers must still be overcome.

Chapter 15 entitled, "Citizen Access and Use of Government Data: Understanding the Barriers" by Richard Heeks of the University of Manchester (United Kingdom) analyses the barriers that need to be understood and addressed if citizen access to government data is to become more of a reality. The chapter discusses the availability of data in the current system and looks at current mechanisms of access. Finally, the chapter looks at ways of increasing both use by citizens and access or availability by the owners of the information.

Chapter 16 entitled, "The Practice of Information Resource Management (IRM) in Australian Government Organizations" by Richard Potger and Graham Pervan of Curtin University of Technology (Australia) reports the results of a study undertaken to determine why the diverse interpretation of what information management really is has kept it from being widely accepted in Australian governmental organizations. The survey of information systems and information technology executives in national and state public organizations revealed that information resources management is not widely undertaken in the Australian public sectors, some mixed success and failures have been achieved and many lack in these organizations lack an awareness of what IRM is and how to implement it.

Chapter 17 entitled, "Business Process Reengineering is not just for Businesses but is also for Governments: Lessons Learned from Singapore's Reengineering Experience" by K. Pelly Periasamy of Nanyang Technological University (Singapore) draws on the experience of Singapore and suggests strategies for Reengineering practice in the pubic sector of developing countries and other nations. The author suggests by implementing and adhering goals of business process reengineering developing nations may be able to progress.

Chapter 18 entitled, "Intelligent Transport Systems (ITS) for Electronic Commerce—A Preliminary Discussion in the Australian Context" by Girija Krishnaswamy of Edith Cowan University (Australia) analyzes the significance of ITS as an enabler to achieve effective electronic commerce by supporting logistics and improving supply chain management. The chapter discusses how information and communication technologies are the unifying elements in ITS and electronic commerce.

Chapter 19 entitled, "Digitization as Adaptation: The Evolution of the Superfund Document Management System" by Steven Wyman and Verne McFarland of the United States Environmental Protection Agency describes how the paper-imaging systems, known as the Superfund Document Management System (SDMS) used by the U.S. Environmental Protection Agency, came to be and achieved institutional acceptance. The chapter discusses how the interactions of two life cycles—records and system development—affected the fitness of the system to its environment.

Chapter 20 entitled, "The Implementation of Electronic Network Systems in Japanese Firms" by Toshio Mitsufuji of Siebold University of Nagasaki (Japan) investigates the implementation process of electronic network systems large Japanese firms. The results reported in the chapter are based on questionnaires sent to large Japanese firms (employing more than 1000 people). Based on these results and interviews, the authors discuss the innovativeness of the firms in the introduction of the electronic network systems and examine why the electronic network systems have come into wide use among these firms.

Chapter 21 entitled, "Outline of a Design Tool for Analysis and Visual Quality Control of Urban Environments" by Predrag Sidjanin of DKS and Waltraud Gerhardt of DBS (The Netherlands) describes a designing tool and its object database system. The design tool discussed improves design practice and analysis within existing and planned urban environments. The chapter also presents a conceptual model of the tool using elements of urban environments and the relationships between the environments and their dependencies.

Chapter 22 entitled, "Nurturing Trust and Reactive Training: Essential Elements in ICT Diffusion Projects" by David Tucker and Pascale de Berranger of Manchester Metropolitan University (United Kingdom) identifies important factors which contribute to successful diffusion projects. The chapter identifies the low adoption rates of information and communications technologies (ICT). By using empirical data collected from a successful diffusion process in the United Kingdom, the chapter reveals the importance of nurturing a trusting relationship with potential

ICT adopters and goes on to show that the provision of reactive training during the diffusion process is vital.

Chapter 23 entitled, "EMS Records and Information Management of Environmental Aspects and Their Associated Impacts with Metadata" by Hans-Knud Arndt, Mario Christ and Oliver Gunther of Humboldt University (Germany) describes an EcoExplorer software package consisting of three closely cooperating programs for the management of XML-based environmental metadata. The chapter focuses on the environmental management information system element in environmental management system documentation and on the information management aspect of these information systems.

Chapter 24 entitled, "The Virtual Web-Based Supply Chain" by Ashok Chandrashekar of IBM Corporation and Philip Schary of Oregon State University (USA) discusses the concept as a juncture of three forces: the virtual organization, Web-based communication and the application service provided. Web-based communication provides access and networks with new institutions and the application service provider makes rapid change flexible and connections feasible. The authors discuss these technologies in a strategic framework of structure, process and organization as a basis for projecting future outcomes.

The Internet has changed society in many ways and is constantly modifying the way organizations organize, present and store information. Virtual communities exist as practically independent entities and have far reaching effects. Leading experts in the fields of virtual communities, librarians, software developers, project managers and business reengineering experts share their experience with a diverse background of applications and environments all brought together by the use of the Internet as a mode of improving their organizations. The authors of this book represent a vast array of countries and organizations, and, from their vast experiences, they outline the road to successful use and application of the Internet and associated technologies in many different scenarios as well as sharing practical tips on how to avoid some of the pitfalls that may lie ahead. This book provides practical guidelines for researchers and practitioners alike. It will prove useful to all who want to better understand the Internet and its implications and apply their understanding to successfully utilizing all the available resources. Teachers, practitioners, researchers and students alike will find the research of this book an excellent resource.

IRM Press
January 2002

Chapter 1

Knowledge Management Strategies for Virtual Organisations

Janice M. Burn and Colin Ash
Edith Cowan University, Australia

Much has been written about the virtual organisation and the impact this will have on organisational forms, processes and tasks for the 21ˢᵗ Century. There has been little written about the practicalities of managing this virtual organisation and managing virtual change. The ability of the organisation to change or to extend itself as a virtual entity will reflect the extent to which an understanding of virtual concepts has been embedded into the knowledge management of the virtual organisation as a Virtual Organisational Change Model (VOCM). Managing these change factors is essential to gain and maintain strategic advantage and to derive virtual value. The authors expand these concepts by using the example of organisations using Information and Communications Technology (ICT) and illustrate the three levels of development mode – virtual work, virtual sourcing, and virtual encounters and their relationship to knowledge management, individually, organisationally and community wide through the exploitation of ICT.

What is a virtual organisation? One definition would suggest that organisations are virtual when producing work deliverables across different locations, at differing work cycles, and across cultures (Gray and Igbaria, 1996; Palmer and Speier, 1998). Another suggests that the single common theme is temporality. Virtual organisations centre on continual restructuring to capture the value of a short term market opportunity and are then dissolved

Previously Published in the *Information Resource Management Journal, vol.13, no.1,* Copyright © 2000, Idea Group Publishing.

to make way for restructuring to a new virtual entity. (Byrne, 1993; Katzy, 1998). Yet others suggest that virtual organisations are characterised by the intensity, symmetricality, reciprocity and multiplexity of the linkages in their networks (Powell, 1990; Grabowski and Roberts, 1996). Whatever the definition there is a concensus that different degrees of virtuality exist (Hoffman, D.L., Novak, T.P., & Chatterjee, P.1995; Goldman, Nagel and Preiss, 1995) and within this, different organisational structures can be formed (Davidow and Malone, 1992, Miles and Snow, 1986). Such structures are normally inter-organisational and lie at the heart of any form of electronic commerce yet the organisational and management processes which should be applied to ensure successful implementation have been greatly under re-searched (Burn and Barnett, 1999; Finnegan, Galliers and Powell, 1998; Swatman and Swatman, 1992).

It could be argued that there is a degree of virtuality in all organisations, but at what point does this present a conflict between control and adaptability? Is there a continuum along which organisations can position themselves in the electronic marketplace according to their needs for flexibility and fast responsiveness as opposed to stability and sustained momentum? To what extent should the organisation manage knowledge both within and without the organisation to realise a virtual work environment?

A virtual organisation's knowledge base is inevitably distributed more widely than a conventional one, both within the organisation and without – among suppliers, distributors, customers, and even competitors. This wide spread can deliver enormous benefits; a wider range of opportunities and risks can be identified, costs can be cut, products and services can be improved and new markets can be reached by using other people's knowledge rather than recreating it. However, this does make it both more important and more difficult to manage knowledge well. It is harder to share knowledge and hence exploit it in a dispersed organisation, and there is an increased risk both of knowledge hoarders and of duplication leading to possible loss of integrity and wasted effort. While competencies and their associated knowledge may be more effectively bought from business partners or outsourced if there are economies of scale, expertise or economic value, care must also be taken to avoid losing the knowledge on which core competencies are based or from which new competencies can be developed quickly.

The ability of the organisation to change or to extend itself as a virtual entity will reflect the extent to which an understanding of these concepts has been embedded into the knowledge management of the virtual organisation as a Virtual Organisational Change Model (VOCM). Managing these change factors is essential to gain and maintain strategic advantage and to derive virtual value. The authors expand these concepts by using the example of organisations using Information and Communications Technology (ICT) to implement an Enterprise Resource Planning (ERP) system and illustrate the three levels of development mode – virtual work, virtual sourcing and virtual encounters and their relationship to knowledge management, individually, organisationally and community-wide.

MODELS OF VIRTUALITY

Despite the growth of online activity many firms are nervous of the risks involved and fear a general deterioration of profit margins coupled with a relinquishment of market control. Nevertheless, as existing organisations are challenged by new entrants using direct channels to undercut prices and increase market share, solutions have to be found that enable organisations to successfully migrate into the electronic market (Burn, Marshall and Wild, 1999). The authors suggest that there are six different models of virtuality which may be appropriate:

- Virtual faces
- Co-alliance models
- Star-alliance models – core or satellite
- Value-alliance models – stars or constellations
- Market-alliance models
- Virtual brokers

Put simply, virtual faces are the cyberspace incarnations of an existing non-virtual organisation (often described as a "place" as opposed to "space" organisation, [Rayport and Sviokola, 1995]) and create additional value such as enabling users to carry out the same transactions over the Internet as they could otherwise do by using telephone or fax (e.g. Fleurop selling flowers or air tickets by Travelocity). The services may, however, reach far beyond this enabling the virtual face to mirror the whole activities of the parent organisation and even extend these Web-based versions of television channels and newspapers with constant news updates and archival searches. Alternatively they may just extend the scope of activities by use of facilities such as electronic procurement, contract tendering, or even electronic auctions or extend market scope by participating in an electronic

Figure 1: The Virtual Face

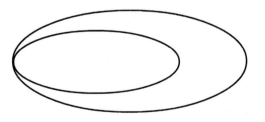

mall with or without added enrichment such as a common payment mechanism.

Co-alliance models are shared partnerships with each partner bringing approximately equal amounts of commitment to the virtual organisation thus forming a consortia. The composition of the consortia may change to reflect market opportunities or to reflect the core competencies of each member (Preiss, Goldman and Nagel, 1996). Focus can be on specific functions such as collaborative design or engineering or in providing virtual support with a virtual team of consultants. Links within the co-alliance are normally contractual for more permanent alliances or by mutual convenience on a project by project basis. There is not normally a high degree of substitutability within the life of that virtual creation.

Figure 2: Co-alliance Model

Star-alliance models are coordinated networks of interconnected members reflecting a core surrounded by satellite organisations. The core comprises leaders who are the dominant players in the market and supply competency or expertise to members. These alliances are commonly based around similar industries or company types. While this form is a true network, typically the star or leader is identified with the virtual face and so the core organisation is very difficult to replace whereas the satellites may have a far greater level of substitutability.

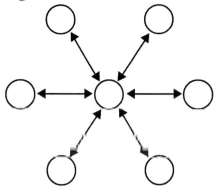

Figure 3: Star -alliance Model

Value-alliance models bring together a range of products, services and facilities in one package and are based on the value or supply chain model. Participants may come together on a project-by-project basis, but generally coordination is provided by the general contractor. Where longer term relationships have developed the value alliance often adopts the form of value constellations where firms supply each of the com-

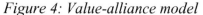
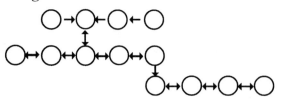

Figure 4: Value-alliance model

panies in the value chain and a complex and continuing set of strategic relationships are embedded into the alliance. Substitutability will relate to the positioning on the value chain and the reciprocity of the relationship.

Market-alliances are organisations that exist primarily in cyberspace, depend on their member organisations for the provision of actual products and services, and operate in an electronic market. Normally they bring together a range of products, services and facilities in one package, each of which may be offered separately by individual organisations. In some cases the market is open and in others serves as an intermediary. These can

Figure 5: Market-alliance Model

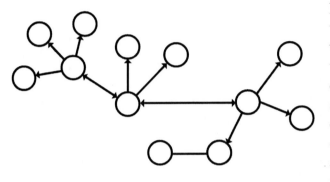

also be described as virtual communities but a virtual community can be an add-on such as exists in an e-mall rather than a cyberspace organisation perceived as a virtual organisation. Amazon.com is a prime example of a market-alliance model where substitutability of links is very high.

Virtual Brokers are designers of dynamic networks (Miles and Snow, 1986). These prescribe additional strategic opportunities either as third party value-added suppliers such as in the case of common Web marketing events (e-Xmas) or as information brokers providing a virtual structure around specific business information services (Timmers, 1998). This has the highest

Figure 6: Virtual Broker

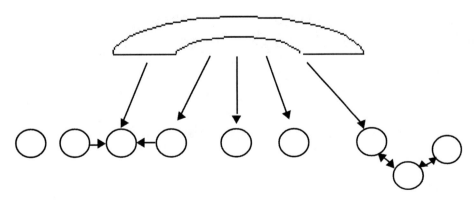

Figure 7: Virtual Alliance Models

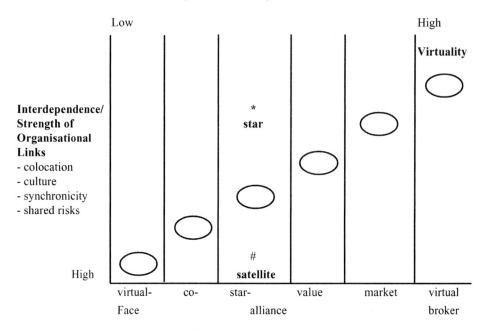

level of flexibility with purpose built virtual organisations created to fill a window of opportunity and dissolved when that window is closed.

As discussed previously each of these alliances carries with it a set of tensions related to autonomy and interdependence. Virtual culture is the strategic hub around which virtual relationships are formed and virtual links implemented. In order to be flexible, links must be substitutable, to allow the creation of new competencies, but links must be established and maintained if the organisation is going to fully leverage community expertise. This presents a dichotomy. The degree to which virtuality can be implemented effectively relates to the strength of existing organisational links (virtual and non- virtual) and the relationship which these impose on the virtual structure. However, as essentially networked organisations they will be constrained by the extent to which they are able to redefine or extend their virtual linkages. Where existing linkages are strong, e.g. co-located, shared culture, synchronicity of work and shared risk (reciprocity), these will both reduce the need for or perceived benefits from substitutable linkages and inhibit the development of further virtual linkages. Figure 7 provides a diagrammatic representation of these tensions and their interaction with the Virtual Alliance Models (VAM).

Table 1: E-Market Ecosystem

EcoSystem Stage	Leadership Challenges	Cooperative Challenges	Competitive Challenges
Birth	Maximise customer delivered value	Find and Create new value in an efficient way	Protect your ideas
Expansion	Attract Critical Mass of Buyers	Work with Suppliers and Partners	Ensure market standard approach
Authority	Lead co-evolution	Provide compelling vision for the future	Maintain strong bargaining power
Renewal or Death	Innovate or Perish	Work with Innovators High Barriers	Develop and Maintain

These six models are not exclusive but are intended to serve as a way of classifying the diversity of forms that an electronic business model may assume. Some of these are essentially an electronic re-implementation of traditional forms of doing business, others are add-ons for added value possibly through umbrella collaboration and others go far beyond this through value chain integration or cyber communities. What all of these have in common is that they now seek innovative ways to add value through information and change management and a rich functionality. Creating value through virtuality is only feasible if the processes that support such innovations are clearly understood.

VIRTUAL ORGANISATIONAL CHANGE MODEL

Virtual organisations all operate within a dynamic environment where their ability to change will determine the extent to which they can survive in a competitive market. Organisational theorists suggest that the ability of an organisation to change relates to internal and external factors (Miles and Snow, 1978), including the organisation's technology, structure and strategy, tasks and management processes individual skills and roles and culture (DeLisi, 1990; Henderson and Venkatraman, 1996) and the business in which the organisation operates and the degree of uncertainty in the environment (Donaldson, 1995). These factors are also relevant to virtual organisations but need further refinement.

Moore (1997) suggests that businesses are not just members of certain industries but parts of a complex ecosystem that incorporates bundles of different industries. The driving force is not pure competition but coevolution. The system is seen as "an economic community supported by a foundation of interacting organisations and individuals —over time they coevolve their capabilities and roles, and tend to align themselves with the direction set by one or more central companies" (p. 26). The ecosystems evolve through four distinct stages:

Figure 8: Information-rich Products and Services by ERP Organisations

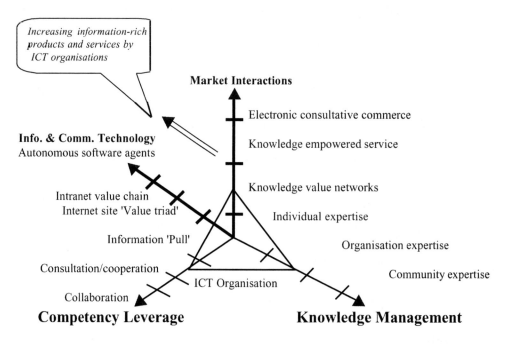

- Birth
- Expansion
- Authority
- Death

And at each of these stages the system faces different leadership, cooperative and competitive challenges.

This ecosystem can be viewed as the all-embracing electronic market culture within which the e-business maintains an equilibrium. The organisational "virtual culture" is the degree to which the organisation adopts virtual organising and this in turn will affect the individual skills, tasks and roles throughout all levels of the organisation .

Henderson and Venkatraman (1996) identify three vectors of virtual organising as:

- Virtual Encounters
- Virtual Sourcing
- Virtual Work

Virtual encounters refers to the extent to which you virtually interact with the market defined at three levels of greater virtual progression:

- Remote product/service experience
- Product/service customisation
- Shaping customer solutions

Virtual sourcing refers to competency leveraging from:
• Efficient sourcing of standard components
• Efficient asset leverage in the business network
• Create new competencies through alliances
Virtual Work refers to:
• Maximising individual experience
• Harnessing organisational expertise
• Leveraging of community expertise

Figure 8 is an adaptation of the 'Virtual Organising' model proposed by Venkatraman and Henderson (1998). The component parts of this paper have been embedded into their original diagram. As a holistic model it summarises the way the four dimensions (activities) work together with synergy, to enable an ICT enabled organisation to deliver information rich products and services for sustainable competitive advantage. Observe the value and complexity increases for each activity as you step up the axes away from the origin.

As organisations step up the 'Information and Communication Technology' axis, there is a cause and effect or pull of 'enabling technologies' on the other axes. This is illustrated in the model by a shift of the small triangle (ICT organisation) away from the origin along this axis. It also means a shift to higher levels in the other three dimensions of competency, management, and market behaviour. Thus migrating the organisation towards an *electronic consultative enterprise*. Furthermore, there is the potential to take the organisation beyond an electronic consultative enterprise, where collaboration and competition are in tension with each other at all levels. To obtain returns on investment the networked organisation or virtual organisation

Figure 9: Virtual Organisational Change Model (VOCM)

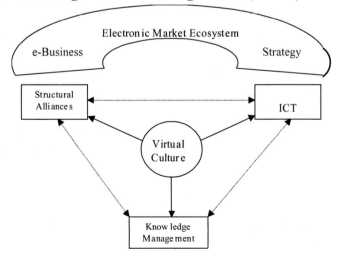

must establish explicit processes to increase collaboration and to facilitate the flow of knowledge throughout the enterprise.

If we view this as the virtual culture of the organisation then this needs to be articulated through the strategic positioning of the organisation and its structural alliances. It also needs to be supported by the knowledge management processes and the ICT. These relationships are depicted in a dynamic virtual organisation change model as shown below.

The degree to which virtuality can be applied in the organisation will relate to the extent to which the VOCM factors are in alignment. When these are not aligned then the organisation will find itself dysfunctional in its exploitation of the virtual marketspace and so be unable to derive the maximum value benefits from its strategic position in the virtual marketspace.

The organisation needs to examine the VOCM factors in order to evaluate effectiveness and identify variables for change according to the virtual culture. Change directions should be value led but there is as yet very little empirical research to identify how value is derived in a virtual organisation and even less to identify how that knowledge should be built into the management of the virtual organisation. For virtual organisations performance measurements must cross organisational boundaries and take collaboration into account but it is also necessary to measure value at the individual level since it is feasible that one could be effective without the other (Provan and Milward, 1995).

VIRTUAL KNOWLEDGE MANAGEMENT STRATEGIES

This new world of knowledge based industries is distinguished by its emphasis on precognition and adaptation in contrast to the traditional emphasis on optimisation based on prediction. The environment is characterised by radical and discontinuous change demanding anticipatory responses from organisation members leading to a faster cycle of knowledge creation and action (Denison and Mishra, 1995).

Knowledge management is concerned with recognising and managing all of an organisation's intellectual assets to meet business objectives. It " caters to the critical issues of organisational adaptation, survival and competence in face of increasingly discontinuous environmental change. Essentially, it embodies organisational processes that seek synergistic combination of data and information processing capacity of information technologies, and the creative and innovative capacity of human beings." (Malhotra, 1997). Knowledge does not come from processes or activities; it comes from people and communities of people. An organisation needs to know what knowledge

Figure 10: Deploying Web Technology

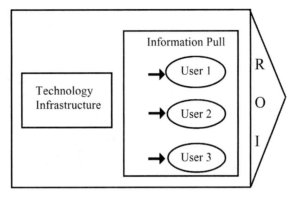

it has and what knowledge it requires – both tacit and formulated, who knows about what, who needs to know and an indication of the importance of the knowledge to the organisation and the risks attached. The goal of a knowledge management strategy should be to understand the presence of knowledge communities and the various channels of knowledge sharing within and between them, and to apply ICT appropriately. This takes place at the level of the individual, networks of knowledge within the organisation and community networks.

EMPOWERING THE INDIVIDUAL

The key characteristic of ICT is it enables a shift in the control of information flow from the information creators to the information users (Telleen, 1996). Individuals using the Web are able to select the information they want, a model of retrieval referred to as information pull. This contrasts with the old 'broadcast' technique of information push where the information is sent to them 'just-in-case,' normally determined by a prescribed list. Such technology empowers individuals. (Figure 10).

For success in deploying ICT management needs to focus on internal effectiveness. In particular, effective integration of the technology into the enterprise infrastructure and a shift in the control of information flow to the users. To be effective and not just efficient (high ROI), requires not only a new information infrastructure, but also a shift in individual attitudes and organisational culture. This can be summarised as in Table 2.

To supplement the ideas expressed in Figure 10, Gonzalez (1998), gives two key factors for successful intranet development. Firstly, the intranet must fulfill its value proposition. Secondly, employees must want to pull content

Table 2: A Summary of Traits of Knowledge Workers (Andriessen, 1998)

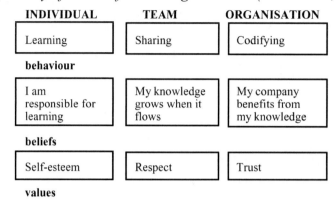

INDIVIDUAL	TEAM	ORGANISATION
Learning	Sharing	Codifying

behaviour

I am responsible for learning	My knowledge grows when it flows	My company benefits from my knowledge

beliefs

Self-esteem	Respect	Trust

values

to themselves. Here the term value proposition is used to expand the requirements for a successful Web site:

- satisfy employees' communication and information needs, e.g. helps me do my job better,
- possess outstanding product features, e.g. intuitive navigation, visually pleasing,
- exhibit operating excellence, e.g. convenient, reliable.

These three elements referred to as the Value Triad, work together to create a value proposition. If any one of the three is weak or fails, then the valuc proposition is reduced.

KNOWLEDGE VALUE NETWORKS

Prior to the development of the Internet, manufacturing companies successfully utilised the value chain approach to increase their ability to compete. Faced with increasing cost pressure from global competitors with significantly more favourable labour costs, companies understood that pure price competition was not a viable option. Through the use of the value chain model, companies determined that speed and service would offer the best hope for continued success and growth. But are they able to sustain their success? The sustainable competitive advantage of the firm derives from the "synergy" of the firm's various capabilities. Porter (1995) proposed a similar concept in his notion of "comple-mentarities." He argued that the various competitive capabilities of the firm should be "complementary" or "synergistic" so that the synergy resulting from them can not be easily imitated by current or potential competitors.

Carlson (1995) uses the idea of synergy to develop a 'totally new' model called the Value Network. This model involves the creation of a shared knowledge infrastructure that enables and "harnesses the flow of knowledge within and between communities." The premise used here is that sustainable competitive advantage can only be attained through a careful integration of activities in a firm's value chain (network) with knowledge being the basis for this activity integration. Whereas a chain implies sequential flow, a network carries a "connotation of multidimensional interconnected-ness." He has developed a model for guiding or managing the change of an old world enterprise through three stages of migration to a knowledge-based enterprise that is able to deliver information-rich products and services, namely:

• **Knowledge Value Networks** - extend the value chain model for competitive advantage to a highly interconnected internet of knowledge flows;
• **Knowledge Empowered Service** - builds on the value network, enabling customer service representatives to become more effective agents of the organization by giving them better access to the shared knowledge;
• **Electronic Consultative Commerce** - creates competitive advantage by taking e-commerce to the next higher plane, where customers have direct access to the organization's intelligence.

The knowledge value network and knowledge empowered service are the first steps towards *electronic consultative commerce*. With electronic consultative commerce a customer would engage in a collaborative process, where human and computer software agents both perform tasks, monitor events, as well as initiate communication.

In Figure 11 the diagram illustrates how the various communication links or channels are assisted by software agents and/or human consultants.

Figure 11: Electronic Consultative Commerce (adapted from Carlson, 1995)

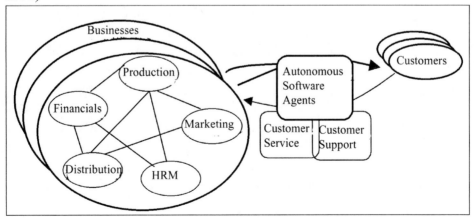

The various channels for doing business are usually categorised as consumer-to-business, business-to-business, and Intranet employee-relationships interactions. Together they contribute to an increasing level of knowledge creation.

Many organisations are expanding the role of consultative customer interaction beyond sales to include consultation in every customer contact and are implementing this through an Enterprise Resource Planning Model (ERP). One such package is SAP, now being implemented widely across the world. For example, SAPNet is SAP's main medium for information and communication between SAP and its customers and partners. SAPNet contains nearly everything you may wish to know about SAP AG, products and processes, partners and solutions, news groups and SIGs. Most of these roles can be supported, at least partially, with a simple Internet site design that includes an underlying information base and a consultative interaction (SAPNet, 1998).

However, more advanced solutions are being developed that employ knowledge-based system technology traditionally found in expert systems, to bring consultative sales directly to the customer through use of *autonomous agents* (software) that provide assistance to users. 'Instead of user-initiated interaction via commands and/or direct manipulation, the user is engaged in a cooperative process in which human and computer agents both initiate communication, monitor events and perform tasks. '(Carlson, 1995)

Market niche players like Radnet provide tools and expertise to develop collaborative enterprise applications that fully leverage relational database technology and the entire range of intranet, extranet, and Internet standards. Radnet's InternetShare products and technology helps companies realise their competitive advantage by bringing advanced Internet-based collaborative features to their core product offerings. (Radnet, 1998)

Autonomous agents can make decisions on a set of options learned from past experiences. So they are fundamentally knowledge-based and belong to the world of artificial intelligence. These agents can be classified in two types: business agents that perform tasks based on business practices, and learning agents that act as electronic teachers. For example, business agents search product catalogs or 'smart catalogs' while learning agents can assist to configure products of all combinations, all accessible via an Internet browser.

It is imperative for organisations to supplement an electronic commerce strategy with human involvement. A software agent underlying the customer's system interface determines when human assistance is necessary and automatically establishes a telephone connection with a service representative. A more advanced use of learning agents for product configuration can be extended to solve problems associated with R/3 installations. Learning agents have the capacity to search out irrelevant detailed information and deliver the most appropriate information for the user to learn —addressing the problem of information overload R/3 installation learning agents which would greatly reduce the time for business consultants to implement R/3 as well as radically change the way industry-specific application are deployed. In response to this problem SAP has developed employee self- service intranet application components that deliver preconfigured access to R/3 application servers, making implementation simple and fast (SAP, 1998).

Ultimately the learning agents will enable the non- technical employees to configure new business processes. This assumes IT specialists and employees come together to perform the activities of the value chain so that it becomes possible for users to have a part in the enterprise re-engineering. Furthermore, this merging of roles represents a change in ownership of the electronic consultative enterprise's business processes.

There are many claims about enabling technologies which can help to capture and leverage knowledge within the organisation but little about explicit knowledge-sharing strategies. Although knowledge is a strategic asset (Eisenhardt and Schoonhoven, 1996; Winter 1987), embedded or tacit knowledge is difficult to transfer and also vulnerable to loss through misfortune or asset transfers and terminations. Such an important asset should be cultivated and measured, but this becomes an impossible task without trust and a close relationship at all levels of the organisation (Scott and Gable, 1997; Badaracco, 1991). This is particularly true of the virtual organisation.

To leverage the benefits of supply chain modeling and management via the internet you need to be aware of the influences beyond your company . Success in exposing your business partners to enterprise systems depends as much on people issues – trust, understanding and communication – as it does on technology (Chirgwin, 1998). This implies a shared vision of culture across all levels of the enterprise.

CONCLUSIONS

The virtual organisation is recognised as a dynamic form of interorganisational systems and hence one where traditional hierarchical forms of management and control may not apply. Little, however, has been written about the new forms that management and control might take other than to espouse a "knowledge management" approach. Managing knowledge about what? In an organisation where change is the only constant then there has to be a system that can capture the organisational core competencies and leverage these to provide strategic advantage. This may be a competitive advantage or a strategic advantage in collaboration with the competition. Knowledge has become the major asset of the organisation, and its recording, communication and management deserve attention. Without the ability to identify who has the key information, who the experts are, and, who needs to be consulted, management decisions are unlikely to be optimal. Both the importance and the difficulty of the issue are magnified by virtuality in the form of decentralisation and dispersion, empowerment and continual change. In interdependent organisations the synergy of knowledge may be the principal benefit of the interdependence and the issue is again magnified.

In dispersed organisations more conscious efforts and explicit procedures are needed. Skills may not be available where they are wanted, data may not be shared and might be used inefficiently or wrongly. New skills need to be developed quickly and employees will have to take personal responsibility for their own knowledge development. This implies that the virtual organisation will need a number of managers with converging expertise in the areas identified within the VOCM. There may no longer be a separate ICT or knowledge management function. Indeed there may no longer be any management function that does not explicitly demand expertise in these areas. The implications for IS professionals are quite frightening. Whole areas of new skills need to be acquired, and these skills are themselves constantly in a process of development, demanding continual updates. We are still struggling with the information age as we are being thrust into the knowledge age but without the intermediation services to support this. Opportunities abound for skilled IS professionals at every level of the organisation but this must be supported by an on-going education programme at the heart of every organisation. The virtual organisation that succeeds will be the learning organisation where people are regarded as their greatest core asset.

REFERENCES

Andriessen, D. (1998). You Can Lead a Professional to Knowledge, *IT Chapter of ICAA*, Issue 22, Spring '98, Australia, 4-5

Badaracco, J.L. The Knowledge Links, in Myers, P.S. (1996). *Knowledge Management and Organisation Design*, Butterworth-Heinemann, USA, 133

Burn, J. M. and Barnett, M. L. (1999). Communicating for Advantage in the Virtual Organisation, *IEEE Transactions on Professional Communication*, 42(4), 1-8.

Burn,J., Marshall, P. & Wild, M., (1999). Managing Change in the Virtual Organisation, *ECIS,* Copenhagen Denmark, Vol. 1, 40-54.

Byrne, J. (1993). The Virtual Corporation. *Business Week*, 36-41.

Carlson, DA (1995). Harnessing the Flow of Knowledge, [http://www.dimensional.com/~dcarlson/papers/KnowFlow.htm]

Chirgwin, R. (1998). The Culture of the Model Enterprise, *Systems,* February, Australia; 14-22.

Davidow, W. H. and Malone, M. S. (1992). The Virtual Corporation, New York: Harper Business.

DeLisi, P. S. (1990). Lessons from the Steel Axe: Culture, Technology and Organisation Change. *Sloan Management Review,*

Denison, D.R. and Mishra, A.K. (1995) 'Toward a Theory of Organizational Culture and Effectiveness', *Organization Science*, 6(2), March-April, 204-223.

Donaldson, L. (1995). American Anti-Management theories of Organisation. Cambridge UK., Cambridge University Press.

Eisenhardt, K M. Schoonhoven, C B (1996). Resource-Based View of Strategic Alliance Formation: Strategic and Social Effects in Entrepreneurial Firms, *Organization Science*, 7(2), March-April, 136-150.

Finnegan, P., Galliers, B. and Powell, P. (1998);. Systems Planning in an Electronic Commerce Environment in Europe: Rethinking Current Approaches. *EM – Electronic Markets,* 8(2), 35-38.

Goldman, S. L., Nagel R. N. and Preiss, K. (1995). Agile Competitors and Virtual Organisations: Strategies for Enriching the Customer, New York: Van Nostrand Reinhold.

Gonzalez, J.S. (1998) *The 21st-Century INTRANET*, Prentice-Hall, N.J. 189-215, 240.

Grabowski, M. and Roberts, K. H. (1996). Human and Organisational Error in Large Scale Systems. *IEEE Transactions on Systems, Man and Cybernetics,* 26(1), 2-16.

Gray, P. and Igbaria, M. (1996). The Virtual Society, *ORMS Today*, December, 44-48.

Henderson, J. C., Venkatraman N., and Oldach S. (1996). Aligning Business and IT Strategies. In *Competing in the Information Age: Strategic Alignment in Practice* (Ed. Jerry N. Luftman), Oxford University Press, 21-42.

Hoffman, D.L., Novak, T.P., & Chatterjee, P. (1995). Commercial scenarios for the Web: Opportunities and challenges. *Journal of Computer-Mediated Communication* [On-line], 1 (3). Available: http://www.ascusc.org/jcmc/vol1/issue3/hoffman.html.

Katzy, B. R. (1998). Design and Implementation of Virtual Organisations. HICSS.

Malhotra, Y. (1997). Knowledge Management for the New World of Business, [http://www.brint.com/km/whatis.htm].

Miles, R. E. and Snow, C. C. (1986). Organisations: new concepts for new forms. *California Management Review* 28, 3, Spring, 62-73.

Moore, J. F. (1997). The Death of Competition: Leadership and Strategy in the Age of Business Ecosystems. New York, Harper Business.

Palmer J. W. and Speier, C. (1998). Teams: Virtualness and Media Choice, Proceedings of HICSS.

Porter, M.E. (1985) *Competitive Advantage*, Macmillan, N.Y., 36-44.

Powell, W. W. (1990). Neither Market nor Hierarchy: Network Forms of Organisation. *Research in Organisational Behaviour*, 12, 295-336.

Preiss, K., Goldman, S. L. and Nagel, R. N. (1996). Cooperate to Compete. New York: Van Nostrand Reinhold.

Provan, K. and Milward, H. (1995). A Preliminary Theory of Inter-Organisational Network Effectiveness: A Comparative Study of Four Community Mental Health Systems. *Adminstrative Science Quarterly*, 14, 91-114.

Radnet, (1998) [http://www.radnet.com/].

Rayport, J. F. and Sviokola, J. (1995). Exploiting the Virtual Value Chain. *Harvard Business Review,* 73 (6), 75-86.

SAP, (1998) [http://www.sap.com/internet/].

SAPNet, (1998) [http://www.sap.com/SAPNet/].

Scott J.E and Gable, G.(1997) Goal Congruence, Trust, and Organizational Culture: Strengthening Knowledge Links, ICIS 97 proceedings, 107-119.

Swatman, P. M. C. and Swatman, P. A. (1992). EDI System Integration: A Definition and Literature Survey. *The Information Society* (8), 165-205.

Telleen, S.L. (1996). Intranets and Adaptive Innovation, [http://www.amdahl.com/doc/products/bsg/intra/adapt.html].

Timmers, P. (1998). Business Models for Electronic Markets. *EM – Electronic Markets*, 8(2), 3-8.

Venkatraman, N. and Henderson, J. C. (1998). Real Strategies for Virtual Organizing, *Sloan Management Review*, Fall, 33-48.

Winter S. G. (1987). Knowledge and Competence as Strategic Assets in Teece, D.J. *The Competitive Challenge*, Harper and Row, 159-184.

Chapter 2

The Competence-Based View on the Management of Virtual Web Organizations

Ulrich J. Franke
Cranfield University, UK

The organizational concept of virtual Web organizations encompasses three organizational elements, namely the relatively stable virtual Web platform from which dynamic virtual corporations derive. Virtual corporations are interorganizational adhocracies that are configured temporally of independent companies in order to serve a particular purpose, such as joint R&D, product development, and production. The third element of this organizational construct is the management organization that initiates and maintains the virtual Web platform as well as forms and facilitates the operation of dynamic virtual corporations. Since the organizational concept of virtual Web organizations is hardly researched this chapter aims to provide readers with a better understanding of the organizational concept of virtual Web organizations and in particular of how such an organizational construct is managed. Based on empirical research the author developed a competence-based management model of virtual Web management organizations. This competence-based view of virtual Web management organizations presents an overview of a set of common sub-competencies underlying the three virtual Web management's main competencies of initiating and maintaining virtual Web platforms and forming dynamic virtual corporations. Furthermore, the developed competence-based management model describes the content of the individual sub-competencies and it explains the purpose, the interrelateness and the temporal dimensions of the virtual Web management's sub-competencies.

Previously Published in *Managing Virtual Web Organizations in the 21st Century: Issues and Challenges* edited by Ulrich J. Franke, Copyright © 2002, Idea Group Publishing.

INTRODUCTION

Since the early 1990s the concept of "virtual organizations," as a particular form of cooperative networks, has been introduced. Despite Mowshowitz (1986) using the term "virtual organization" in 1986 for the first time, the academic world paid little attention to this new organizational network approach. Only since Davidow and Malone published their book *The Virtual Corporation* in 1992 as well as the landmark *Business Week* article of Byrne in 1993 about virtual corporations was published, have academics around the world become interested in this topic.

Since them, the organizational concept of "virtual organization" has been researched and a number of real "virtual organizations" have been established in practice. However, many authors have created a variety of different terms and definitions to describe this new form of network organization that has caused confusion about the term "virtual organization" and its underlying organizational concept, i.e., terms such as virtual company (Goldman and Nagel, 1993), virtual enterprise (Hardwick et al., 1996), and virtual factory (Upton and McAfee, 1996). Moreover, most of the contributions in the literature of virtual organizations are conceptual and descriptive and some authors even tend to advocate the concept of virtual organizations in a rather idealistic and speculative way.

Basically, one can constitute that the "virtual organization" is a partnership network enabled and facilitated by modern information and communication technology (ICT). The term "virtual" originates from the Latin word "virtus" which basically means "proficiency, manliness" (Scholz, 1994), it defines an attribute of a thing, which is not really existing, but would have the possibility to exist (Scholz, 1996). What does that mean in the context of organizations? Scholz (1997) distinguishes the virtual organization into an intra-organizational and inter-organizational perspective.

Whereby the intra-organizational perspective on virtual organizations refers to a particular form of organization within defined boundaries of a firm (hierarchy), the inter-organizational perspective is about the exchange of resources between firms. The inter-organizational perspective is divided into virtual markets (market transactions) and virtual corporations (transaction through networking). Virtual markets mean e-commerce market transactions between actors using sophisticated ICT, i.e., the Internet. In contrast, virtual corporations are basically partnership networks of independent companies.

Thus, Byrne (1993) defines the virtual corporation as follows: *A Virtual Corporation is a temporary network of independent companies–suppliers, customers, and even rivals–linked by information technology to share skills, costs, and access to one another's markets. This corporate model is fluid and flexible–a group of collaborators that quickly unite to exploit a specific opportunity. Once the opportunity is met, the venture will, more often than not, disband. In the concept's purest form, each company that links up with others to create a virtual corporation contributes only what it regards as its core competencies. Technology plays a central role in the development of the virtual corporation. Teams of people in different companies work together, concurrently rather than sequentially, via computer networks in real time* (pp. 36-37).

Having a closer look at this definition, it basically means that independent actors, such as companies, are allocated on short-term notice and contribute their best (core competencies) to a partnership of strangers. Furthermore, the constant alternation of the value chain configuration does certainly not improve the level of trust between the acting partners and the willingness to share their knowledge and resources to be exploited by others. In theory, it sounds perfect to switch between the best in class, to constantly alternate the value chain as needed, and to design the perfect value chain to achieve the common goals. But, who is "common;" who carries the benefits away? Is this totally free system of assignment and reassignment of companies to tasks feasible; is it realistic if one considers that each company can be out of the game any time? Does a company contribute its best to a partnership in such an uncertain and turbulent environment? It seems to be fairly obvious that this would not be the case. Hence, the following four fundamental key difficulties have to be addressed in respect to the organizational concept of virtual corporations.

- The search for suitable partner companies that keep the complementary core competencies in order to design a successful value chain.
- The organizational fit of the selected partner companies, technologically and sociologically.
- The necessary level of trust between the partner companies in order to accelerate the partnering process, to shorten the time to market process and to reduce transaction costs.
- The needs for cooperation management in order to coordinate the activities of the dispersed partner companies and to build trustworthy relationships between the partnering companies.

Therefore, Goldman et al. (1995) proposes the organizational concept of "virtual Webs." They define the "Web" as an open-ended collection of pre-qualified partners that agree to form a pool of potential members of virtual corporations. The success of the virtual organization model is tied to the ability of "real" companies to form virtual organizations rapidly to meet an emerging time-based opportunity. The ability to work intensively with other organizations and to be able to trust them from the start of the project is enhanced by prequalification agreements based on company attributes and contractual commitments (Goldman et al., 1995). Basically, the virtual Web organization consists of three organizational elements. First, the virtual Web platform is a pool of independent companies that have agreed to cooperate. This virtual Web platform is a rather stable company network from which dynamically virtual corporations derive. Virtual corporations are inter-organizational adhocracies that are configured temporally of independent companies in order to serve a purpose, such as joint R&D, product development, and production. The third element of this organizational construct is the management organization that initiates and maintains the virtual Web platform as well as forms and facilitates the operation of dynamic virtual corporations.

Since the organizational concept of virtual Web organizations is hardly researched this chapter aims to provide readers with a better understanding of the organizational concept of virtual Web organizations. In particular, this chapter introduces a competence-based view on the management of virtual Web organization. Thus, the author introduces a competence-based management model of virtual Web organizations that has been derived from empirical research. However, first this chapter reviews the organizational concept of virtual Web organizations (VWO); it briefly outlines the theoretical approach of the competence-based view and presents the research methods that were used for the development of the competence-based management model of VWOs. The chapter concludes with a brief discussion about the introduced competence-based management model and its implications on the establishment of virtual Web organizations in practice.

THE ORGANIZATIONAL CONCEPT OF VWOS

Goldman et al. (1995) define the virtual Web platform as an open-ended collection of pre-qualified partners that agree to form a pool of potential partner companies for the formation of virtual corporations. They state, one can imagine organizing a large number of supplier companies into a resource pool from which to draw the number of companies, and the kind of companies, that would be required to provide comprehensive customer services in any industry and that would compete directly with the largest single companies in that industry (Goldman et al., 1995).

Klüber (1997) proposes a two-level model of abstraction to distinguish the virtual Web platform from virtual corporations. The virtual Web platform is basically regarded as the organizational framework on a macro-organizational level, whereby virtual corporations are the actual performing units on the micro-organizational level. On the macro organizational level the virtual Web platform is the institutional framework of companies and their resources, which facilitates the formation of virtual corporations according to market needs. Therefore, it is

Figure 1: The virtual Web organization, Franke and Hickmann (1999)

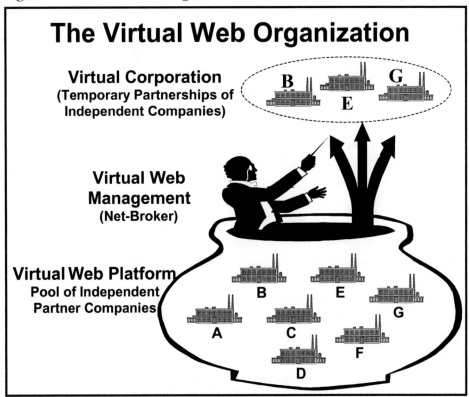

proposed that the organizational concept of virtual Web organizations consists of three organizational elements. First, the virtual Web platform is a relatively stable network, it can be compared with a resource, capability, and core competence warehouse from which the necessary items are employed to meet customer expectations and market opportunities. Second, a virtual Web management organization (net-broker organization) manages the virtual Web platform and the formation of virtual corporations. The third organizational element is dynamic networks, virtual corporations that derive from the pool of independent companies, which are consolidated on the virtual Web platform. Figure 1 illustrates the concept of virtual Web organizations and its three interrelated organizational elements.

The Virtual Web Platform

In general, one can state that the main purpose of the virtual Web platform is to facilitate the formation of virtual corporations. Therefore, the virtual Web platform is regarded as a relatively stable company network that aims to provide a cooperative environment for its partner companies. The focus of the virtual Web platform is to prepare the conditions for the coordination of virtual corporations, such as to define the flow of information and to agree on coordination mechanisms. In addition, the virtual Web platform is supposed to provide the environment in which trust between partner firms can develop. In general, the virtual Web platform fertilizes the development of cooperation and cooperative behavior of partner firms and their individual employees.

The Virtual Web Management Organization

In the academic literature this central management function of virtual corporations has been interchangeably named as broker, net-broker (Franke, 1999, 2000a) or network broker (Hatch, 1995), network coach (Schuh, 1998), information broker (Upton and McAfee, 1996), network intermediaries (Perry, 1996), and the virtual general manager (Warner and Witzel, 1999). For the purpose of this chapter this central management function is interchangeably named as "net-broker" or the "virtual Web management organization." However, Reiß (1997) assumes that the foremost role of the net-broker of a virtual Web organization is primarily the management of synergy. Hatch (1995) defines the net-broker as a facilitator and catalyst. Net-brokers help companies to form strategic partnerships, organize network activities and identify new business opportunities. Their task is to spread the network concepts, promote cooperation, organize groups of firms, and connect them to the product designers, marketing specialists, training providers, and industry service programs they need to compete successfully. Karnet and Faisst (1997) propose that the net-broker is also the primary point of contact for the customer. The net-broker proposes a suitable virtual corporation configuration and monitors their performance. They suggest that during the operation of a virtual corporation the net broker acts as moderator and helps resolve possible conflict between partner companies. In respect to virtual Web organizations the management, the net-broker organization, does not only focus on the formation of virtual corporations, but also manages the virtual Web platform. Therefore, the virtual Web management organization takes care of the cooperation management on the stable virtual Web platform and facilitates the formation of dynamic virtual corporations.

The rather normative statements regarding the management of virtual Web organizations (net-brokers) indicate that the view on net-broker organizations is merely based on assumptions rather than on empirical research. Therefore, this chapter presents the competence-based view on the management of virtual Web organizations that is grounded in empirical research.

The Deriving Virtual Corporations

Basically, virtual corporations are temporary partnerships of independent actors, such as individuals, companies, research institutes, etc. The major difference

Figure 2: The virtual Web organization, Franke (1998)

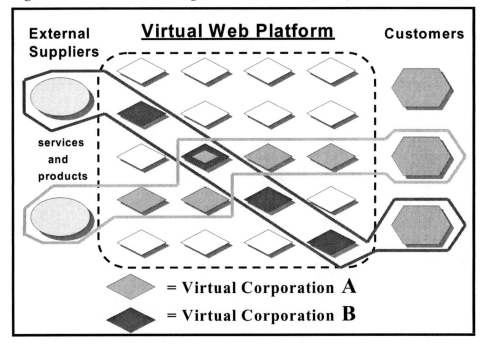

between totally free configured virtual corporations and virtual corporations deriving from virtual Web platforms is that partner firms have established a pre-partnership relationship prior to working together for the first time. Thus, the virtual Web platform can be viewed as a hub of potential partner firms that are selected according to an actual need in order to carry out a given task on a temporary basis. In general, such virtual corporations are value-added partnerships of independent virtual Web partner firms, but depending on their purpose and given circumstances, such deriving virtual corporations also might integrate customers and external suppliers into the temporary value-adding partnership. Figure 2 illustrates a virtual Web organization, the virtual Web platform and its partner firms that form virtual corporations and integrate customers and virtual Web external suppliers.

Furthermore, virtual Web partner companies can be involved in more than one virtual corporation at the same time. However, as soon as the joint project is completed or the customer orders are executed the virtual corporation disbands and the individual partner firms fall back into the pool of companies consolidated on the virtual Web platform. Virtual corporations are value-added partnerships, which can either comprise the vertical or horizontal value chain, or both (Franke, 2000b). In addition, virtual corporations are expected not to be limited to a particular sector or industry. Virtual corporations can be formatted from the service or manufacturing sector, or mix, the partner firms can originate from one and the same industry or partner firms from different industries join their forces. Neverthe-less, the direction of virtual corporations might depend on the vision and mission of the virtual Web organization, which means it depends on the kind of companies that are aggregated on the virtual Web platform. Furthermore, it is suggested that besides joint manufacturing or the joint provision of services, the purpose of virtual corporations can also be joint R&D and innovation project (Bund, 1997) or joint learning and education partnerships (Stuart et al., 1998).

In summary, the virtual Web organization and its organizational concept can be defined as follows:

The organizational concept of "virtual Web organizations" encom-passes three interrelated organizational elements, namely the virtual Web platform, the virtual Web management and virtual corporations. The virtual Web platform is a stable company network of pre-qualified independent partner firms that have generally agreed to cooperate in virtual corporations. The virtual Web platform establishes a coopera-tive environment and prepares the conditions for the formation and operation of dynamic virtual corporations. The management of virtual Web organizations takes care of the cooperation management on the virtual Web platform and facilitates the formation and operation of virtual corporations.

THE COMPETENCE-BASED VIEW

The idea of looking at firms as a broader set of resources goes back to the seminal work of Penrose (1959). She argues that a firm is more than an administrative unit; it is also a collection of productive resources, the disposal of which between different uses and over time is determined by administrative decisions. The essence of the resource-based view of a firm is not to see the firm as a portfolio of products, i.e., Daimler-Chrysler and its product range of cars, trucks and buses. The resource-based theory identifies the firm as a pool of resources, capabilities and competencies needed to accomplish a task, i.e., physical products or intangible services.

The "Resource-Based Theory" literature is mainly divided into two differ-ent streams, one group of researchers are concerned with the internal and external resources of a firm, the economic perspective of market, hierarchies and networks, or the different implications of transaction cost theory. The other group of researchers emphasize how to make the best use of the available resources, i.e., core competence theory (Prahalad and Hamel, 1990), asset stock accumulation and sustainability of competitive advantage (Dierickx and

Cool, 1989), or the relationship between the firm's resource base and competitive advantage (Grant, 1991).

For the purpose of this chapter the resource-based theory is used as an analytical framework in order to describe the tasks and duties virtual Web management organizations perform. Grant (1991) states that resources and capabilities are the input to a transformation process. On its own, only a few resources and capabilities are productive. To be productive as a team of inputs they need cooperation and coordination. Competencies are the capacity for a team of resources and capabilities to perform some task or activity. In simple terms, competencies are the combination of capabilities and resources. Therefore, a competence is the capacity of combining and coordinating resources and capabilities in a way that it leads to a desired outcome.

To build competencies is not simply a matter of pooling resources; competencies involve complex patterns of coordination between people, knowledge and other resources. To understand the anatomy of a firm's competencies, Nelson and Winter's (1982) concept of "organizational routines" is illuminating. Organizational routines are regular and predictable patterns of activity, which are made up of a sequence of coordinated actions by individuals. Thus, a competence is, in essence, a routine, or a number of interacting routines (Grant, 1991). Furthermore, Grant (1991) states that organizations themselves are a huge network of routines. This statement implies that firms' competencies are employed within a network of many competencies and that the competencies interrelate to each other.

Thus, the competence-based view on virtual Web management organizations portrays the organizational routines, the tasks and duties performed by virtual Web management organizations into order to manage VWOs.

THE RESEARCH METHOD

The competence-based management model of virtual Web management organizations presented in this chapter is based on six case studies conducted about virtual Web organizations and their management. The qualitative data collection contained semi-structured interviews with manager of virtual Web management organizations as well as virtual Web partner firms. The authors conducted more than 40 interviews as well as spent more than six months with a management organization of a virtual Web organization (participant observation case study). Based on the empirical data the author conducted a number of cross-case analyses and constructed the competence-based management model presented in this chapter.

Figure 3: Main competencies of virtual Web management organizations

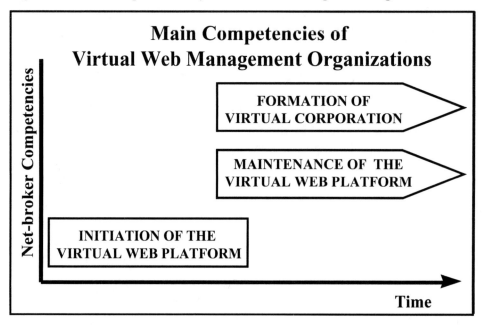

THE COMPETENCE-BASED FRAMEWORK OF VIRTUAL WEB MANAGEMENT ORGANIZATIONS

Besides a theoretical and analytical framework (the competence-based view), the author developed a conceptual competence-based framework for the research project as well. Grant (1991) states that a firm (organization) consists of a network of competencies. Such a competencies network can be structure in main competencies, sub-competencies and so on. Thus, this conceptual–competence-based framework aims to predetermine the main competencies in order to facilitate the investigation of the underlying level of sub-competencies. The three identified main net-broker competencies derived deductively from the literature review on virtual Web organizations. Thus, the predetermined conceptual framework of main virtual Web managements' competencies provided an initial structure for the empirical field research, data analysis, and the competence-based management model building process. Figure 3 illustrates the developed conceptual framework. The presentation of the competence-based management model of virtual Web management organizations follows this section.

- **Initiation** of the virtual Web platform. The purpose of this main competence is the ability to perform the process of establishing a stable network organization of independent companies. The performance of the initiation competence lays the foundation for the succeeding operation of the virtual Web organization, the maintenance and formation competencies.

- **Maintenance** of the virtual Web platform. This net-broker's competence enables the net-broker to maintain the stable virtual Web platform consisting of independent partner firms. Thus this competence keeps the independent partner companies together and is concerned with the further development of the virtual Web organization. In general, the net-brokers' maintenance competence manages the virtual Web platform and prepares the ground for the dynamic formation of temporary virtual corporations.
- **Formation** of virtual corporations. The purpose of this net-broker's competence is the ability to form and operate virtual corporations, which are timely or purposely limited partnerships of independent virtual Web partner companies. Based on the literature, the net-broker allocates a purpose for the formation of virtual corporations, whether it is a market opportunity, a customer inquiry, or an opportunity to conduct joint R&D. The net-brokers' main task is to configure a virtual corporation that is based on the virtual Web partners' resource-bases in order to match the allocated opportunity.

THE COMPETENCE-BASED VIEW ON VIRTUAL WEB MANAGEMENT ORGANIZATIONS

Based on the empirical data collected, the author conducted a series of cross-case analyses. The result of the research work is a set of 21 sub-competencies commonly employed by virtual Web management organizations. These sub-competencies support the performance of the three main competencies identified, namely the initiation of virtual Web platforms, the maintenance of virtual Web platforms and the formation and operation of dynamic virtual corporations. In addition, the author identified the temporal dimensions of the sub-competencies employed by virtual Web organizations. Figure 4 illustrates the set of 21 sub-competencies underlying the three main competencies employed by virtual Web management organizations. Additionally, Figure 4 indicates the temporal employment of the individual sub-competencies on an imaginary timescale. This temporal bracketing of virtual Web management organizations' sub-competencies portrays the point of time, the sequence and the duration of sub-competencies employed by virtual Web management organizations.

The following description of each individual sub-competence explains the content and the purpose of each sub-competence. Furthermore, it summarizes the set of sub-competencies underlying each main competence using the predetermined structure of the conceptual competence-based framework introduced in the previous section. The summary of each main competence employed by virtual Web management organizations also states the interrelation between the individual sub-competencies as well as the interrelation between the three main competencies.

Figure 4: Temporal Bracketing of Virtual Web Management Organization's Sub-Competencies

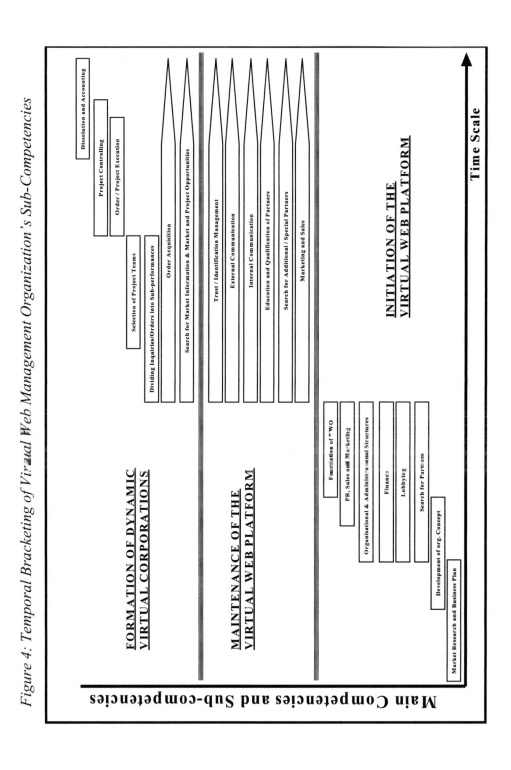

Initiating Sub-Competence: Market Research
and Business Plan

This sub-competence entails the ability of the VWO management organizations / initiators to conduct market research and to develop a business plan. For the market research the VWO initiators search for information about the markets (national and/or international), market potentials, competitors, and customers. Furthermore, this sub-competence includes the ability to conduct a structure analysis about the industry, the business field in which the future VWO should be established. In addition, VWO initiators carry out a feasibility study, an assessment which is supposed to indicate the possibility to establish a VWO in the identified business field. Based on this market research information the VWO initiators develop a business plan, which determines the strategic planning of setting up a VWO, the future operation of the VWO as well as defining business and marketing goals. The purpose of the VWO business plan is to guide the establishment and later operation of the VWO.

Initiating Sub-Competence: Development of
Organizational Concept

This sub-competence is about the ability of VWO initiators to design an organization concept that is feasible and practical so that it can be operationalized through the participation of partner firms. Thus, this sub-competence is concerned with the design of a new VWO organizational concept and / or the modification of an already existing VWO concept. The VWO initiators have to consider the particular circumstances and the environmental conditions of the emerging VWO. The developed VWO concept describes, for instance, the defined organizational structure, conditions (rules and regulations), and the planned operation of the stable virtual Web platform, the virtual Web management organization as well as the deriving dynamic virtual corporations. This sub-competence serves several purposes. One purpose of developing a new VWO concept or adjusting an existing VWO concept to the particular circumstances is to have guidance for the initiation and a blueprint for the operation of the emerging VWO. The second purpose of the organizational concept is to present it to possible partner firms and to convince them to participate in new VWOs. Furthermore, the developed organizational concept can be used to convince private or public investors to provide financial resources for the initiation and operation of VWOs and / or to gain support of different stakeholder groups (lobbying).

Initiating Sub-Competence: Search for Partners

This sub-competence entails the VWO initiators' ability to attract, select, discuss and convince potential partner firms to join the VWO. The sub-competency "search for partners" consists of a number of different tools. First, the VWO initiators define a group of companies they seek to attract. For the selection of partner firms they determined criteria, such as particular industries, geographical limitations, or particular qualification criteria. Secondly, they present the organizational concept and other possible advantages to potential partner firms at information events/workshops or through other media, such as newspapers, journals, or sending out information material to potential partner firms. In addition, they contact potential partner firms directly by telephone or through personal contacts. Thirdly, the VWO initiators get in a personal contact with the candidates, and try to persuade them to join the VWO. Furthermore, the VWO initiators assess the candidates and decide whether the candidates are admitted to become a partner firm of the VWO. The main reason for VWO initiators to employ this sub-competence is to find suitable partner companies that are willing to cooperate with other firms in temporary partnerships. Thus, they search for and select partner firms with similar interests, such as firms from a similar or the same industry, which are willing to contribute their competencies, whether they are similar or complementary, to temporary partnerships, i.e., value-added partnerships, or joint R&D project teams. The purpose of applying qualification criteria for the assessment of candidates is to secure a certain quality standard on the virtual Web platform as well as to admit companies to the virtual Web platform that have the ability to cooperate with other firms. However, the overall aim of this sub-competence is to collect a pool of partner firms on the virtual Web platform from which dynamic virtual corporations can derive.

Initiating Sub-Competence: Lobbying

This sub-competence entails the ability of the VWO initiators to communicate and to convince key persons of stakeholder groups about the VWO concept and visions. Therefore, they present, advertise and convince different stakeholder groups, such as politicians, ministries, industry and trade associations, and chambers of commerce, about the concept and visions of the new VWO. They use different communication channels to stakeholder groups, i.e., meetings and events to present their VWO concept, press conferences and press releases, and in particular, personal meetings with opinion makers in industry and politics. The main objective of this sub-competence is to receive support and 'goodwill' from the different stakeholder groups. This support and/or goodwill is supposed to help with obtaining public funding, implementing long-term relationships with key persons, as well as supporting the credibility of the new VWO in order to ease the search for partners and to establish customer relationships.

Initiating Sub-Competence: Finance

Basically, this sub-competence concerns the ability of the VWO management to obtain and administrate financial resources for the initiation and maintenance of the virtual Web platform. There are a variety of different financing possibilities. For example, the VWO initiators can obtain their venture capital by selling shares to their partner firms and cover the operation costs during the maintenance phase through commissions for executed orders. Another possibility is to obtain public funding and/or to generate income through membership fees partner companies pay to the VWO association. Therefore, the VWO initiators calculate the financial needs of the VWO and determine the yearly membership fees. Besides obtaining financial resources, this sub-competence also involves the ability to make financial plans for the expenditures of the VWO, to develop VWO budgets and long-term financial strategies. The purpose of this sub-competence is to obtain the financial resources and to plan the VWO's financial requirements (budgets) during the initiation and maintenance phase. Such VWO budgets are needed to obtain financial resources such as public funding, membership fees, shareholder capital, and commissions on orders. These financial resources are required in order to cover the costs for providing partner firms with VWO services and, if necessary, to generate profits. Therefore, the overall purpose of this sub-competence is to plan the financial needs (budgeting) and to obtain the financial resources needed to operate the VWO.

Initiating Sub-Competence: Organizational and Administrative Structures

On the one hand, this sub-competence is concerned with implementing and setting up the virtual Web management organization and its infrastructure. Therefore, the VWO initiators search for suitable employees, and purchase, rent or lease infrastructure, such as office space, office furniture, computer hardware and software, telecommunication infrastructure, etc. On the other hand, this sub-competence is concerned with the development, adjustment and implementation of business processes, job descriptions, roles and responsibilities for the virtual Web management organization as well as for the maintenance of the virtual Web platform and the formation and operation of dynamic virtual corporations. The aim is to install an office infrastructure for the virtual Web management organization, as well as to define and implement VWO rules and regulations (processes, roles, responsibilities, etc.) for the management of the virtual Web platform and the deriving dynamic virtual corporations.

Initiating Sub-Competence: PR, Sales and Marketing

The VWO initiator's sub-competence "PR, sales and marketing" consists of performing a number of different activities, such as writing and publishing articles in the daily press and specialized journals and placing advertising campaigns in newspapers. Moreover, this sub-competence entails presenting the VWO at events and trade fairs, showing physical products of the VWO to customers, designing and developing corporate identity (branding), and organizing training for sales representatives of partner firms to enable them to sell VWO products and services. This sub-competence aims to make the emerging VWO known, to present and advertise their product range and to build up an image and reputation (branding) within the target markets and among stakeholder groups. In addition, the early sales activities aim to provide partner companies with a sense of achievement, which is basically supposed to keep or even to increase the level of motivation of partner firms to contribute to the further development of the VWO. Furthermore, the training provided to partners' sales personnel seeks to integrate partner firms into the VWO PR and marketing activities as well as to encourage them to sell the VWO product range, which is intended to be produced by deriving dynamic virtual corporations.

Initiating Sub-Competence: Foundation of VWO

This VWO initiator's sub-competence entails the ability to develop (together with partner firms) a legal framework for the VWO and to register the VWO as a legal entity. Whether the VWO is established as a non-profit organization or as a shareholding company, the VWO initiators (together with partner firms) develop and realize a legal framework for the VWO, such as defining a constitution for the VWO or a partnership agreement, and register the VWO as a legal entity officially. Furthermore, this sub-competence entails the ability to organize an official and formal foundation ceremony of the VWO. The foundation of a legal entity serves several purposes. First, it enables the VWO and its management organization, to do business officially, i.e., to sign contracts with customers and suppliers. Secondly, the VWO as a legal entity enables the VWO initiators to set up the net-broker organization, which means, for example, to rent office space, to lease cars, to invest in office equipment, and to employ a management team. Thirdly, the VWO as a legal entity provides the legal framework for the dynamic formation of temporary virtual corporations. Furthermore, the organization of a foundation ceremony serves as the initial general meeting of members, partners or shareholders in order to apply legal obligations, such as to agree on a constitution or a partnership agreement for the VWO and to elect an executive committee, a supervisory board and/or board members for the virtual Web management organization. Another purpose of the foundation ceremony is to demonstrate the official launch of the VWO. This can be communicated to the external environment (i.e., the press, stakeholder groups) and on the other hand, it is supposed to create a kind of partner's identification with the VWO. Moreover, it is also a social event where partner firms can meet in order to get in touch with each other and to make initial contacts.

Summary of Initiating Sub-Competencies

In summary, the main competence of 'initiating the virtual Web platform' entails the ability of VWO initiators to employ a number of different sub-competencies. The aggregation of the distinct individual sub-competencies aims to establish a virtual Web platform from which dynamic virtual corporations can be formed. Thus, the performance of the initiating sub-competencies lays the foundation for the subsequent maintenance of the virtual Web platform and consequently, for the deriving dynamic virtual corporations. The overall objective of the initiating sub-competencies is to create a stable interorganizational company network (virtual Web platform) that provides a suitable environment and favorable conditions for the dynamic formation of temporary virtual corporations. All individual sub-competencies employed by VWO initiators interrelate each other. Some sub-competencies need the completion, or at least partial completion, of other sub-competencies before they can be employed. Furthermore, some sub-competencies are sequential whereas some others, such as "search for partners," "lobbying," "finance," and "organizational and administrative structure," are employed in parallel (see also Figure 4). In general, one can conclude that all initiating sub-competencies are one-off sub-competencies, interrelating with each other, whereas their employment is partly sequential and partly parallel. The initiation phase of virtual Web platforms is completed with the legal foundation, marked by the foundation ceremony. Moreover, the set of sub-competencies employed during the initiation phase has a strong and direct impact on the succeeding maintenance phase of virtual Web platforms and the formation of dynamic virtual corporations.

Maintaining Sub-Competence: Marketing and Sales

This sub-competence concerns the ability of the virtual Web management organization to do marketing and sales of VWO products and services as well as to support the marketing activities of its partner firms. Thus, the virtual Web management organization has to be able to use a variety of different marketing tools, such as press and advertising campaigns, setting up a VWO homepage, design and development of information material (brochures), direct mailing, attending trade fairs and exhibitions, establishing contacts for partners to customers, designing a VWO logo (branding) and organizing events and presentations. Furthermore, this sub-competence entails the ability of VWO managements to motivate partner firms to do sales and marketing for the VWO. Thus, for example, virtual Web management organizations establish working groups together with partner firms that deal with the sales and marketing activities for VWO products and services. The aim is that the VWO becomes better known to improve its reputation, to inform externals about the VWO and to communicate its potentials. The ultimate purpose of this sub-competence is to sell VWO products and services which consequently leads to the formation and operation of dynamic virtual corporations.

Maintaining Sub-Competence: Search for Additional/Special Partners

Basically, the sub-competence "search for additional/special partners" employed during the maintenance phase by virtual Web management organizations is about the ability to attract additional partner firms, to assess them and to introduce them to the VWO and its partner firms. In general, one can distinguish between an active and passive partner search. Passive partner search basically means that companies contact the VWO management in order to become a member/partner firm. Active partner search means that the VWO management searches actively for new partner firms with particular attributes or distinct competencies. Thus, the virtual Web management organization determines attributes and competencies which are needed on the virtual Web platform. If the VWO managers have detected a suitable candidate they get in contact with this company and try to convince the company to become a partner firm. However, whether a candidate contacts the VWO management or is approached by it, the virtual Web management conducts a candidate assessment and seeks acceptance of the other partner firms, or the executive committee. Furthermore, new partner firms have to attend a seminar where they learn more about the VWO, its structure, rules and regulations. The objective of this sub-competence is to enlarge and to improve the scope and scale of the virtual Web platform with the final aim to improve the competitiveness of the VWO as a whole and its deriving virtual corporations. Furthermore, VWO managers search for new partner firms with specific, additional and complementary competencies in order to substitute partner firms which left the virtual Web platform. In its final consequence, this sub-competence improves the quality of the virtual Web platform and its available scope and scale as well as increases the possible number of combinations for the dynamic formation of virtual corporations.

Maintaining Sub-Competence: Education and Qualification of Partners

This sub-competence concerns the ability of virtual Web management organizations to analyze education and qualification needs of partner firms, to keep contact with universities and research institutes in order to keep updated regarding the latest developments, and to provide partner firms with education and qualification events. The virtual Web management organization might install a working group consisting of partner firms that analyze the need for training programs. Furthermore, this sub-competence consists of planning, organizing, moderating and conducting different kinds of education and qualification events, such as seminars about the VWO organizational structure and culture, seminars about the Internet and the VWO intranet, seminars for marketing and sales managers of partner firms, or seminar with special technical topics. Moreover, the VWO management team organizes so-called workshops in which interested partner companies meet, search for synergies and might initiate a consultant or R&D project. Another kind of event is regional group meetings, which are supposed to facilitate the exchange of information and experiences between partner firms but also where particular topics are presented and discussed. In addition, virtual Web management organizations might organize continuous training programs for partner firm's employees, such as a "business English seminars." The purpose of this sub-competence is to facilitate the cooperation between partner firms and to improve competitiveness of the individual partner firms and consequently of the VWO as a whole. Furthermore, this sub-competence aims to achieve synergies in the area of education and qualification and to develop ideas for the formation of new virtual corporations, i.e., joint R&D projects or value-added partnerships. Another aim is to make partner firms familiar with the VWO organization, its structures and culture, and to fertilize cooperation on the virtual Web platform and to accelerate the formation of virtual corporation.

Maintaining Sub-Competence: Internal Communication

In general, this sub-competence is about the distribution of information from the virtual Web management organization to the partners and the communication between VWO management and partner firms, but also between partner firms. In order to perform this sub-competence, virtual Web management organizations develop a number of communication tools. For example, the virtual Web management organizations maintain an Intranet from which partner firms can retrieve information about the VWO, present projects and project tenders, training and education events, a calendar, partner's profiles and competencies, and so on. Furthermore, the VWO management organizations send regular newsletters by e-mail or postal mail to their partner firms and inform them about VWO news. In addition, virtual Web management organizations organize regular partner meetings or work group meetings in which a smaller group of partner firms meet in order to exchange information and experiences. Besides the regular partner meetings in smaller groups, virtual Web management teams might also organize experience exchange meetings for all partner firms of the VWO every three months. Another tool to improve the communication between partner firms is that virtual Web management teams organize company tours, which means, that one partner company invites other VWO partners to visit its production facilities and learn more about the partner firm. In short, this sub-competence includes the ability to develop and maintain suitable communication tools, such as intranet, newsletters, partner meetings, company visits, etc. One purpose of this sub-competence is to keep all partner firms at the same level of information about the VWO and its activities to inform them about market news and opportunities, new technical possibilities and technical innovations, new project tenders, projects and orders. The second purpose is to establish trust and communication between the virtual Web management organization and the individual partner firms to exchange information, experiences, ideas, proposals and critique. The third purpose of this sub-competence is to establish trust and communication between partner firms in order to improve the cooperation on the virtual Web platform and the formation and operation of virtual corporations.

Maintaining Sub-Competence: External Communication

The sub-competence "external communication" describes the ability of virtual Web management organizations to establish communication and relationships with stakeholder groups other than customers. Virtual Web management teams maintain relationships with universities and other research institutions in order to keep themselves updated about the latest developments, but also to make use of the resources (i.e., expert knowledge for seminars and R&D projects) provided by external institutions. In addition, they establish and maintain relationships with stakeholder groups, such as other lobbying groups, institutions and associations, the press, politicians and financial institutions. The basic tools underlying this sub-competence are PR and lobbying activities as well as personnel contacts. Furthermore, virtual Web management organizations inform their partner firms about the external communication (lobbying) activities. In principle, virtual Web management organizations employ this sub-competence in order to pursue the VWO business goals, such as to do lobbying for their partner firms, to improve the conditions for their particular industries, to secure access to external knowledge, and to improve the virtual Web platform potentials and the competitiveness of deriving virtual corporations.

Maintaining Sub-Competence: Trust/Identification Management

The sub-competence "trust/identification management" concerns the ability of virtual Web management organizations to facilitate and to fertilize the development of trust among all VWO players as well as to achieve that partner firms identify themselves with the vision and mission of the VWO. On the one hand, this sub-competence consists of establishing an information and communication infrastructure that keeps partner firms updated and provides occasions for f2f (face-to-face) meetings, such as regular partner meetings and company visits. Furthermore, this sub-competence also includes joint activities on the virtual Web platform, such as working groups, workshops, and seminars. Another tool to facilitate the development of trust among the VWO players is a clear and transparent VWO concept as well as that partner firms understand and incorporate the VWO's visions and missions. Such a VWO concept defines roles and responsibilities, predetermines business processes, states a code of conduct and provides rules and regulations for the cooperation of partner firms on the virtual Web platform and deriving virtual corporations. Furthermore, this sub-competence also includes the coaching of passive partner firms in order to integrate them into the VWO. The main purpose of this sub-competence is to create a trustworthy environment on the virtual Web platform from which dynamic virtual corporations can derive. Thus, the virtual Web management organization aims to establish a cooperative culture on the virtual Web platform by generating positive experiences partner firms gain through the cooperation with other partners by working together in working groups or other partner meetings. Hence, the objective of this sub-competence is to create the environmental conditions on the virtual Web platform in order to achieve competitive advantages through fast and flexible configuration and close and smooth cooperation in temporary virtual corporations.

Summary of Maintaining Sub-Competencies

The main competence of "maintaining the virtual Web platform" entails the ability of virtual Web management organizations to employ a number of different sub-competencies that aim to establish an environment from which dynamic virtual corporations can be formed. In general, one can distinguish the individually employed sub-competencies into two groups. One group of sub-competencies, such as "search for additional/special partners," "education and qualification of partners," "internal communication," and "trust and identification management" aim to maintain and improve the quality and potentials of the virtual Web platform as a whole and to fertilize the ability and willingness of partner firms to cooperate. On the other hand, the maintaining sub-competencies of "marketing and sales," and "external communication" aim to bridge the VWO towards the external environment. However, all maintaining sub-competencies focus on creating an environment and conditions for the dynamic formation and smooth operation of virtual corporations. The overall purpose of the maintaining sub-competencies employed by virtual Web management organizations is to improve the competitiveness of the individual partner firms for either their own and individual businesses, or, more importantly in respect to the VWO, for their participation in dynamic virtual corporations. In general, all virtual Web managements' maintaining sub-competencies are permanently employed during the maintenance phase of virtual Web platforms whereby some sub-competencies might fluctuate in their intensity depending on the need they are required at certain times. However, all six common maintaining sub-competencies identified are employed in parallel and interrelate with each other. The maintaining sub-competencies start with the completion of the initiation phase and continue until the VWO eventually disbands. In summary, all maintaining sub-competencies aim to maintain or improve the environmental conditions, whether internally or externally, with the objective to facilitate the formation and operation of dynamic virtual corporations.

Forming Sub-Competence: Search for Market Information & Market and Project Opportunities

This sub-competence entails the virtual Web management organization's ability to search for market information, such as market trends and opportunities, local and international tenders, information about political and other environmental changes, public support and subsidies for projects, and technical innovations, and to distribute it to its partner firms. Furthermore, this sub-competence also refers to the ability to detect possible cooperation projects or to develop cooperation ideas based on the information gathered, and to search and find partner companies, which are interested to participate in such joint cooperation projects. There are different ways to allocate VWO cooperation projects. For example, based on the observation of markets and customer contacts, the virtual Web management organization develops ideas for possible cooperation projects and presents those to partner firms. Another possibility is that external experts (i.e., consultants) submit project proposals to the virtual Web management and they decide whether to go ahead with the project proposals. A third possibility is that one or a group of partner firms submits an idea for a cooperation project. If required, the virtual Web management team assists to find other interested partner firms for joint cooperation projects.

Forming Sub-Competence: Order Acquisition

In principle, each partner firm is encouraged to sell VWO products and services. However, this sub-competence concerns the ability of the virtual Web management organization to acquire and analyze customer inquiries, to consult customers and develop customer solutions, to calculate the costs, and to prepare and present quotations to customers. Additionally, this sub-competence involves the ability to negotiate and complete contracts with customers. On the other hand, this sub-competence also refers to the ability of the virtual Web management organization to motivate and encourage partner firms to do sales for the VWO, as well as to employ external sales brokers. Whether partner companies, external sales brokers, or the virtual Web management organization itself acquires inquiries/ orders and submits quotations, the purpose of this sub-competence performed by the virtual Web management organization is to complete contracts with customers in order to form and operate virtual corporations.

Forming Sub-Competence: Dividing Inquiries/Orders

This sub-competence refers to the ability of the virtual Web management organization to divide inquiries or orders into a set of different sub-services/sub-performances. These sub-services/sub-performance are then described individually in order to be sent as tenders to partner firms, which keep the required competencies. These partner firms are supposed to submit quotations according to the specifications of tenders sent out. For example, the virtual Web management organization places a tender on the VWO intranet and all partner firms are requested to submit offers for the part of the whole inquiry that they are able to perform. Another possibility is that the virtual Web management team contacts partner firms directly and requests them to submit a quotation. However, based on partners' quotations the virtual Web management organization prepares one quotation to the customer that includes all sub-services/sub-performances. If necessary, the partners' quotations are renegotiated. In addition, this sub-competence also includes the organization of seminars for partner firms regarding the kind of supply chain thinking that is needed to oversee the virtual Web potentials and therefore the sales of complete value chains configured from the pool of competencies available on the virtual Web platform. The purpose of this sub-competence is to make use of the virtual Web platform potentials and to allocate the dispersed potentials available on the virtual Web platform. By dividing complete inquiries/orders into separate performance areas the VWO aims to define smaller and more specialized work units that can be carried out by virtual Web specialists. The use of a tender system aims to allocate virtual Web potentials. The virtual Web management organization applies market mechanisms to the VWO in order to identify the best suitable and most economical partner firm for a particular suborder. However, the definite aim is that the aggregation of suborders, carried out by specialists, provides an economic and qualitative competitive advantage for virtual corporations compared to traditional companies and value chains.

Forming Sub-Competence: Selection of Project Teams

This virtual Web management's sub-competence refers to the ability to search for and to select the most appropriate team of partner firms for a particular order or project. There are different ways project teams' configurations of virtual corporations are determined. Either the virtual Web management organization selects the partner firms that they think are capable to participate in particular projects, or every interested partner company is invited to join the cooperation project, i.e., in the case of joint R&D projects. However, if a project idea is put forward, the virtual Web management team provides assistance in defining the project aims and objectives, development of a detailed project plan, and agreeing on a cooperation contract. A third possibility is that the virtual Web management organization applies a tendering system. Then, the virtual Web management organization administers the tender process and observes the deadlines. Since several partners normally submit offers for one sub-service, the partners' offers are compared and the best offer is selected to be included in the final quotation to the customer. Furthermore, the virtual Web management might benchmark internal quotations against external quotations in order to evaluate their competitiveness. Whether the virtual Web management organization or a partner firm takes over the virtual corporation management, the virtual corporation manager subcontracts the selected partner companies, or if necessary, external suppliers as well. However, virtual Web management organization provides assistance in setting up the virtual corporation. The overall aim of this sub-competence is to search for and to select the most appropriate team of partner firms for the formation and operation of virtual corporations.

Forming Sub-Competence: Order/Project Execution

In general, virtual Web management organizations are not directly involved, as a value-adding partner, in the execution of orders or projects. However, the virtual Web management organization provides the overall project management, which means that they coordinate and monitor all activities along the value chain. The actual order/project execution is performed by the virtual corporation partner companies. There is an appointed virtual corporation manager, either an employee of the virtual Web management organization or a partner firm, who coordinates the activities along the value chain that involves VWO partner firms, external suppliers and eventually customers as well. The virtual corporation manager (a virtual corporation partner firm or the virtual Web management organization) signs a contract with the customer and is liable for the delivery of virtual corporation products and services. Furthermore, the virtual corporation manager signs the contracts with the participating VWO partners and external suppliers. The main reason for the virtual Web management organization to employ this sub-competence is to provide general project management to virtual corporations. The overall aim of the virtual Web management organization is the successful completion of orders and projects. Successful, executed orders/projects improve the reputation of the VWO as a whole, which might lead to additional order/projects. Furthermore, this sub-competence clarifies the legal issues/relationships between the involved parties, such as customers, partner firms, and external suppliers.

Forming Sub-Competence: Project Controlling

This sub-competence refers to the ability of the virtual Web management organization to monitor and control the performance of its virtual corporation and its participating parties. This means that they monitor the quality, keeping the schedule and project plan, as well as cost control. This controlling might involve keeping track of and controlling project interim reports, interim reviews and the final project reports, or joining project meeting without pre-notice. Since the virtual Web management organization has a neutral role, it intervenes only in cases where the project or order execution is interrupted or the defined objectives are not achieved, or in case of conflicts between the participating partner firms. Then, the virtual Web management organization facilitates to solve the problems, so that the project or order can be completed. Furthermore, the virtual Web management organization measures the satisfaction of externals, using such tools as customer surveys, with the performance of virtual corporations and reports the results back to the partner firms. The overall purpose of this virtual Web management's sub-competence is to monitor and control the performance of virtual corporations in order to safeguard the achievement of the defined project objectives and/or the delivery of the agreed products/services to the customers. Furthermore, the virtual Web management organization measures the performance/customer satisfaction after delivery in order to learn and to improve the performance of future virtual corporations.

Forming Sub-Competence: Dissolution and Accounting

Basically, this sub-competence employed by virtual Web management organizations is about the ability to disband virtual corporations when a project is completed or an order is executed and delivered to the customers. Thus, this sub-competence is concerned with the dissolution of virtual corporations and the accounting. In general, the partner firms submit their invoices to the virtual Web management organization or the virtual corporation manager, whereby on the other hand, they submit their invoices for the whole project/order to the customer. This accounting mainly involves bookkeeping and credit control. Furthermore, this sub-competence also includes the distribution of project results, i.e., of R&D projects to other virtual Web partner firms. The overall aim of this sub-competence is the smooth dissolution of virtual corporations, so that no negative implications for future virtual corporations arise. The purpose of making project results available to other virtual Web partner firms is to provide them with a good example of a successful complete project and to make the new/additional knowledge available to other partner firms so that other partner firms can benefit from joint virtual Web partner projects.

Summary of Forming Sub-Competencies

The main competence of "forming virtual corporations" concerns the ability of virtual Web management organizations to form, operate and dissolute dynamic virtual corporations. Certainly, there is a difference between virtual corporations which are temporary value-added partnerships or, for example, temporary R&D partnerships. However, in both cases it is a partnership of independent companies that agreed to cooperate for a limited period of time. Therefore, the individually employed forming sub-competencies aim to facilitate the formation, to ease the operation and to smooth the disbanding of dynamic virtual corporations. The main interest of virtual Web management organizations is the successful completion of virtual corporations. In sum, the aggregation of all forming sub-competencies cover the lifetime of temporary virtual corporations, from the initial idea or market opportunity to dissolution of the partnership and the settlement of invoices. In general, the purpose of the virtual Web management's main competence of "formation of dynamic virtual corporations" is to lead virtual corporations to a positive outcome in order to generate positive examples for others and to improve the VWO's reputation for further projects and/or orders. Thus, there is a strong interrelation between the main competence of "maintaining virtual Web platforms" and "forming and operating virtual corporations." On the one hand, the formation and operation of dynamic virtual corporations depends heavily on the groundwork laid on the virtual Web platform. On the other hand, the performance of dynamic virtual corporations reflects back on the virtual Web platform and, thus, has a strong impact on a number of sub-competencies employed during the maintenance of virtual Web platform. Apart from the two initial sub-competencies, which are employed continuously, all other sub-competencies employed during the formation and operation of virtual corporations are related to individual projects, customer inquiries and/or orders. Therefore, these sub-competencies are employed sequentially as one-off sub-competencies for each project, customer inquiry or order separately and, consequently, are repeated for each formation and operation of virtual corporations.

CONCLUSION

The introduction of this chapter identified four fundamental key difficulties associated with the organizational concept of virtual corporations that are configured as adhocracies of strangers. Thus, in order to overcome such inhibitors and obstacles regarding the formation of dynamic virtual corporations the virtual Web concept has been evolving within the last few years. The organizational concept of the virtual Web organization and its three encompassing organizational elements provides a possible way for the dynamic formation of temporary value chain and/or other temporary limited cooperations of independent companies, such as joint R&D projects. The virtual Web platform, as a stable company network, provides the environmental certainty necessary to establish favorable conditions for the dynamic formation of temporary limited cooperations. The groundwork laid on the virtual Web platform determines the formation and operation process of virtual corporations and consequently their competitiveness and the business success of each individual partner firm. However, besides the stable and the dynamic company networks, the management organization is the third organizational element of virtual Web organizations. Based on six empirically conducted case studies the author developed a competence-based management model of virtual Web management organizations. This competence-based view on the management of virtual Web organizations provides an overview of the sub-competencies employed by virtual Web management organizations to initiate and maintain virtual Web platforms and to facilitate the formation and operation of dynamic virtual corporations. Basically, this competence-based management model describes the content of the individual sub-competencies and it explains the purpose, the interrelateness and the temporal dimension of the virtual Web management's sub-competencies.

In respect to the four identified difficulties of totally free configured virtual corporations, the virtual Web management organization searches for suitable partner companies for the stable virtual Web platform that keep the complementary core competencies in order to be selected for the formation of dynamic virtual corporations. The virtual Web management organization searches for and selects partner firms according to predefined qualification criteria for the virtual Web platform that fit technologically and sociologically with the VWO and its partner firms. In addition, the virtual Web management organization develops and improves the technological and social fit of each individual partner firm and the group of collaborators in general. Furthermore, the virtual Web management organization implements an internal communication infrastructure and conducts trust and identification management in order to fertilize the development of trust between the partner companies, to accelerate the partnering process, to shorten the time to market process and to reduce transaction costs. Finally, the virtual Web management organization provides cooperation management on the virtual Web platform and for dynamic virtual corporations, in order to coordinate the activities of the dispersed partner companies and to build trustworthy relationships between them.

REFERENCES

Bund, M. (1997). Forschung und Entwicklung in der virtuellen Unternehmung. *Wirtschaftsmanagement,* 5, 247-253.

Byrne, JA. (1993, February 8). The virtual corporation. *Business Week,* February 8, 98-102.

Davidow, W. H., and Malone, M. S. (1992). *The Virtual Corporation: Customization and Instantaneous Response in Manufacturing and Service, Lessons from the World's Most Advanced Companies.* New York: HarperCollins.

Dierickx, I., and Cool, K. (1989). Asset stock accumulation and sustainability of competitive advantage. *Management Science,* 35(12), 1504-1514.

Franke, U. J. (1998). The evolution from a static virtual corporation to a virtual Web–What implications does this evolution have on supply chain management. *VoNet: The Newsletter,* 2(2), 59-65. Retrieved MD,Y from the World Wide Web: http://virtual-organization.net.

Franke, U. J. (1999). The virtual Web as a new entrepreneurial approach to network organizations. *Entrepreneurship & Regional Development,* 11(3), 203-229.

Franke, U. J. (2000a). The knowledge-based view (KBV) of the virtual Web, the virtual corporation, and the Net-broker. In Y. Malhotra (Ed.), *Knowledge Management and Virtual Organizations* (pp. 20-42). Hershey, PA: Idea Group.

Franke, U. J. (2000b). Virtual logistics: The vertical co-operation of virtual corporations. In *Conference Proceedings of the International Manufacturing, International and Strategic Network Development* University of Cambridge, UK, September.

Franke, U. J. and Hickmann B. (1999). Is the Net-broker an entrepreneur? What role does the net-broker play in virtual Webs and virtual corporations? *Workshop: Organizational Virtualness and Electronic Commerce,* Zurich, Switzerland. *Proceedings of the 2nd International VoNet-Workshop,* September, 117-134.

Goldman S. L., and Nagel R. N. (1993). Management, technology and agility: The emergence of a new era in manufacturing. *International Journal of Technology Management, 8* (1-2), 18-38.

Goldman S. L., Nagel R. N., and Preiss K. (1995). *Agile Competitors and Virtual Organizations: Strategies for Enriching the Customer.* New York: Van Nostrand Reinhold.

Grant, R. M. (1991). The resource-based theory of competitive advantage: Implications for strategy formulation. *California Management Review,* 33(3), 114-135.

Hardwick, M., Spooner, D. L., Rando, T., & Morris, K. C. (1996). Sharing manufacturing information in virtual enterprises. *Communications of the ACM,* 39(2), 46-54.

Hatch, C. R. (1995). The network brokers handbook. Gaithersburg, MD: U.S. Department of Commerce, National Institute of Standards and Technology, Manufacturing Extension Partnership.

Kanet, J. J. and Faisst, W. (1997). *The Role of Information Technology in Supporting the Entrepreneur for the Virtual Enterprise: A Life-Cycle-Oriented Description.* Working paper, Clemson University, SC.

Klüber, R. (1997). The need for the function of the promotor. *VoNet: The Newsletter*, 1(4), 3-9. Available on the World Wide Web at: http://virtual-organization.net.

Mowshowitz, A. (1986). Social dimensions of office automation. In M. Yovits (Ed.), *Advances in Computers*, 25, 335-404.

Nelson, R. R. and Winter S. G. (1982). *An Evolutionary Theory of Economic Change.* Cambridge, MA: Harvard Business Press.

Perry, M. (1996). Research note: Network intermediaries and their effectiveness. *International Small Business Journal*, 14(4), 72-79.

Prahalad, C. K. and Hamel, G. (1990). The core competence of the corporation. *Harvard Business Review*, 68(3), 79-91.

Reiß, M. (1997). Virtuelle Organization auf dem Prüfstand. *VDI–Zeitschrift*, 139(1), 24-27.

Scholz, C. (1994). Die Virtuelle Organisation als Strukturkonzept der Zukunft. Arbeitspapier Nr. 30. Lehrstuhl für Betriebswirtschaft. Universität des Saarlandes, Saarbrücken, Germany.

Scholz, C. (1996). Virtuelle Organisationen: Konzeption und Realisation. *Zeitschrift für Organisation*, (4), 204-210.

Scholz, C. (1997). Das Virtuelle Unternehmen–Schlagwort oder echte Vision? *Bilanz Manager*, (1), 12-19.

Schuh, G. (1998). *Virtuelle Fabrik: Neue Marktchancen Durch Dynamische Netzwerke.* München, Germany: Carl Hanser Verlag.

Stuart, I., Deckert, P., McCutcheon, D., and Kunst, R. (1998). Case study: A leverage learning network. *Sloan Management Review*, 39(4), 81-93.

Upton, D. M. and McAfee, A. (1996). The real virtual factory. *Harvard Business Review*, 74(4), 123-133.

Warner, M. and Witzel M. (1999). *The Virtual General Manager.* Working Paper 15/99. The Judge Institute of Management Studies, University of Cambridge, England.

Chapter 3

The Virtual Corporation and Trust: Balancing Between Identity and Innovation

Wendy Jansen, Hans P. M. Jägers and Wilchard Steenbakkers
Royal Netherlands Military Academy, The Netherlands

It is ironic that trust, often criticized by managers as a soft and unmanageable concept, is nevertheless a necessary condition for achieving the competitive advantages related to strategic and structural innovations (Whitener, Brodt, Korsgaard and Werner, 1998)

Virtual corporations are seen as new organisational forms to ensure knowledge sharing and innovation. In this chapter the reason for the knowledge-creating competence of virtual corporations is explained. A shared identity and mutual trust of the participants are of paramount importance to innovation. Virtual corporations are in fact balancing on a tightrope. They have to create an identity which is strong enough for the participants to trust each other. At the same time the identity shared by the participants of the virtual corporation must not become so strong that very promising innovative avenues are blocked. ICT will fulfil an important function here which is mainly aimed at the support of the social relation between the participants.

INTRODUCTION

Why do organizations work together more and more often in the form of networks in general and virtual corporations in particular? Why are terms such as trust, knowledge sharing and innovations used more and more frequently when organizing (virtual) cooperation between organizations? What is the relation between these concepts and from which angle can cooperation between organizations be considered?

We shall examine this in more detail in this chapter and try to shed light on the complex pattern that is related to exchanges between parties and individuals. We maintain that 'trust' is the keyword in cooperation in networks in general and in virtual corporations in particular. This trust, however, is based in the shared identity of those concerned. We shall describe which aspects are important in obtaining and keeping mutual trust in organizations, but especially in virtual corporations. This chapter contains an analytical model, in which the relations between these different aspects of trust are represented. In the discussion of this model in the following paragraphs we shall argue that the virtual corporation is a successful form of organization for operating in an uncertain environment with a high degree of competition. On the one hand we see the traditional organizational form, in which innovation is hampered by the internal hierarchic supervision and the strong organizational culture and identity.

On the other hand, the exchanges of organizations take place on the free market, where the absence of a common culture and identity hampers the sharing of knowledge and the realization of innovation. Virtual corporations have the best of both worlds. However, this does mean that sufficient attention needs to be paid to the issues of trust and identity, which are often labelled as "soft."

RELEVANT APPROACHES

In this paragraph three lines of approach are described for the organization of activities and the relations between the individuals and/or parties concerned here.

The lines of approach are, successively:

- the transactional costs approach;
- the organizational capability approach;
- the social exchange approach.

The transactional costs approach has been chosen because it is a much-discussed theory in the literature to provide an explanation for the organization of activities. Trust, although not mentioned explicitly, plays an important part in this approach. The organizational capability approach embroiders on this. It contends that the transactional costs approach does not suffice for this explanation. Attention to knowledge is necessary as a supplement to the transactional costs approach. Examination from a social exchange point of view instead of the transactional costs theory sheds a clearer light on the dynamic aspects of relations (Whitener et al., 1998). This point of view helps to explain why people are still inclined to trust the other party instead of resorting to control.

The Transactional Costs Approach

The difference between the internal organization of activities and obtaining goods or services by way of the market can be made clear by means of the transactional costs theory (Williamson, 1975). The point of departure here is that if the transactional costs are higher than the (internal) coordination costs, activities will take place within the organization. If the transactional costs are low, goods or services will be acquired by way of the market. As the uncertainty increases, the chance that parties behave differently from what has been predicted also increases. This is also denoted as the principle of discretionary powers. In the event of a high degree of uncertainty trust is necessary to offer resistance to opportunist behaviour. Uncertainty may be defined as the difference between the information that is needed and the information that is present/available (Galbraith, 1976). This information is possibly held by other parties. In the transactional costs theory this is called information asymmetry (Williamson, 1975). One party knows more than another party. For the other party it is difficult to get that information or the cost for the other party is so great that the advantages of having that information make no odds against the chance that it gets more certainty. Imbalance in the information which parties have will also lead to opportunist behaviour of the party which has the most information. Information asymmetry and opportunism are directly interrelated. Both influence each other and lead to uncertainty. Opportunism and information asymmetry are used in the transactional costs theory to explain why activities take place in organizations or by way of the operation of the market mechanism.

Trust decreases the transactional costs, because there is less (fear of) opportunist behaviour (Granovetter, 1985, 1992; Gulati, 1995). This opportunist behaviour of partners becomes most obvious when sharing knowledge. The party with knowledge at its disposal has a position of power based on this in comparison with the other party. Sharing knowledge, one of the main resources of organizations (Hertog and Huizenga, 1997; Weggeman, 1997; Jansen, Jägers and Steenbakkers, 1998) requires a great deal of trust.

The Organizational Capability Approach

The organizational capability (OC) approach embroiders on the transactional costs approach, but attempts to diminish the shortcomings of the latter approach. An organization is no longer seen as a "bundle of transactions or contracts," but as a "bundle of knowledge and the processes on which it is based." This view of knowledge is an important nuance on the transactional costs approach, which assumes that economic activities can always take place by way of the market. Knowledge is unique and not so easy to trade. This partly explains the growing importance of collaborations and in particular of virtual corporations. The decision about the organization of economic activities (within the organization/hierarchy), by way of the market or collaborations) is not only based on the minimization of the (transactional) costs. Certain unique capabilities and knowledge of organizations which enable them to create value must also be taken into account in the decision-making process (Madhok, 1996).

The Social Exchange Approach

This approach is based on the social relationships, contrary to the economic approach with contracts as it takes place in the transactional costs approach. The basic assumption here is that an individual performs something with which he obliges another party to reciprocate. Trust therefore plays a role as a pattern of expectations. Initially, this can produce problems. After all, how can anyone know whether the other party can be trusted? Blau (1964) contends that two factors account for this basis of trust, that is, the fact:

- that relationships often have a repetitive character;
- that achievements increase in importance in the course of time.

The "social exchanges" differ fundamentally from the contractual relationships in the transactional costs approach. In the social exchange approach, also intrinsic advantages can be the subject of the relationship. It does not concern direct economic advantage here, but for example support or friendship. Beside that, the performances in the social exchange approach have not been laid down formally or contractually. This means that trust should be seen in a social context here. Identification of social relationships requires that they are approved of by shared values and standards. Consequently, these relationships are strengthened and sustained.

Just like the organizational capability approach complements the more limited point of view of the transactional costs approach, the social exchange point of view complements both approaches. The strong point of the social exchange approach is not only the attention to the cultural context in which the exchanges between parties take place, but especially the fact that trust is considered as part of the dynamic process of exchange in this. This point of view pays attention to the given that successful exchanges influence the perceptions with respect to the risks of not fulfilling agreements and expectations (opportunism) and mutual trust. The social exchange approach explains why parties which have a strong social bond, built up on the basis of a process of successful exchanges, perceive less of a risk of opportunism than parties to which this does not apply (Whitener et al., 1998, p.515). The creation of such a social bond is therefore of paramount importance in the development and functioning of virtual corporations.

In this chapter our basic assumption is that in relationships among parties within and among organizations, economic factors, knowledge considerations, as well as aspects in the field of values and standards and mutual trust play an important role. Only by considering exchanges from several perspectives will there be a view of the whole.

TRUST AND RISK

Trust in and among organizations is generally considered as especially important (Handy, 1995; Jarvenpaa, Knoll & Leidner, 1998; Jarvenpaa & Shaw, 1998; Lewicki, McAllister & Bies, 1998; Grabowski & Roberts, 1998). Yet one can barely speak of coherent research in the field of trust. One of the reasons for this is that definitions of the concept of trust have brought about more confusion than clarity in the course of time. Among other things, trust has been described as a type of behaviour, an attitude, an expectation, a contingency variable, a structure variable, a social agency variable and an interpersonal variable (McKnight et al., 1998). For some authors trust is a static variable for others trust is the outcome of a process.

In short, the concept of trust is a container concept, in which anyone can find something they like. In this chapter we approach trust from the point of view of the design of organizations. We distinguish four important aspects of trust, the relational aspect, the aspect of the dynamics, the aspect of the mutual dependence and the aspect of dealing with risks. As a starting point, we take the following definition of trust, whereby these aspects come up for discussion:

Trust is the mutual willingness of parties (individuals and/or organizations) to take up a position of mutual dependence with a feeling of relative security, even if negative results are possible.[1]

The Relational Aspect

Trust is not only an attitude of one party vis-à-vis another one, but exists in the relationship between the parties (Whitener, 1998, p. 514). By considering trust as an essential part of a relationship between parties and not a one-sided aspect or a process, justice is done to the fact that all parties must make efforts to develop trust and to deepen it. Beside that, with this we shed light on the fact that the basis of the trust must be shared by the parties. In this chapter we contend that the shared identity of the parties in general and the virtual corporation in particular is of crucial importance for its effective functioning.

The Dynamics Aspect

In paragraph 2 in the discussion of the social exchange approach, attention was already paid to the fact that exchanges between parties and the role of trust in this constitute a dynamic process. Many authors point to the fact that in most cases trust only grows after a considerable period of time and can be lost very quickly (Dasgupta, 1988; Luhmann, 1988). Trust should therefore be considered a dynamic concept, whereby the key question is: "How does trust come about at the beginning of the relationship between parties, what is trust based on and how can it be deepened?" (McKnight et al., 1998).

The Aspect of the Mutual Dependence

Trusting is about dependence. If parties in a relationship do not depend on each other it is not necessary to trust each other. The concept of dependence brings trust into the design theory. Trust is an important "mechanism" to shape the dependence and is even considered to be the new coordination mechanism by some authors (Jarvenpaa & Shaw, 1998). Furthermore, within this framework trust and the coordination mechanism of "control" have been represented as a continuum by a number of authors. On the one hand the dependence can be managed by using stringent control instruments, while on the other hand the control is not necessary if there is sufficient trust (McKnight et al., 1998; Whitener et al., 1998; Das & Teng, 1998).

Dealing With Risks

The possibly negative consequences which trust entails are sometimes called "risks" or "uncertainty" (Gambetta, 1988; Lewicki et al., 1998; McKnight et al., 1998). Precisely because negative consequences are possible, successful exchanges and relationships make trust necessary.

In exchanges between parties a distinction can be made between two types of risks (Ring & Van de Ven, 1994, p. 94; Das & Teng, 1998, p. 25), namely performance risks and relational risks. In exchanges there is always the risk that the other party fails to perform what is expected or agreed.

Performance risk is related to the possibility that the strategic goals of the collaboration cannot be achieved. In virtual corporations, focussed on structural innovation, the outcome of the process is not known beforehand. There is a chance that new products or services can be developed, but this can also fail. The uncertainty about the outcome of the (innovation) process means that trust is necessary between the parties that participate. Trust is then related to the belief in each other's abilities/skills and in the products/services that are to be developed. These skills/abilities which organizations "offer" in interorganizational collaborations can usually be reduced to knowledge (Das & Teng, 1998, p. 23). Trust in each other's performances is also based on the experiences of the participating parties with each other in the past (Thorelli, 1986).

Relational risks are the risks which parties run when the interpersonal relationship cannot progress according to expectations.

Relational risk has to do with the relationships between the cooperating individuals and/or organizations and has direct consequences for the cooperation. Trust between persons, as representatives of the organization, strengthens the common standards and values and simplifies the communication. Consequently, the cooperation takes place more smoothly. Not surprisingly, the risk is more related to the relations between people than to the outcomes of the process. The relational risk exists particularly in interorganizational cooperation (Das & Teng, 1998, p. 26) because this is directly related to opportunist behaviour. This behaviour is focussed on maximizing self-interest, even if this is at the expense of the common interest which parties have in cooperation (Williamson, 1983, 1985; Gulati, 1995). Trust, the conviction that a mutually satisfying relationship continues (Thorelli, 1986), decreases the relational risk and the opportunism (Ring & Van de Ven, 1992; Zaheer & Venkatraman, 1995, p. 379; Kraut, Steinfield, Chan, Butler & Hoag, 1998).

THE ROLE OF TRUST IN HIERARCHIES, MARKETS AND VIRTUAL CORPORATIONS

In this paragraph we present our conceptual model. In this model the role of trust in hierarchies, markets and virtual corporations is highlighted. In each of the three forms, however, the interpretation of the model differs. Discussion of the market as well as the hierarchy is important for the line of reasoning. Therefore, the interpretation of this model for these two situations will come up for discussion for these two situations subsequently. The core of this chapter, however, lies in the discussion of the interpretation of the model for the virtual corporation (see Figure 4). The starting point here is that trust is a necessary condition for knowledge sharing and innovation. It concerns structural innovation here, whereby new knowledge is created, and not so much incremental improvements. Up until now attention has been paid to the need for trust, but the risk that is perceived in virtual corporations has mostly been interpreted as a performance risk. This "top" of the model has been widely discussed in the literature about virtual corporations, among other places in the discussion about the combination of core skills, knowledge sharing, and the power to innovate of virtual corporations (Have et al., 1997; Travica, 1997). We contend that the 'bottom' of this model is at least as important for the successful functioning of the virtual corporation. Trust is the upshot of a social process. The aspects of identity and communication are inextricably bound up with trust. Relational risk and trust go hand in hand here. We will go into that in more detail in the following paragraphs.

Hierarchies

Identity Leads to Knowledge Sharing

An organization (hierarchy) differs from a market because coordination, communication and learning have not only been brought together physically in one location, but also mentally in an identity. Organizations provide the normative field with which members identify themselves. This identification is often described as a process of self-characterization, characterized by distinctive, central and enduring qualities (Kogut & Zander, 1996, p. 509). The identity, which is obtained in a continuous process and is kept in place, is extremely important for organizations. First of all, the identity determines the habits and rules by means of which individuals in the organization coordinate their behaviour and decision making. People know what to expect from the others and what the other members expect from the organization. Identity sees to it that problems are solved in a similar way and that making decisions takes place in the same way and based on the same assumption. Identity, not surprisingly, has the reduction of uncertainty as an important function. (Schein, 1992, Van Hoewijk, 1988)

A second and even more important function is fulfilled by the shared identity in organizations in the process with which learning is developed (Kogut & Zander, 1996, p. 506).

Individuals (participants) share cognitive models of the world based on the same categories through a common identity. Although these images are enduring and robust, this does not mean that these shared images of reality cannot be changed. Organizations can learn and it is easier to learn based on common understanding. Communication between participants who share cognitive models is fruitful because new learning is promoted because of the fact that there is a certain basic knowledge with fixed categories (Kogut & Zander, 1996, p. 510). For this basic knowledge various terms are used, such as meta-knowledge, background knowledge and accepted knowledge protocols (Coleman, 1999, p. 37). In the model represented in Figure 1 the relationship between the concepts is portrayed

Figure 1: The role of trust in hierarchies

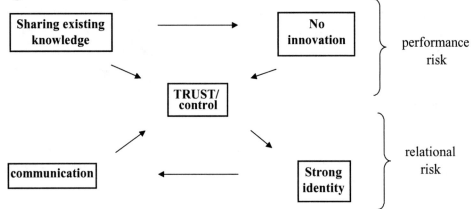

diagrammatically. There is a process in which the aspects mutually reinforce each other. Identity causes communication through learning. After all, the shared categories (the cognitive models) are acquired through learning and knowledge sharing. As a result of the shared identity, communication, and thereby learning (i.e., knowledge sharing) is made easier, while the common identity is reinforced again through learning and knowledge sharing.

Trust is a crucial aspect in this. Due to the shared identity that is present, with shared expectations and shared understanding, the members of the same organization "know" that the relational risks are limited and that sharing knowledge is supported and welcomed.

Identity Hampers Innovation

Innovation, the creation of new knowledge, does not take place in a vacuum, in an absence of already existing knowledge and skills. Merging, or the increase of the combining capacity is the only way to create new knowledge from existing knowledge (Davenport and Prusak, 1998, Volberda, 1998, Jansen et al., 1998).

Although identity leads to order on the basis of which people can transfer knowledge and learn more easily within organizations, this knowledge sharing and knowledge increase nevertheless remain limited to the existing knowledge.

The fact of the matter is that identity creates order but also lays down rules regarding exceptions. Identity implies that some ideas, logic, or practices are not allowed to come up for discussion in the organization because they do not fit in with the notions which are shared in the identity. That is why there are disadvantages inherent in a shared identity which can cancel out the advantages. Because identity demands consistency, potentially attractive ways for innovation and creativity are kept outside the organization that way.

Identity not only provides a feeling of a shared central character, but also of distinction, what does and does not belong to the domain of the organization.

Precisely because learning is guaranteed in the shared identity, it is impossible for many organizations to innovate. This is also called the problem of the inertia of knowledge (Kogut and Zander, 1992).

The holding on to existing knowledge and patterns of knowledge is explained by the way in which organizations deal with knowledge. Although new information (whether or not in the form of new employees) comes into organizations, in most cases the existing principles of the organization of knowledge and the existing relational structures in the organization are not changed. Organizations are nevertheless open to flows of data, but they are basically closed systems with regard to information and knowledge). What keeps the innovative search limited to the existing knowledge is the fact that knowledge and technologies which fit in with the organizational knowledge and capabilities do not require any changes in the

Figure 2: The role of trust in markets

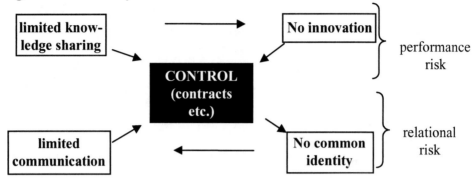

"recipes" for the organization of research and in the organization's meta-knowledge (Kogut & Zander, 1992, p. 392).

The Role of Trust in Markets

There is No Knowledge Sharing in Markets

Trust plays no concrete role in markets. The transactions which have come about through the market mechanism are based on goods or services which are obtained in a competitive situation. This means that the same goods or services can also be supplied by different suppliers. The absence of trust renders knowledge sharing impossible. After all, parties do not trust each other and are afraid that the other party "runs off with the knowledge." As a result of the absence of knowledge sharing, innovation within the relationship between market parties is not possible. Products or services are very easy to specify and contracts will give substance to all aspects which are important for the transaction (terms of delivery, price, quality aspects etc.).

The contracts arrange for the transaction (see Figure 2). Parties therefore do not need to have a common identity because the contracts do not leave anything to be desired with regard to clarity. Not even a common framework of concepts is necessary, because the contract normally specifies the concepts which are important for the transaction. Communication is therefore not necessary to deepen the trust. Performance of the transaction, after all, is not guaranteed by trust, but by contracts and control of them.

The knowledge of an organization or hierarchy has an economical value which rises above market transactions in the sense that identity leads to social knowledge, with which coordination and communication is supported. If an organization considers innovation to be important, a different form shall need to be chosen for the organization of activities. Markets are not suitable for this. With innovations it is hard or impossible to specify the exchanges in advance. Consequently, specified contracts cannot be drawn up; as a result of which, control is not possible. If trust and control are seen as the ends of a continuum, markets are to be positioned on the side of control.

A qualification is in order here. The fact that trust is not a necessary condition for the achievement of the goals of the organization does not mean that trust plays no role at all in markets. Based on experiences in the past, trust also plays a role in transactions which come about by way of the market mechanism (people also often go back to the same shops, etc.), but it does not play a dominant role in it. The fact of the matter is that there is no obligation to have the next transaction take place in the same way. Subsequent transactions can come about with other parties.

The Role of Trust in Virtual Corporations

Activities can also be organized in other ways than through a hierarchy or market (Das & Teng, 1996, p. 829). Network organizations are a way to cooperate without the hierarchic relations of traditional organizations being necessary for this and without

Figure 3: Networks: Between markets and hierarchies

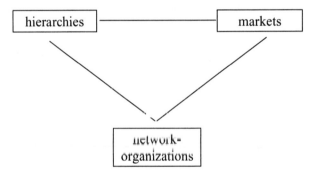

Figure 4: The role of trust in virtual corporations

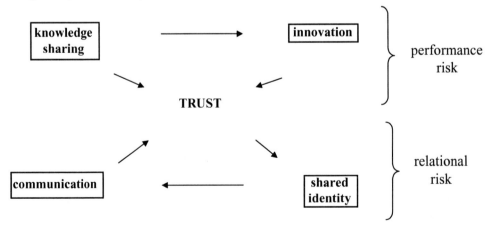

market operation fulfilling its role (Jones, Hesterly & Borgatti, 1997). Albertini (1998) argues that the dependence between organizations keeps becoming greater and this leads to a "variety of hybrid organizational forms ... between markets and hierarchies. This wide population of intermediate structures has been called networks."

Network organizations (Figure 3) are located between markets and hierarchies (Thorelli, 1986; Albertini, 1998). The degree in which opportunism and, directly related to this, the attention to trust play a role depends on the type of network organization. In a virtual corporation the chance of opportunism is great and trust plays a dominant role (Jarvenpaa & Shaw, 1998; Jägers, Jansen, & Steenbakkers, 1998). An important network form is the virtual corporation.

Characteristics of the Virtual Corporation

A virtual corporation is a combination of several, geographically dispersed, parties (persons and/or organizations) that through the combination of mutually complementary core activities and means attempt to achieve a common goal. This virtual corporation has an equal distribution of power of participants. The coordination of these activities is supported by electronic connections (an ICT infrastructure). The virtual corporation can be found in situations of great uncertainty. Participants of the virtual corporation do not try to decrease this uncertainty by means of control or regulation (for example, by means of contracts), but by sharing information and knowledge. An example of this is the cooperation between KPN multimedia and the temporary employment agency START, which was the only temporary employment agency with the courage to share information during the creation of a virtual labour market (the so-called Jobbing Mall) (Jong, 1997).

There is a high degree of mutual dependence between the participants in the virtual corporation. Without the skills and means of the partners the end product or the services cannot be realized. Sharing knowledge takes place because the participants know that they depend heavily on each other and that sharing this is necessary to be able to continue participating in the network (Have et al., 1997).

Trust and Identity

Virtual corporations operate in environments that lack certainty. Often they operate on new markets, of which it is uncertain whether the existing knowledge of the individual organizations is applicable. In such situations the organizations are deterred from developing the available knowledge or from imitating the knowledge of other organizations because the organizing principles (i.e., the underlying codes, the meta-knowledge) cannot easily be identified (Kogut & Zander, 1992, p. 395). Beside that, an important characteristic of virtual corporations is that the participants are not physically together.

This combination of (extreme) uncertainty and distance seems an insurmountable barrier to knowledge sharing and innovation. Effective virtual corporations, however, meet an essential condition of knowledge sharing. Contrary to participants in a market situation, participants in an effective virtual corporation have a common identity. This identity offers the virtual corporation support in communication and knowledge sharing but is not so strong that the disadvantages of the identity in the more traditional organizations (hierarchy) occur in the form of knowledge inertia and barriers to innovation (see Figure 4). An (often implicitly) common goal of virtual corporations, not surprisingly, is to experiment with new ways in which relationships are structured. The most important function of the shared identity, however, is that this constitutes the basis for the relational trust. Relational trust is a requirement in situations of information asymmetry.

Information Asymmetry

Traditionally, information asymmetry plays an important role in the variety of approaches to organizing. As mentioned earlier, a high degree of information asymmetry has been a reason to keep knowledge sharing within the organization from times immemorial. Virtual corporations are interesting phenomena, because, for the first time, in this way of organizing there is no decrease of information asymmetry or decrease of the related risks of uncertainty (Galbraith, 1976; Williamson, 1975, 1983). It is inherent in the concept of virtual corporations (the sharing of knowledge and the combination of core skills) that information asymmetry exists and is in some cases even promoted. Knowledge sharing in situations of information asymmetry, however, is only possible if there is trust. This trust extends further than merely the expectation of each other that people fulfil agreements and perform. For true knowledge sharing relational trust is essential. There has to be a certain basis of values and standards and of accepted knowledge protocols.

COMMUNICATION AS A POINT OF ACTION

We hold the view that through improvement of the communication, the process of increasing trust and reinforcing the identity can be initiated.

Several "measures" are possible to build up or reinforce a common identity in virtual corporations through communication. Organizational as well as technological (ICT) measures can contribute to this.

Organizational Measures

First of all personal contact can and should be considered. In a virtual corporation the participants will have to get together regularly. The formal as well as the informal meetings will contribute to the common identity. The common identity finds the origin and results in "shared dreams" (Steenbakkers et al., 1998). Since virtual corporations jointly develop a product or service, or introduce it on the market, brands can reinforce the identity ('branding'). The organization of "customer"-days is another possibility to reinforce the common identity. These times offer good possibilities to "make everyone fall into line" in the content-related field, while thoughts can be exchanged also in an informal atmosphere.

Employees who have left the organization (and who have often established companies themselves) can continue to be involved with the organization. They can become a part of the virtual corporation. They know the standards and values of the organization and have partly internalised them.

A virtual corporation does not come to bloom by itself. It is necessary to have a number of "initiators" or "boosters" for this. Who these are is not so important. However, it is important that this group is spirited and passionate about the subject. The "boosters" have to invest a lot of energy in the motivation of the other participants in the virtual corporation.

Training and/or education of participants that are, or are going to, function in a virtual corporation is also a possible measure. Learning a common repertory of concepts can constitute an important part of such training. This could also be applied in a situation in which suppliers and/or customers participate in a virtual corporation.

Technological Measures

Information and communication technology (ICT) plays an increasingly important role in the way organizations function and collaborate. Yet the application of ICT seems to be limited to the support of existing physical processes. Many organizations try to reduce uncertainty that way with the help of ICT. The decrease of information asymmetry is often seen as a goal of the application of ICT in organizations. Also the applications which are developed for knowledge management (intranets and other systems) are usually based on this idea. However, ICT can also play a role in the "bottom" of the model, that is to say the promotion of the communication and the reinforcement of the identity and thereby the trust. This is a condition for cooperation, particularly in virtual corporations.

Because the participants in a virtual corporation are in most cases geographically dispersed, ICT plays an essential role in the realization of the identity, which, however, differs in nature from the often-described role of ICT in innovation. After all, in many virtual corporations ICT is applied in order to support the content-related aspect, the exchange of knowledge and information itself.

Phillips Alaska, for example, a large oil company, has developed a system ("Alaska Drilling Knowledge Transfer") whereby employees, customers, suppliers, and external experts can share knowledge about oil drilling. Not only is knowledge shared by experts within the organization, but also experts outside the organization are involved in the improvement of the processes for oil drilling. Also the experiences of "operators" play a role in the improvement of the drilling process (Pfister, 2000).

Also the applications which are developed for knowledge management (intranets and other systems) are usually based on this idea. Examples of the use of ICT are applications such as e-mail, groupware, and videoconferencing are all focussed on the promotion of the communication and not so much on the content-related aspects.

ICT measures can therefore reinforce the identity. These alone, however, are insufficient to turn a virtual corporation into a success. A mistake which is often made is looking for solutions in technology. Participants in the virtual corporation are responsible for knowledge sharing and keeping the community "lively," not technology. Therefore, when applying ICT, attention shall not only have to be focussed on the establishment of a virtual corporation. This is an important point of attention for the brokers who try to bring the parties in a virtual corporation together, and especially try to keep them together and to help them develop a common identity. In practice it turns out that successful brokers indeed make very great efforts in this field (Bremer et al., 1999). Beside the organizational measures already mentioned ICT can offer possibilities to facilitate and support social relationships within the virtual corporation.

CONCLUSION AND MANAGEMENT CONSEQUENCES

In the discussions of virtual corporations, attention has long been focussed on the aspects of knowledge sharing and innovation. ICT has been considered an important support in this, particularly for the content-related exchange of information between the participants. In this chapter we have indicated that the aspects which are often characterized as the softer aspects of cooperation are playing an increasingly important role. Virtual corporations are the ideal form for optimal knowledge sharing and innovation. They are balancing on a tightrope. They have to have an identity which is strong enough to trust each other and to provide enough meta-knowledge to innovate. At the same time this shared identity cannot become so strong that very promising avenues are blocked, because these require or create knowledge which does not fit in with the collective knowledge models. Those participating in the virtual corporation shall have to become aware of this necessary balance. In the beginning stage of the virtual corporation the shared identity shall have to be created and reinforced. Next, very close attention must be paid to the realization of a shared identity of the network in which their organizations function and to the communication necessary for this. ICT will fulfil a different function here which is mainly aimed at the support of the social relation between the participants in the cooperation. But the participants in the virtual corporation must also keep sufficient freedom to preserve their own separate identities. Only then will the virtual corporation achieve the ideal balance between identity and innovation.

ENDNOTE

[1] This definition is largely based on the definition of trust of Knight et al. (1999), in which a party's willingness to adopt a dependent position towards another party is discussed. In this chapter the relational aspect has been added to this definition.

REFERENCES

Albertini, S. (1998, July). *Inter-organizational networks: The conceptual approach and the analytical framework*. Paper presented at the EGOS-14th Colloquium, Maastricht, The Netherlands.

Blau, P. M. (1964). *Exchange and Power in Social Life*. New York: Wiley.

Bradach, J. L., and Eccles, R. G. (1989). Markets versus hierarchies: From ideal types to plural forms. In W.R. Scott (Ed.), *Annual Review of Sociology* (pp. 97-118). Palo Alto, CA.

Bremer, C. F., Mundim, A. P. F., Michilini, F. V. S., Siqueira, J. E. M., and Ortega, L. M. (1999). New product search and development as a trigger to competencies integration in virtual enterprises. In P. Sieber & J. Griese (Eds.), *Organizational Virtualness and Electronic Commerce*: (pp. 205-215). *Proceedings of the 2nd International VoNet Workshop*. Bern, Switzerland: Simowa Verlag.

Das, T. K. and Teng, B. S. (1996). Risk types and inter-firm alliance structures. *Journal of Management Studies, 33*, 827-843.

Das, T. K. and Teng, B. S. (1998). Resource and risk management in the strategic alliance making process. *Journal of Management*, 24, 21-42.

Dasgupta, P. (1988). Trust as a commodity. In Gambetta, D. (Ed.), *Trust*, 49-72. New York: Basil Blackwell.

Davenport, T. and Prusak, L. (1998). *Working Knowledge: How Organizations Manage What They Know*. Boston, MA: Harvard Business School Press.

Galbraith, J. R. (1976). Designing complex organizations. Reading, MA: Addison-Wesley.

Gambetta, D. (1988). *Trust: Making and Breaking Cooperative Relations.* New York: Basil Blackwell.

Grabowski, M. and Roberts, K. H. (1998). Risk mitigation in virtual organizations. *Journal of Computer Mediated Communication*, 3. Retrieved M D, Y from the World Wide Web: http://jcmc.huji.ac.il/vol3/issue4/grabowski.html.

Granovetter, M. S. (1973). The strength of weak ties. *American Journal of Sociology*, 78, 1350-1380.

Granovetter, M. S. (1985). Economic action and social structure: A theory of embeddedness. *American Journal of Sociology*, 91, 481-510.

Granovetter, M. S. (1992). Problems of explanation in economic sociology. In Nohria, N. and Eccles, R. (Eds.), *Networks and Organizations: Structure, Form and Action*. Boston, MA: Harvard Business School Press.

Gulati, R. (1995). Does familiarity breed trust? The implication of repeated ties for contractual choice in alliances. *Academy of Management Journal*, 38, 85-112.

Handy, C. (1995). Trust and the virtual organization. *Harvard Business Review*, 41-50.

Have, S. ten, Lierop, F. van, and Kühne, H. J. (1997). Hoe virtueel moeten we eigenlijk zijn? [Virtuality: To what extent?]. *Nijenrode Management Review*, 85-93.

Hertog, J. F. den, and Huizenga, E. (1997). *De Kennisfactor, Concurreren als Kennisonderneming [The Knowledge Factor: Competing as a Knowledge Corporation]*. Deventer: Kluwer Bedrijfsinformatie.

Hoewijk, R. van. (1988). De betekenis van de organisatiecultuur. Een literatuuroverzicht, (The meaning of organization culture: A literature survey), *M&O*, 42.

Jägers, H. P. M., Jansen, W. and Steenbakkers, G. C. A. (1998). Characteristics of virtual organizations. In Sieber, P. and Griese, J. (Eds.), *Organizational Virtualness*, 65-77. Bern: Simowa Verlag.

Jansen, W., Jägers, H. P. M. and Steenbakkers, G. C. A. (1997). Kennis, macht en informatietechnologie in netwerkvarianten, (Knowledge, power and ICT in network forms). *Management en Informatie*, 5, 4-12.

Jansen, W., Jägers, H. P. M. and Steenbakkers, G. C. A. (1998). Kennismanagement en organisatie-ontwerp, (Knowledge management and organization design). *Management & Informatie*, 6, 30-43.

Jarvenpaa, S. L., Knoll, K. and Leidner, D. (1998). Is anybody out there? Antecedents of trust in global virtual teams. *Journal of Management Information Systems*, 14, 29-64.

Jarvenpaa, S. L., and Shaw, T. R. (1998). Global virtual teams: Integrating models of trust. In Sieber, P. and Griese, J. (Eds.), *Organizational Virtualness*, 35-53. Bern: Simowa Verlag.

Jones, C., Hesterly, W. S. and Borgatti, S. P. (1997). A general theory of network governance: Exchange, conditions and social mechanisms. *Academy of Management Review*, 22, 911-945.

Jong, S. de. (1997). Virtuele arbeidsmarkt geopend, (Creation of a virtual employment market). *Computable*, 11.

Kogut, B. and Zander, U. (1992). Knowledge of the firm, combinative capabilities, and the replication of technology. *Organization Science*, 3, 383-397.

Kogut, B. and Zander, U. (1996). What firms do? Coordination, identity and learning. *Organization Science*, 7, 502-518.

Kraut, R., Steinfield, C., Chan, A., Butler, B. and Hoag, A. (1998). Coordination and virtualization: The role of electronic networks and personal relationships. *JCMC*, 3. Available on the World Wide Web at: http://jcmc.huji.ac.il/vol3/issue4/kraut.html.

Lewicki, R. J., McAllister, D. J. and Bies, R. J. (1998). Trust and distrust: New relationships and realities. *Academy of Management Review*, 23, 438-458.

Luhmann, N. (1988). Familiarity, confidence, trust: Problems and alternatives. In Gambetta, D. (Ed.), *Trust*, 94-107. New York: Basil Blackwell.

Madhok, A. (1996). The organization of economic activity: Transaction costs, firm capabilities, and the nature of governance. *Organization Science*, 7, 577-590.

McKnight, D. H., Cummings, L. L. and Chervany, N. L. (1998). Initial trust formation in new organizational relationships. *Academy of Management Review*, 23, 473-490.

Pfister, M. (2000, May). Lecture presented at the *IRMA Conference*, Anchorage, AK.

Provan, K. G. (1993). Embeddedness, interdependence, and opportunism in organizational supplier-buyer networks. *Journal of Management*, 19, 841-856.

Ring, P. S. and Ven, A. H. van de. (1992). Structuring cooperative relationships between organizations. *Strategic Management Journal*, 13, 483-498.

Ring, P. S. and Ven, A. H. van de. (1994). Developmental processes of cooperative interorganizational relationships. *Academy of Management Review*, 15, 90-118.

Schein, E. H. (1992). *Organizational Culture and Leadership*. New York: Jossey-Bass.

Steenbakkers, G. C. A., Jägers, H. P. M. and Jansen, W. (1998). Prolion: A case study of a virtual organization. Paper presented at the *3rd EGOS Conference*, Maastricht, The Netherlands.

Thorelli, H. B. (1986). Networks: Between markets and hierarchies. *Strategic Management Journal*, 7, 37-51.

Travica, B. (1997). The design of the virtual organization: A research model. *Proceedings of the Americas Conference on Information Systems*, USA, Vol., 417-419.

Volberda, H. W. (1998). *Blijvend Strategisch Vernieuwen: Concurreren in de 21e Eeeuw*, (*Continuing Strategic Renewal: Competing in the 21st Century*). Deventer: Kluwer.

Weggeman, M. (1997). *Kennismanagement*, (*Knowledge Management*). Schiedam: Scriptum Management.

Whitener, E. M., Brodt, S. E., Korsgaard, M. A. and Werner, J. M. (1998). Managers as initiators of trust: An exchange relationship framework for understanding managerial trustworthy behavior. *Academy of Management Review*, 23, 513-530.

Williamson, O. E. (1975). *Markets and Hierarchies*. New York: Free Press.

Williamson, O. E. (1983). Credible commitments: Using hostages to support exchange. *American Economic Review*, 73, 519-540.

Williamson, O. E. (1985). *The Economic Institutions of Capitalism*. New York: Free Press.

Zaheer, A. and Venkatraman, N. (1995). Relational governance as an interorganizational strategy: An empirical test of the role of trust in economic exchange. *Strategic Management Journal*, 16, 373-392.

Chapter 4

Exploring the Common Ground of Virtual Communities: Working Towards a 'Workable Definition'

Vanessa Dirksen and Bas Smit
University of Amsterdam - AIM, The Netherlands

INTRODUCTION

A great deal of the literature on virtual communities evolves around classifying the phenomenon[1] while much empirically constructive work on the topic has not been conducted yet. Therefore, the research discussed in this paper proposes to explore the *actual field* of the virtual community (VC). By means of a comparative ethnographic research, virtual communities are to be defined in terms of their inherent social activity, the interaction between the groups of people and the information and communication technology (ICT), and the meanings attached to it by its members.

This chapter will report on the initial propositions, research questions and approach of the explorative research of working towards a "workable definition" of virtual communities. It will also present its "work to be done" which will ultimately form the basis of moving beyond defining virtual communities, i.e., actually designing and deploying one.

CONCEPTS AND ISSUES

For now we will postulate that all virtual communities at least consist of, on the one hand, groups of people – in this chapter referred to as "community of practices"[2] – and, on the other hand, information and communication technology. However, it should be noted that we do not make any distinction between for instance commercial and non-commercial communities of practice.

Previously Published in *Managing Information Technology in a Global Economy,* edited by Mehdi Khosrow-Pour, Copyright © 2001, Idea Group Publishing.

Virtual Community?

In order to derive at a workable definition of virtual communities, we need to first explicate the constituent parts of the terms: "virtual" and "community." This "what's-in-a-name exercise" will lead the way to some basic understandings of: The extent to which virtual communities refer to physical phenomena, and what it is that makes a virtual community a *community* to begin with.

According to the 9th edition of *The Concise Oxford Dictionary*, "virtual," in the case of computing, refers to "not physically existing as such but made by software to appear to do so." This definition implies that the virtual space created and mediated by ICTs is evolving as a completely new world. Adherents to this view assert for instance that the virtual space will become a placeless space in which hierarchical differences are negligible and in which more democratic inter-personal relations exist. Instead, we contend that the virtual consists of more or less the same features as does its real life (RL) counterpart, e.g., in terms of gen-der (see Boudourides and Drakou, 2000). What will emerge in the virtual will be the extension of present forms and practices of interaction and construction of meaning.[3] If any, the virtual space could conceal or, the opposite, act as a magni-fying glass of certain features and attributes of communities of practice such as their mode of interaction (or, lack of interaction); prevalent power struggles, and issues such as openness and trust. Hence, we assert that in exploring virtual com-munities we should not "disembed" them from their offline reality.

"Community," the other constituent of the term virtual community, entails most of all that its members have something in common with each other and hold a specific "sense of belonging" (see Cohen, 1985). Hence, in investigating virtual communities we should gain an understanding of this common ground, that is; peoples' individual experience of participating *in* and their attachment *to* the com-munity.

Situated "Interactional" relationship

We hold that a virtual community is and becomes what its participants[4] per-ceive it to be (*interpretation*) and how they use it accordingly (*practice*). Apart from the conviction that people's perception *of* and behaviour *in* the virtual com-munity affects its development, we hold that, it is in turn also the ICT that affects people's behaviour in it. This means that the ICT is supporting and enabling[5] as well as transforming the social behaviour of the people engaged in the virtual com-munity.[6]

Central to our approach, therefore, is the conviction that a virtual community must be perceived as an outcome of the "interactional relationship" of ICT and the socio-cultural formation in which it is deployed. Understanding virtual communities entails the realisation that the ICT and its socio-cultural context affect each other simultaneously (not necessarily proportional though).

Altogether, we contend that a virtual community is a constellation of attributes[7] - not a simple equation or just a random constellation of properties -, given a *specific* context and a *specific* community of practice interacting with a *specific* ICT. In the proposed study as such we are exploring the attributes of various virtual communities and their situated character (of design, development, use and interpretation) in order to, ultimately, built a socially and culturally embedded virtual community that fully exploits the possibilities of contemporary ICTs. This quest requires explicating the "visible" as well as the "invisible" attributes of virtual communities; that is, of both its community of practice and its ICT. The visible, or first level attributes refer to their superficial characteristics such as form, structure and the kinds of applications used. The invisible attributes refer to the underlying structures and the social processes of virtual communities such as the unwritten rules, routines, rituals and power struggles existing within the community as well as inscribed in the applied ICT.

Control, cultivation or spontaneous commitment[8]?

One issue that we come across in the literature on virtual communities is the issue of sustaining, or maintaining, a virtual community. Supposedly, a virtual community is *self-organised* in that "… it is *not created by managerial mandate* and may not even begin with the intention of becoming a group" (Prusak, 1997: 15). [emphases are ours] For this reason it has often been asserted that the virtual community as a tool of, for example, knowledge management, is a paradox of management. For, the real value of the virtual community is said to lie in the spontaneous gathering of people with shared interests or aims, that is, the self-organising principle. Thus, actively managing the formation of such constellations would go against the very grain of its principle.[9]

Since participant-generated content and interaction are of prime importance it is often said that "… a radically different approach to management must be followed in which a high degree of autonomy is ceded to members, and managers display a "gardener's touch" (Hagel and Armstrong in Werry, 1999). Although we do argue that albeit a large degree of self-organisation is necessary, sporadic direct intervention is requisite in order to sustain a viable community. Hafner (1997), for example, describes an incidence of a woman being expelled from the Well. The woman had a long history of abusing participants, and flaming them. Initially, the moderators did not react because they wanted the community to handle the problem by itself. But also because the many outrageous posts made by the woman incidentally enhanced the sense of belonging within the community. However, for reason of intrusion on privacy of the participants were the moderators forced to expel the woman after all. And, in this case, external intervention thus appeared to be ineluctable.[10]

How to create and sustain commitment of participants without interfering with the natural growth of the virtual community but with preventing it from dying a slow death, requires to be researched in the various contexts. How and by what are people motivated to interact, generate content and share information in a virtual community? And would the solution lie in a moderator or content "manager" gardener's- style?

In any case, apart from focussing on the virtual community as a constellation of certain attributes, we should above all perceive and investigate virtual communities as dynamic phenomena; requiring constant monitoring and feedback, and adaptation of the ICT involved.[11]

APPROACH

In order to investigate both the situated attributes of virtual communities and the way to keep them viable, needed is: (1) an evaluation of the involved ICT and its "workings;" (2) a characterisation and assessment of the social dynamics of the community of practice and; (3) an understanding of the interpretative flexibility of the virtual community (that is to say, of both the ICT and the community of practice). Accordingly, the research activities will be directed towards: explicating the descriptive (*what and how*), functional (*use and purpose*) and normative definition (*ascribed meanings*) of both the community of practice and the deployed ICT.[12] Defining virtual communities functionally, descriptively and normatively will enhance our comprehension of what they consist of, their purpose, how people perceive them and what people want them to become.[13]

To begin with, the descriptive definition of virtual communities contains the most obvious or superficial - first order - features of the community of practice and the deployed ICT and will be constructed according to its texts, e.g.:

- *Community and membership profiles.* These will provide us information such as the amount of participants involved, their educational and working background, gender, and nationality. Other documents like 'business' plans and all will provide us with the first insights into the rules, regulations and procedures about what is expected to be proper conduct in the virtual community.
- *Plan of requirements of the ICT infrastructure and the documentation of the design and deployment of the ICT.* On the basis of these texts, we will be able to draw up a (historical) reconstruction of the information and communication technology; its structure, the kinds of applications and the preceding decision-making processes.

Secondly, the functional definition will be derived at from an introspection of the community in terms of its actual practice (*social activity*). Such an introspection should incorporate, amongst others, the manners and degrees of socialisation of the participants of the community; their actual conduct of interacting as well as a reconstruction of their "interactional" history (to be deducted from the log files, or in technical terms "referrer"). This will ultimately reveal issues such as: the degree of openness; the unwritten rules of conduct, routines, habits, rituals and; the prevailing power structures and struggles (deduced from such things as the ways of addressing each other and well possibly the division of space).

Thirdly, the normative definition of the virtual community will be constituted according to the so-called 'narrative infrastructure'; that is, the stories people tell about themselves and others, as well as about the virtual community and the way they relate to it.[14] The narrative infrastructure will reveal what meanings people attach to the virtual community and may also reveal how "story-lines may structure action before the fact and how *prospective structure* emerges" (Van Lente and Rip, 1999: 217).

Altogether, a characterising of the virtual community will be drawn by means of its *texts*, *practices* and *narratives*. This involves the following research methods:

- The study of archives and documentation *on* and observation *in* the virtual community;
- participant observation and description *in* and *of* the actual practice in the virtual community in order to recognise patterns and regularities (the purpose of which is to reveal 'what actually is instead of what ought to be') and;
- conducting unstructured interviews with the various participants involved in the virtual community.

  "When direct observation and description are involved the term ethnography is often referred to. Ethnography – in the sense used by anthropologists - entails participant-observation, frequent and often informal interviews, and the cultivation of insiders known as 'informants'" (Hess, 1992: 21).

In addition to meeting the participants of the virtual community, the informants, online, that is conducting a *Virtual ethnography* (Hine, 2000; Markham, 1998; Paccagnella, 1997), face-to-face meetings will be conducted as well.

THE WEBGRRLS CASE

WebGrrls[15] is a community with a relatively long history. It started in 1995 and has grown into a world-spanning community. An interesting aspect of this community is that its participants are empowered to shape their community themselves. In fact, the community is built by its members from the very beginning. A group of likewise minded "Grrl's" met (New York city, 1995) and decided that there was a need to create a platform for: "… women from diverse backgrounds, talking up a storm about our big common interests – the internet and the World Wide Web".[16] More importantly, they wanted to create an online place for women to help each other in making their entrance to the new medium (the Internet); in using the technology, and in learning to find jobs and to network.[17]

The meetings, like the first one, in which they decided to start an online community, continued and in half a year they had over 200 participants. In 1997 they officially went international and organised an event in which women from all over the world participated through online chat[18]. That meeting also initiated the start of the various international "Chapters." And, within four years after the start there were more than 100 Chapters.[19] These Chapters are actually based in the various different (RL) countries and regions. They are part of the WebGrrls community but have complete freedom in creating their own website and range from simple pages with only information to fully interactive websites with many features[20].

Most of the participants are tied to the internet professionally, as can be seen by browsing through the "WebGrrl of the Week" archive.[21] They participate by sending in content for the website, going to the community meetings, and eventually also by setting up their own local Chapter of WebGrrls. It is abundantly clear that the participants not only look for information but also actively support the notion of the 'helping hand'. As one of them said: "*I got my job through WebGrrls, before that it helped me to stay informed and inspired about working on the web, WebGrrls was my support group.*"[22]

CONCLUDING REMARKS

Analysing 'grrls' actual behaviour by participating ourselves, analysing the log files and interviewing the participants will be the next steps in our research. At the same time we will start with the ethnography of at least one other virtual community in order to provide the comparative data. This will be a community which has different ways of getting participants to co-operate than does Webgrrls.

REFERENCES

Benschop, A. (1998). Virtual Communities: Networks of the Future, <http://www.pscw.uva.nl/sociosite/WEBSOC/network.html> [accessed: 12-jan-2001].

Boudourides, M. A. & Drakou, E. (2000). Gender@cyberspace, *Proceedings of the 4th European Feminist Research Conference*, September 28 - October 1, Bologna, Italy.

Cohen, A.P. (1985). *The Symbolic Construction of Community*, Chichester: Ellis Horwood.

De Moor, A. (1999). Empowering Communities: A Method for User-Driven Specification of Network Information Systems. Doctoral thesis.

Escobar, A. (1994). Welcome to Cyberia: Notes on the Anthropology of Cyberculture, *Current Anthropology: a World Journal of the Sciences of Man*, 25 (3), 211-232.

Hafner, K. (1997). The Epic Saga of The Well. <http://www.wired.com/wired/archive/5.05/ff_well_pr.html> [accessed: 12-jan-2001].

Hanseth, O. (1996). Information Technology Infrastructure, Gothenburg Studies in Informatics, Report 10, Department of informatics, Göteborg University.

Hess, D. J.(1992). Introduction: The new Ethnography and the Anthropology of Science and Technology. *Knowledge and Society: The Anthropology of Science and Technology*, 9, 1-26, JAI Press Inc.

Hine, C. (2000). *Virtual Ethnography*, London: Sage Publication.

Jansen, W., Steenbakkers, C. A., & Jägers, H. P. M. (1999). Knowledge Management and Virtual Communities, PrimaVera Working Paper 99-18.

Klang,M. & Olson, S. Virtual Communities. Göteborg, Viktoria Institute, University of Göteborg.

Markham, (1998). *Life Online: Researching Real Experience in Virtual Space*, Walnut Creek, CA: Altamira.

McInnes, A. The Agency of the Infozone: Exploring the Effects of a Community Network, <http://www.firstmonday.dk/issues2_2/mcinnes/index.html> [accessed: 12-jan-2001].

Paccagnella (1997). Getting the seats of your pants dirtyL strategies for ethnographic research on virtual communities. *Journal of Computer Mediated Communities* 3(1), <http://www.ascusc.org/jcmc/vol3/issue1/paccagnella.html > [accessed: 12-jan-2001].

Prusak, L. (1997). *Knowledge in Organisations*, Boston, MA: Butterworth-Heinemann.

Rheingold, H. (1994). The Virtual Community, <http://www.www.well.com/user/hlr/vcbook/index.html> [accessed: 12-jan-2001].

Valauskas, E. J. Lex Networkia: Understanding the Internet Community, <http://www.firstmonday.dk/issues/issue4/valauskas/index.html> [accessed: 12-jan-2001].

Van Lente, H. & Rip, A. (1999). Expectations in technological developments: an example of prospective structure to be filled in agency, in *Getting New Technologies Together: Studies in Making Sociotechnical Order*, Disco and Van der Meulen (eds.), Berlin/New York, pp.203-229.

Wellman, B. & Gulia, M. (1999). Virtual Communities as Communities: Netsurfers don't ride alone. In Smith, M. A. & Kollock, P. (eds), *Communities in Cyberspace*, pp.167-194.

Wenger, E. C. (1998). *Communities of Practice: Learning, Meaning and Identity*, Cambridge University Press.

Wenger, E. C. & Snyder, W. M. (2000). Communities of Practice: The Organizational Frontier, *Harvard Business Review*, January-February.

Werry, C. (1999). Imagined Electronic Community: Representations of Virtual Community in Contemporary Business Discourse, <http://www.firstmonday.dk/issues/issue4_9/werry/index.html> [accessed: 12-jan-2001].

END NOTES

[1] Classifying virtual communities as 'The Forum', 'The Club', 'The Shop' or 'The Bazaar'(Klang and Olson). Also in Jansen et al. (1999) we read about the Chat virtual community, the Expert virtual community and the Innovative virtual community.

[2] Communities of practice "... in brief, are groups of people informally bound together by shared expertise and passion for a joint enterprise ..." (Wenger. & Snyder: 2000: 139).

[3] "A virtual community comprises all dimensions of a community: economic, political, social and cultural ones" (Benschop: 7).

[4] We deliberately speak of participants, instead of users. The reason for both is that: The virtual community is in constant transformation (we are not making any distinction between the phases of virtual community development); by participating the community the users transform it in turn and; most 'end-users' are also designers.

[5] "A virtual community is a community in which most interactions are *enabled by information technology*" (De Moor, 1999: 3) [emphases are ours]

[6] This 'enabling and constraining view' is derived from Anthony Giddens' Structuration Theory and has exhaustively been discussed in the IS literature.

[7] An attribute is "a quality regarded as a natural or typical part of sb/sth" (Oxford Advanced Learner's dictionary,1995: 66).

[8] See Wellman and Gulia (1999).

[9] The virtual community as a tool of knowledge management becomes in that case a rather artificial and frightening tool geared towards the distillation of the so-called tacit knowledge of people. This relates to Werry's critique of some of the ways in which contemporary business models seek to commodify community, to organize and regulate social interaction, and to control practices of online knowledge production" (Werry 1999: 13).

[10] A lesson learned from this is that in order to make a community you may need some kind of conflict or a confrontation with outsiders. Since, when confronted with the 'Other', the group will posit itself as a whole.

[11] This, to underline the fact that we contend that the ICT involved should be completely at the disposal of the groups of people working with it.

[12] See Hanseth (1996) for approach.

[13] This is what Van Lente and Rip (1999) refer to as the 'script of expectation statements'.

[14] We tend to define ourselves through defining the 'Other' – the Other referring to other members of the community, other communities and the technology.

[15] http://www.webgrrls.com

[16] http://www.webgrrls.com/history

[17] http://www.webgrrls.com/history

[18] Internet Relay Chat

[19] http://www.webgrrls.com/faq/#1

[20] See for instance the Austrian chapter at http://www.webgrrls.at/index.phtml, and the New Zealand chapters at http://www.webgrrls.org.nz/.

[21] http://webgrrls.cybergrrl.com/wfs.jhtml?/archives/wotw/index2.html

[22] Martina Kauter, Senior Producer and Designer, Cybergrrl.Inc.

Chapter 5

Virtual Transactional and Relational Exchanges: The Enabling Effects of Information Technology

Andrew Gaudes and Mary Brabston
I. H. Asper School of Business
University of Manitoba, Winnipeg

The transactional and relational components of virtual organizing are evaluated and compared against the transactional and relational exchange-enabling characteristics of various forms of information technology. The findings suggest that further examination of this linkage in relation to organizational performance outcomes would be beneficial.

INTRODUCTION

A new form of organic organization known as virtual organization requires the application of information technology (IT) and provides organizations with greater interaction, agility, and flexibility (Byrne, 1993; Metes et al., 1998; Miller et al., 1993; Palmer, 1998). However, virtual organizations exhibit the relational difficulties of multiple agency that occur when individuals and groups from different organizations with different competencies band together across distances (Fulk and DeSanctis, 1995). An appropriate approach is to recognize a virtual organization as a process of *virtual organizing*. This changes the concept from a stagnant organizational form to a dynamic method of organizational management. Virtual organizing is, in part, the establishing and maintaining of a web of relationships between agents.

Previously Published in *Managing Information Technology in a Global Economy,* edited by Mehdi Khosrow-Pour, Copyright © 2001, Idea Group Publishing.

We argue that the approaches to virtual organizing can vary and that the approach taken can be defined by the transactional and relational characteristics of the exchange as well as the IT environment in which they occur. First we discuss the requisite conditions that enable virtual organizing and the common approaches taken by organizations that apply virtually organized exchanges (telework, outsourcing, alliances). We then present the two key components – the transactional and relational – that define the relationship between agents. Virtual organizing approaches are then evaluated based on their transactional and relational exchange content and distributed on a two-by-two matrix. Various types of information technology are then evaluated based on their ability to support these transactional and relational exchanges and plotted on the same matrix, followed by a discussion of our findings.

VIRTUAL ORGANIZING

Three different approaches are most common to virtual organizing: forming alliances, outsourcing, and teleworking. An alliance "connects members and partners in pursuit of specific project objectives" (Palmer, 1998, p. 72). Outsourcing is the divesting of extraneous departments within a corporation while maintaining the corporation's core focus. An integral part of outsourcing is governance through a contract agreement that tends to have explicit and comprehensive deliverables. Telework uses remote work locations for individuals who would otherwise work in a more central location (Gordon, 1988). The arrangements in telework are often at the individual level.

Transactional/Relational Ties in Virtual Organizing

Each of these three approaches to virtual organizing share the same requisite conditions: interdependent relationships, physical dispersion, and computer-mediation. However, each fosters a different type of relationship between the virtually organized agents. Relationships involve ties that are comprised of transactional (or instrumental) and relational (or social) components that have been regularly examined in the study of psychological contracts.

Transactional ties are best represented in contracts or relationships that "focus on short-term and monetizable exchanges" (Rousseau 1995, p. 91). The transactional represents that which is explicit and agreed upon. Relationships that are task-specific, involve explicit economic incentives, predetermined time frames, limited flexibility without renegotiation of a contract, or utilization of worker skills without future development are all examples of contract terms deemed highly transactional (Rousseau, 1995).

In contrast, the relational component emphasizes social exchange and interdependence. However, it should not be confused with relational attributes that are deemed "communal." In an exchange relationship, the relational component still anticipates reciprocation and is best represented by "open-ended relationships involving considerable investments by both employees and employers" (Rousseau, 1995, p. 92). Contract terms that are deemed highly relational are those with open-ended time frames, written and unwritten terms, and/or dynamic relationships that are subject to change or involve personal growth and development.

Virtual organizing relies heavily upon information technology and computer-mediated exchanges to facilitate both transactional and relational aspects of the relationship. Since IT filters out many of the social context clues that exist in face-to-face encounters, Nohria and Eccles (1992) believe continuing to have face-to-face interaction may be critical to the viability and effectiveness of electronic interaction. On the other hand, it can be argued that IT filters out the "noise" that can often distort the message in a face-to-face exchange. Travica (1998) feels that IT contributes to "relatively uninhibited behavior, social equalization, decision shifts, and the creation of new ideas" (p. 1227). Invariably, in a virtual organizing approach, IT is a critical contributor towards determining the outcome of transactional and relational ties between agents.

Different approaches to virtual organizing (telework, outsourcing and alliances) have different transactional and relational compositions. For example, it could be argued that an outsourcing arrangement is more explicit and has a more specific time frame than an alliance and that a telework arrangement will affect an individual's relational life more than an outsourcing relationship. Because virtual organizing relies heavily on IT to support the relational and transactional components of an exchange, providing an appropriate technological environment for these different exchange compositions is necessary to produce the desired outcome.

We hypothesize that each approach to virtual organizing is comprised of a different and relatively consistent set of transactional and relational components. The approach adopted between two or more agents can be classified as containing exchange characteristics that are low or high in *transactional* content and exchange characteristics that are low or high in *relational* content. The different approaches to virtual organizing can be distributed among four quadrants within a two-by-two transactional/relational matrix. Table 1 presents each virtual organizing approach with a discussion on its transactional and relational make up.

Alliances

High Transactional: The central motivation for alliances to form is resource complementarity – when shared resources of two or more members create greater economic value than when left separate (Barney and Hesterly, 1999). This mandates a high transactional environment maintained through contracts and arrangements that have specific time frames (Mohrman, 1999).

Table 1: The transactional/relational composition of virtual organizing approaches

High Transactional - Low Relational	High Transactional - High Relational
Outsourcing	Alliances
Low Transactional - Low Relational	High Relational - Low Transactional
	Teleworking

High Relational: At the same time, alliances rely on trust between their members (Barney and Hesterly, 1999), reducing the threat of cheating among members. Alliances may also form to explore opportunities that are not clearly defined, resulting in emergent activities where specific outcomes and time frames are not clearly known at the outset.

Outsourcing

High Transactional: The primary motivation for outsourcing has also been to reduce costs (Watkins, 1998). The outsourced relationship is clearly transactional with explicit contracts and deliverables.

Low Relational: Outsourcing is largely a transactional exchange. Both organizations function in an opportunistic fashion.

Telework

Low Transactional: Telework programs were originally developed for cost reduction and productivity increases (Hill et al., 1998; Kaplan, 1995). Today, the prime objectives have turned to other, more intangible benefits, including an improved work/life balance, increased flexibility, reduced stress, improved recruiting, and greater employee retention, (Blanc, 1988; Cascio, 1999; Gaudes, 1998).

High Relational: A teleworking exchange is high in relational content because of the types of exchange possible from a home office. Intangible benefits include those mentioned above, all relational benefits.

Because virtual organizing has different transactional and relational compositions, we posit that these different approaches to virtual organizing will also require different IT environments. In order to determine which IT environments are appropriate for each quadrant, the enabling characteristics of the various information technologies used to support these virtual organizations must be assessed.

INFORMATION TECHNOLOGY AND ORGANIZATIONS

Information technology is the marriage of computing and communicating abilities. While communication technology supports the exchange of information, computer technology enables the transformation of that information.

According to DeSanctis et al. (1999), IT can be viewed as "the rich background, or milieu, in which interdependencies are enacted" (p. 98). Our question here is drawn from this perspective of IT as part of a social context, an integrated, ecological environment that fosters the development and maintenance of virtually organized relationships. From the social context perspective, it is critical to ensure that there are few, if any, obstacles to the quality of the exchange between agents. For instance, if a telework relationship requires high relational content, then the IT selected should support these relational aspects. Otherwise, a less than optimal exchange will occur, producing potentially less than desired outcomes. Virtual organizing requires a blend of various types of IT to close these gaps.

Whether different virtual organizations require the implementation of different information technologies has been examined in the past. Palmer (1998) found that the use of IT differs based upon the type of virtual organization employed. Palmer's categorization differs from ours and does not offer much in the way of generalizability across all organizations.

We propose that the enabling characteristics of each form of IT can be categorized by its ability to support transactional and relational exchanges. Each form of IT can contribute to an environment where two or more agents can engage in a virtual relationship, providing low or high support in transactional exchanges and low or high support in relational exchanges. The transactional/relational enabling characteristics of information technology may be used in distributing IT within the same two-by-two matrix created above for virtual relationships.

There are three ways that information technology can be categorized as high in support of transactional exchanges. First, IT that is high in supporting transactional exchanges must be able to support the exchange of quantifiable goods or services (Williamson, 1981; Gibbens, 1998). Second, IT that facilitates compensating suppliers for their goods or services can be classified as high in supporting transactional exchanges (Gibbens, 1998). Third, a transactional exchange occurs when there is a specific task undertaken between agents; IT can enable that task to be performed.

To categorize the enabling characteristics of information technology as low or high in relational exchanges, we use media richness theory (Trevino et al, 1990). Daft and Lengel (1986) proposed that communication media have different abilities to reduce ambiguity and facilitate understanding and can be classified as "rich" or "lean". The criteria used to determine media richness are 1) the availability of instant feedback; 2) the capacity of transmitting multiple cues through the medium; 3) the personal focus of the medium, and 4) the use of natural language (Trevino et al, 1990). Because all the information technologies we examine in this paper support the use of a natural language, we have not included it as one of our criteria.

Monge et al. (1998) discuss the creation of public goods when alliances form interorganizational communication and information systems that create two generic public goods for members of an alliance – connectivity and communality. Connectivity is the "ability of partners to directly communicate with each other" and communality is "the availability of a commonly accessible pool of information to alliance partners" (p. 411). We find that connectivity and communality have relational characteristics as defined by Rousseau (1995), involving open-ended relationships with considerable investments by members of the alliance.

Although Daft and Lengel developed a hierarchy of media based upon the richness of their capacity to reduce ambiguity, we will categorize IT into the four quadrants created in the transactional/relational matrix. We believe that each category provides valuable support for organizations and that they are not necessarily ordinal. We now present common and emerging forms of IT along with their ability to support transactional and relational exchanges (see Table 2).

Facsimile (Fax)

High Transactional: Because a fax machine is able to send complete documents and illustrations, it supports the exchange of goods or services provided by one agent for another. A fax machine is also able to transmit payments, such as credit card numbers and signatures. They can provide for task-specific exchanges.

Low Relational: Although a fax machine supports a personal focus, a fax machine does not provide a good means of immediate exchange between individuals. Returning the response via the same medium can take considerable time relative to a face-to-face exchange. Also, a fax machine is not very good for conveying multiple cues.

Voice-mail

High Transactional: Although not likely to be the transactional medium of choice, voice-mail could support the exchange of payment between agents. It is possible for individuals to leave transactional/payment advice and information via voice-mail.

High Relational: Voice-mail provides the same benefits as conventional telephone conversations other than the immediacy of the exchange (Trevino et al., 1990). Users of voice-mail can recognize multiple cues through inflections and emotion in the voice of the sender; voice mail supports a personal focus.

E-mail

High Transactional: E-mail can enable the exchange of goods or services either within the message or as an attachment. Also, e-mail facilitates the exchange of payment for goods or services and can be used to send instructions for tasks to be performed.

High Relational: While limited in its immediacy compared to telephone and face-to-face media (Trevino et al., 1990), e-mail has a greater level of immediacy than other computer-mediated exchanges. While e-mail has also been ranked lower in richness than phone and face-to-face channels, Sarbaugh-Thompson and Feldman (1998) have argued that individuals make up for the loss of cues by inserting their own symbolic, punctuation, format, and salutation cues in e-mail messages. Today's use of formatting and multimedia within email messages provides richness cues. Electronic mail also supports a personal focus.

Electronic bulletin boards (EBB) / newsgroups

Low Transactional: The public nature of bulletin boards and newsgroups would likely inhibit their use as means of direct task-specific exchanges with specific agents or groups.

Low Relational: Unlike a medium such as e-mail, electronic bulletin boards and newsgroups do not notify users when there is a message. This makes the immediacy of the medium quite low. While the number of multiple cues is equivalent to e-mail, electronic bulletin boards and newsgroups are not a good medium for providing a personal focus.

Mailing lists / list servers

Low Transactional: A mailing list or list server is a way of exchanging ideas and information among individuals who share some common interest. Similar to electronic bulletin boards, they do not provide good support for the exchange of quantifiable goods or services, nor are they a good means of payment or task-specific exchange.

Low Relational: Mailing lists or list servers do not provide the availability of instant feedback. The immediate relevance by individuals receiving a broadcast message is assumed to be low (Wang, 1997). Multiple cues are the same as e-mail. The message itself is broadcast, limiting the capacity to personalize the content to a specific individual.

Group decision support systems (GDSS) / group support systems (GSS)

High Transactional: These group technologies support decision making by individuals who can interact from distributed locations. Although GDSS and GSS enhance group activity over distance, they do not support the exchange of a quantifiable good or service, but they can support task-specific exchanges.

Low Relational: The very nature of GDSS and GSS makes them strong in supporting instant feedback. Multiple cues, however, are not supported because the immediacy of the exchange and limitations in format presentation diminish the opportunity to generate alternative cues. They are also limited in supporting a personal focus.

Audio and video teleconferencing

High Transactional: Both audio and video teleconferencing are able to support the exchange of a good or service, particularly if the session is used as a billable consultation between one agent and another. Both conferencing methods are also able to support a task-specific exchange. Support for payment via these IT, however, is less typical.

High Relational: Both forms of teleconferencing provide instant feedback with video supporting more cues, making it the richer of the two media. Both also support a personal focus.

Screen sharing/whiteboarding

High Transactional: Screen sharing enables two or more individuals to work on the same monitor from different work stations. White boarding allows individuals to work from a mutually shared virtual "whiteboard". In both cases, individuals can insert text, generate graphics, and make a variety of changes while being viewed or revised by the other participating individuals. Individuals need to use other supportive technologies, such as video, telephone, or e-mail in order to support their dialogue while using these technologies. Both technologies provide a good means of working on a specific task, but they do not offer a good method for exchanging a quantifiable good or service. Finally, they are not a good mechanism for exchanging payment for a good or service.

High Relational: Screen sharing and whiteboarding support immediate feedback; however, they are limited in the number of cues they present. Both media also support exchanges that have a personal focus.

Integrated technologies / groupware (e.g., Lotus Notes)

High Transactional: Integrated technologies incorporate several applications across time and space. Because these technologies integrate some of the applications that were assessed above, they take on the exchange supporting attributes of those individual applications. These integrated technologies can support the exchange of and payment for a quantified good/service as well as short-term task oriented exchanges.

High Relational: Likewise, integrated technologies support the high relational attributes of their integrated applications. One caveat for integrated technologies; although they provide the ability for both high transactional and high relational, this ability is dependent upon the bundled applications and how they are used.

Table 2: The transactional/relational composition of virtual organizing approaches and enabling characteristics of information technology

High Transactional - Low Relational	High Transactional - High Relational
Outsourcing Fax EDI and IOS Group Decision Support Systems	*Alliances* Voice-Mail E-Mail Audio/Video Teleconferencing Screen Sharing / White Boarding Integrated Technologies (Lotus Notes) Intranets / Extranets / LANs, WANs... Internet
Low Transactional - Low Relational	**Low Transactional - High Relational**
Electronic Bulletin Boards / Newsgroups List Servers / Mailing Lists	*Teleworking*

Interorganizational systems (IOS) and electronic data interchange (EDI)

High Transactional: By their very nature, both IOS and EDI support the exchange of and payment for a quantifiable good or service.

Low Relational: Both IOS and EDI are primarily transaction-specific media, yet they provide connectivity and communality, which are relational components. IOS and EDI also provide immediacy in exchange. However, the feedback received is normally data processing related. These systems are largely informational, providing little in the way of interaction. Both are low in personal focus and social cues.

Intranet / extranet / local area networks / wide area networks / value added networks / virtual private networks

High Transactional: These networks have been grouped together because they provide a vehicle for exchange relationships and some form of exclusivity, albeit to varying degrees. These networks support the exchange of and payment for a quantifiable good or service as well as task-specific exchanges.

High Relational: All of these networks provide support for immediate feedback in a natural language. Multiple cues are also supported with the number of cues being largely dependent upon the bandwidth of the network. A personal focus is also supported by all network types, mostly through the use of other IT, such as email. Finally, connectivity and communality are attributes created by each of these networks.

The Internet

High Transactional: The Internet supports all transactional exchanges, the exchange of quantifiable goods or services, payment, and task-specific exchanges.

High Relational: The Internet also supports relational components of an exchange. It supports immediate feedback and enables multiple cues and personal focus. However, the open-to-everyone nature of the Internet diminishes its exclusive connectivity and communality value.

CONCLUSION
Overview of Findings

When these technologies are plotted on the same transactional/relational two-by-two matrix as virtual organizing, we find some interesting results. Distribution over the entire matrix is not balanced. IT appears to be concentrated in the high transactional/high relational quadrant. The information technologies in this quadrant comprise the most recently developed and evolving systems. The most notable are those that capitalize on the growth of the Internet. This may suggest that developers are currently focusing on IT that supports both high transactional and high relational exchanges. The cluster in this quadrant may also suggest that any IT which supports more than a text or numeric based exchange can support a high level of both relational and transactional exchange.

In contrast to the concentration of IT in the high transactional and high relational area is the lack of any IT in the low transactional and high relational area. This suggests that a particular IT with the level of richness necessary to support a high relational exchange has an inherent ability to satisfy a high transactional exchange, a "leaner" form of exchange, but it could also suggest that IT development has focused upon supporting transactional exchanges. IT that support high relational exchanges will not be developed unless they already provide a high level of transactional support.

The uneven distribution of IT in the matrix may require current information technologies presently in one quadrant provide support for other quadrants as well. For example, the use of teleconferencing may be focused more on relational support in order to fit into the requirements mandated by the low transactional - high relational quadrant.

Teleworking has clearly drawn the shortest straw with respect to support by IT. Although there are technologies that support low-transactional/high relational exchanges, none that we assessed are developed with this specific intent. While we cannot say that this has had any direct impact upon teleworking, we can comment on the comparatively disappointing growth that telework has experienced, compared to outsourcing and alliances.

Implications for Practice

Almost every organization has the ability to implement a virtual organizing strategy. Managers need only focus on the act of virtual organizing – the development and maintenance of relationships that cross regions and time zones through interaction via computer-mediation – as the means to begin reaping the benefits of virtual organizations. Managers must also understand the relational and transactional exchange demands of different virtual organizing strategies. Deficits or surpluses in the content of the two exchange components will result in less than optimal exchange relationships. Information technology can provide support for transactional and relational exchanges. Managers must be aware of the type of virtual organizing relationship they are establishing when building their IT environment in order to avoid exchange gaps. They need to implement the information technologies that we have grouped with the particular virtual organizing approach they wish to adopt. If a manager is already virtually organizing, our matrix can be used to determine if the right information technologies are being used. Although much of the new IT supports both high transactional and high relational interactions, it may be necessary to focus on the transactional or relational supporting attributes when creating an environment for an outsourced or teleworking relationship.

Directions for Future Study

Assessing and placing information technologies and virtual organizing approaches within the matrix have been carried out with the broadest of brushes and require a more rigorous approach. We found that various information technologies, although clustered in the same quadrant, have different relational attributes in which they excel. A more detailed assessment might result in some information technologies being deemed marginal in their current quadrant while others might be quite high.

Each of the information technologies assessed here should be viewed more closely and evaluated on a more rigorous scale for their transactional and relational attributes. Evaluation of the information technologies should also be undertaken by IT managers as Palmer (1998) did because they play a critical role in the development of virtual relationships (Davidow, 1992). This may elicit subtle differences that have presently been lost by grouping these information technologies together in the same quadrant. In addition, other emerging forms of IT, such as expert agents, should be included in a more detailed assessment.

Finally, our assignment of the transactional and relational exchange attributes of virtual organizing approaches has also been undertaken with a broad brush. Conducting a more detailed assessment of the transactional and relational exchange characteristics using criteria developed in the psychological contract literature (McLean-Parks et al., 1998) would provide a greater contribution. These criteria could then be applied to existing organizations that engage in any of the three virtual organizing approaches in order to assess where each of them fall on the transactional/relational matrix. This study might show that there is an overlap and possibly a migration of outsourcing and teleworking approaches toward the quadrant occupied by alliances. Comparing the virtual organizing approach and IT used by an organization to standard organizational outcomes (performance, productivity, absenteeism, organizational commitment) could reveal relationships between the virtual organizing IT environment and organizational performance.

The objective of this study was to determine if the three virtual organizing approaches are supported differently by different types of information technology. Our findings warrant further examination of the linkages between virtual organizing and the various emerging forms of IT.

REFERENCES

Barney, J. B. & Hesterly, W. (1999). Organizational economics: Understanding the relationship between organizations and economic analysis. In S. R. Clegg & C. Hardy (Eds.) *Studying organization: Theory and method* (109-141). Thousand Oaks, CA: SAGE Publications.

Blanc, G. (1988). Autonomy, telework and emerging cultural values. In W. B. Korte, S. Robinson, & W. J. Steinle (Eds.), *Telework: present situation and future development of a new form of work organization* (189-200). North-Holland: Elsevier Science Publishers B.V.

Byrne, J. A. (1993). The virtual corporation: The company of the future will be the ultimate in adaptability. *Business Week*, February 8, 98-103.

Cascio, W. F. (1999). Virtual workplaces: Implications for organizational behavior. In C. L. Cooper & D. M. Rousseau (Eds.), *Trends in organizational behavior volume 6: The virtual organization* (1-14). Chichester, England: John Wiley & Sons.

Daft, R. L., & Lengel, R. H. (1986). Organizational information requirements, media richness and structural design. *Management Science*, 32(5), 554-571.

Davidow, W. H. (1992). Postmodern information forms. *Computerworld*, Oct. 5, 1992, 29.

DeSanctis, G., Staudenmayer, N., & Wong, S. (1999). Interdependence in virtual organizations. In C. L. Cooper & D. M. Rousseau (Eds.), *Trends in organizational behavior volume 6: The virtual organization* (81-104). Chichester, England: John Wiley & Sons.

Fulk, J., & DeSanctis, G. (1995). Electronic communication and changing organizational forms. *Organization Science*, 6(4), 337-349.

Gaudes, Andrew J. (1998) *Optimizing Mobility to Marginalize Interruption,* [unpublished thesis], University of Manitoba Winnipeg, MB.

Gibbens, M. (1998). *Financial Accounting: An Integrated Approach*, Scarborough, ON: International Thomson Publishing.

Gordon, G. E. (1988). The dilemma of telework: Technology vs. tradition. In W. B. Korte, S. Robinson, & W. J. Steinle (Eds.), *Telework: Present situation and future development of a new form of work organization* (113-136). North-Holland: Elsevier Science Publishers B.V.

Hill, E. J., Miller, B. C., Weiner, S. P., & Colihan, J. (1998). Influences of the virtual office on aspects of work and work/life balance. *Personnel Psychology, 51*(3), 667-683.

McLean Parks, J., Kidder, D. L., & Gallagher, D. G. (1998). Fitting square pegs into round holes: Mapping the domain of contingent work arrangements onto the psychological contract. *Journal of Organizational Behavior*, 19, 697–730.

Miller, D. B., Clemons, E. K., & Row, M. C. (1993). Information technology and the global virtual corporation. In S. P. Bradley, J. A. Haisman, & R. L. Nolan (Eds.), *Globalization, technology and competition: The fusion of computers and telecommunications in the 1990s*. Boston, MA: Harvard Business School Press.

Monge, P.R., Fulk, J., Kalman, M.E., Flanagin, A.J. (1998). Production of collective action in alliance-based interorganizational communication and information systems. *Organization Science*. 9(3), 411-433.

Nohria, N., & Eccles, R.G. (1992). Face-to-face: Making network organizations work. In N. Nohria & R.G. Eccles (Eds.), *Networks and Organizations. Structure, form, and action* (288-308). Boston, MA: Harvard Business School Press.

Palmer, J. W. (1998). The use of information technology in virtual organizations. In M. Igbaria & M. Tan (Eds.), *The virtual workplace* (71-85). Hershey, USA: Idea Group Publishing.

Rousseau, D. M. (1995). *Psychological contracts in organizations.* Thousand Oaks, CA: SAGE Publications.

Sarbaugh-Thompson, M., & Feldman, M.S. (1998). Electronic mail and organizational communication. Does saying 'hi' really matter? *Organization Science*. 9(6), 685–698.

Travica, B. (1998). Information aspects of new organizational designs: Exploring the non-traditional organization. *Journal of the American Society for Information Science,* Nov. 1998, 1224-1244.

Trevino, L. K., Daft, R. L., & Lengel, R. H. (1990). Understanding managers' media choices: A symbolic interactionist perspective. In J. Fulk & C. Steinfield (Eds.) *Organizations and communication technology* (71-94). Newbury Park, CA: SAGE Publications.

Wang, S. (1997). Impact of information technology on organizations. *Human Systems Management,* 16(1997), 83-90.

Watkins, W.M. (1998). *Technology and business strategy: Getting the most out of technology assets.* Westport, CT: Quorum Books.

Williamson, O. E. (1981). The economics of organization: The transaction cost approach. *The American Journal of Sociology*, 87(3), 548-577.

Chapter 6

Requirements Engineering During Virtual Software Development: Towards Balance

Jo Hanisch
School of Accounting and Information Systems
University of South Australia, Adelaide

There has been growing interest in virtual teams, and more specifically in virtual software development. Requirements engineering, which is seen as a crucial phase in software development provides another dimension when software development occurs in a virtual setting. While formal software development methods are the obvious first choice for project managers to ensure a virtual information system project team remains on track, the social aspects of requirements engineering cannot be ignored. These social aspects are especially important across different cultures, and have been shown to affect the success of an information system. This chapter proposes a framework indicating that project managers need to encourage a balance between formal methods and social aspects in requirements engineering to suit the virtual team members.

INTRODUCTION

Within contemporary organisations it is usual to find an array of computer-based information systems which support their business processes and assist the organisations to achieve their business goals. Businesses have changed as predicted by Drucker in 1988. Organisations have a flatter structure with "decentralized and autonomous units" including the extensive use of "task forces" (Drucker,

Previously Published in *Managing Information Technology in a Global Economy,* edited by Mehdi Khosrow-Pour, Copyright © 2001, Idea Group Publishing.

1988). Given the new organisational structure in business, and the more recent emergence of the global economy and global markets (Karolak, 1998), there is a change in both the type of work being performed and the way work is developed. For example, many companies operate entirely using the Internet capabilities (Laudon and Laudon, 2000).

As businesses have changed, so have their information systems. Information systems (IS) still support organisations as they achieve their business goals, however both the type of systems being developed and the nature of software development have changed. There is evidence of change from locally developed software to virtual (or global) software development (Carmel, 1999). As the technology now exists to enable collaborative team work over distance and time, virtual teams, in which virtual software development occurs, are becoming more recognised as the rule rather than the exception (Kimball, 1997). There is no doubt that virtual software development teams present some challenges to organisations. However, with improved understanding of the influences during virtual software development, organisations have the opportunity to develop strategies and techniques to manage this type of development. This in turn can help reduce the risk of failure of the systems being developed.

As Kuiper (1998) states, one of the greatest challenges for business is defining its needs for a new information system. Kuiper (1998) continues that the complexity and factors to be considered in developing a new information system is often overwhelming to business. Added to this is the realisation that the success or failure of the new information system, often determines whether the business succeeds or fails. Therefore ensuring the needs of business are clearly determined and communicated is important in the process of developing an information system.

One particularly crucial phase in software development that requires clear communication is the requirements definition (engineering) phase (Darke and Shanks, 1997). This phase has been said to impact directly on the success or failure of new IS in organisations (Byrd et al., 1982; Davis, 1990). Requirements engineering occurs early in the software development process, where the requirements for an information system are defined and expressed in the form of a systems requirements specification (Greenspan et al., 1994).

The main purpose of this chapter is to explore some of the influences associated with the requirements engineering phase of the software development process as it occurs in a virtual setting. The chapter first reviews the concept of virtual teams and virtual software development, then the requirements engineering phase of software development is reviewed, followed by a discussion of requirements engineering in virtual software development. This chapter is offered as a starting point for debate concerning two opposing forces perceived in the IS literature within requirements engineering and virtual software development

VIRTUAL TEAMS AND VIRTUAL SOFTWARE DEVELOPMENT

Jarvenpaa and Ives (1994) describe successful organisations as those that are moving towards a dynamic network structure. They suggest that "dynamic network organisations are spun from small, globally dispersed, ad hoc teams or independent organisational entities performing knowledge or service activities"(Jarvenpaa and Ives 1994:26). In this way organisations can respond quickly and efficiently to customer demands or changes in the external environment. Hacker and Kleiner (1996) support the notion that the extent to which an organisation is dynamic in an agile, competitive environment will affect its success.

Many organisations are already planning to operationalise the necessary human and information technology resources to cultivate the growth of the virtual environment (Greenbaum, 1998). Grenier and Metes (1995) state that some of the factors driving the trend towards virtual teams include mergers, corporate acquisitions, downsizing and increased use of new technology. As a result of downsizing on a global scale by the organisation, much of their expertise becomes spread throughout the organisation across a number of countries or regions, so virtual teams may form. Significantly many of the mergers and acquisitions involve international offices, and this also spawns the development of virtual teams with members potentially from many different cultures. When business requires certain projects to be undertaken in the organisation, virtual teams are established utilising expertise from any area of the organisation without the necessity for re-location of staff (Melymuka, 1997; Hacker and Kleiner, 1996).

Hacker and Kleiner (1996:196) believe that virtual teams have progressed from the status of a "good idea" to "a critical strategy for many organisations." From these authors, it appears that virtual teams are now being considered as a natural option to address business problems when team members are geographically separated. Melymuka (1997) supports the idea that virtual teams have been touted as one way to circumvent problems associated with re-location of team members to a central business site. This has been particularly evident with software development as there has been a dearth of skilled IS specialists globally over the past five years (Carmel, 1999).

What are virtual teams and why are they important to management? "Virtual teams are groups of people working closely together even though they may be separated by many miles, even continents" (Beger, 1995:36). Hartman and Guss (1996:185) more fully define virtual teams as *"a temporary network of independent professionals, separated by geographic, temporal and psychological distance, whose use of telecommunications tools for business communication is interdependent, to satisfy the business requirement of sharing skills and working to meet a common goal."*

Virtual teams are characterised by members who are physically isolated, who interact mainly through the use of computer-mediated communication technologies and who rarely or never meet face-to-face (Jarvenpaa and Leidner, 1997). Virtual teams are said to be functional units of an organisation which are flexible, and which both quickly and professionally "execute multiple projects, anywhere and anytime" (Hartman and Guss, 1996:185). They are characterised by short-term (i.e., 6 months) project based work and by their nature virtual teams lend themselves to ad hoc teams or "task-force" work groups which come together for specific project objectives and disband once these have been fulfilled (Jarvenpaa and Leidner, 1997).

There is recognition of barriers to virtual teams, such as, information overload and its associated stress, decreased informal communication capabilities, resistance to new work methods, uncertainty with requirements, and uncertainty with security, control, power and information when working with external organisations (Grenier and Metes, 1995).

While there are barriers to virtual team work, there are advantages such as the decrease in time and cost of travel, the ability to select expertise from the whole organisation regardless of employees' locations and the speed and flexibility at which project teams can be formed and disbanded (Lipnack and Stamps, 1997).

Virtual (or global) software development teams are but one type of an array of possible virtual teams. Knowledge in the area of virtual software development is increasing, however this is recognised as an emerging field of research (Carmel, 1999). Issues which appear most frequently in the limited literature concerning virtual software development include loss of communication richness (Jarvenpaa and Leidner, 1997, Carmel, 1999), cultural differences (Carmel, 1999), loss of identity with the team (Karolak, 1998; Carmel, 1999) and lack of management support (Karolak, 1998).

There are more questions and issues than answers at this stage, and many more questions will no doubt present themselves over the next decade, particularly when implementation and maintenance of the software newly developed by virtual teams stands the test of time. At this point, many organisations are still questioning whether this type of development is suitable for them, or whether they should wait to determine the success of the software developed by virtual teams.

Studies concerning the management of virtual software development (Carmel, 1999; Karolak, 1998) indicate that formalising the software development methods is essential in virtual software development. Other researchers (Jones, 1994; Meadows, 1996; Grenier and Metes, 1995) concur that virtual work requires a more formalised regime of work plans, deliverable progress reports and mandatory meeting schedules to assist the team to remain on track and focused for the delivery of the product. Researchers in the area of computer-based communication media (Damian et al., 2000; Prabhakar, 1999; Jarvenpaa and Leidner, 1997) also consider that formalised procedures aid in the success of communication between virtual team members and in the ultimate success of the project.

Given the research concerning the management of virtual teams and that of computer-based communication technologies, it appears that formal software development methods are not only essential, but of utmost priority, in ensuring the successful delivery of a new information system in an organisation. However, before stating the proposition that formal techniques are the ultimate project management tools for virtual software development and that project managers should be rigorous in their applications of formal methods, the influencing factors during requirements engineering (as part of software development) need to be considered.

REQUIREMENTS ENGINEERING

Requirements engineering has been defined as "the disciplined application of scientific principles and techniques for developing, communicating, and managing requirements" (Christel and Kang, 1992:3). This definition of requirements engineering is supported by the well known definition from Loucopoulos and Karakostas (1995), which is defined as:

"...the systematic process of developing requirements through an iterative co-operative process of analysing the problem, documenting the resulting observations in a variety of representation formats, and checking the accuracy of the understanding gained." Loucopoulos and Karakostas (1995:13)

Requirements engineering therefore covers "all the activities of discovering, documenting, and maintaining a set of requirements for building a computer-based information system" (Thanasankit and Corbitt, 1999; Sommerville and Sawyer, 1997). During requirements engineering, the requirements engineer (or systems analyst) needs to be mindful of the objectives/outcomes of the requirements engineering phase and implement appropriate processes or techniques which will help to avoid failure of the IS (Macauley, 1996). But the failure of many of these IS development projects is due not just to the inadequate requirements (Boehm, 1981) in general, but more specifically to the social, political and cultural factors associated with the project (Goguen and Linde, 1993).

The development of an "effective IS requires thorough analyses of user information needs prior to IS design" (Byrd et al., 1992:117). Requirements engineering, which is concerned with understanding the needs of the client (user) and determining the systems requirements which satisfy these needs, given any identified constraints and exclusions (Carroll and Swatman, 1997), is a crucial phase in the software development process (Greenspan et al., 1994).

So why is the requirement engineering phase so important to IS specialists and users? As Carroll and Swatman (1997:2) state, any "inconsistencies, omissions and errors in the requirements specification have significant impact upon the ability of the developed systems to meet customers' needs." The implication is that the client is less likely to accept and use the system that has been developed (Hocking, 1996) when there are problems with either the communication or agreement of the requirements (Urquhart, 1997). In project management terms of delivery of the system on time, within budget and meeting the users' requirements (McLeod and Smith, 1996), the system is said to have failed to deliver. Laudon and Laudon (2000) attribute this to failure of the organisation to meet its goals. Further, most errors found later in the systems development process can be retraced to the requirements specification, which either contains errors in the requirements or misinterpretation of the requirements (Liou and Chen, 1994).

The significance is that early detection of errors or misinterpretations decreases the cost of their rectification later in the process (Boehm, 1981; Park, Kim and Ko, 2000) and improves the quality of the system being developed (Darke and Shanks, 1997a). As Thanasankit (1999) has shown, these costs can be substantial to an organisation. According to Park et al. (2000:429), 5% of the total cost of a major system is spent on its design and development, while "70% of the ability to influence the quality comes from this meager amount." They state that errors in the requirements which are left uncorrected early in the software development cycle, ultimately end up as maintenance problems in the delivered software. It transpires that 5% of the total effort expended on requirements analysis leverages 50% of the total influence on improved quality of the system (Park et al., 2000).

Within the social context, it is necessary for IS specialists to understand communication and cooperation, as well as social complexity during requirements engineering (Thanasankit, 1999). Requirements engineering research has traditionally been positivist in its approach, largely focusing on the methods and tools used in the gathering elicitation and validation of requirements. Many researchers conclude that the more formal the techniques used, the more likely that the requirements will be clearly defined and understood. However, as Thanasankit (1999) states, organisations need to consider the emotions and culture of users and IS specialists. It has been shown that different cultures will perform tasks not only because they are responsible for the task, but because they wish to maintain surface harmony and trust between the group (Thanasankit, 1999) and this often inhibits formal sign offs of requirements specifications, which in turn causes delays and potential failure of the project. In these cases, the imposition of formal, often western philosophies and methods, have a negative impact on the requirements gathering process (Thanasankit, 1999).

REQUIREMENTS ENGINEERING IN VIRTUAL SOFTWARE DEVELOPMENT

There may occur a dilemma for project managers who are responsible for the requirements engineering phase during virtual software development. When systems analysts use more formalised tools and techniques for gathering requirements, as these tools are deemed to assist in the process of virtual communications, there may occur a negative impact on the social process of gathering of the requirements.

There may arise tension between the two forces and therein lies the interest and motivation for this discussion. Virtual work and virtual teams have been shown by previous research (Carmel, 1999; Karolak, 1998; Jones, 1994; Meadows, 1996; Grenier and Metes, 1995) to benefit from a more structured approach to the working environment. Therefore it would be logical to deduce that the requirements engineering phase of systems development in a virtual environment would also benefit from a more structured approach.

However, western ideologies created requirements engineering foundations (Odedra, 1993) and many of these processes were formalised and structured to suit western philosophies. Jirotka and Goguen (1994) argue that requirements engineering should be developed in an environment which suits both the social and technical concerns of the requirements. These structured methods may not be suitable for members of a virtual team who are likely to be situated in regions and cultures where social processes are deemed more significant in the requirements gathering process, rather than utilising structured tools and techniques (Thanasankit, 1999).

Figure 1: A Framework of Requirements Engineering in Virtual Software Development (adapted from McLeod and Smith, 1996:6)

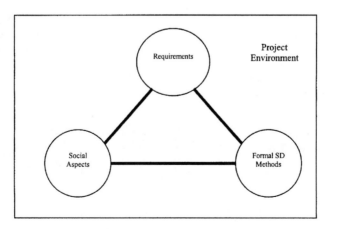

From the reviews above, many virtual teams include members who are from different cultural and social backgrounds. They will come into the team with different experiences in the formal techniques of software development and the way they have been used in their region previously. This will affect the way they communicate the requirements of the system and the extent to which formal method are used. Requirements engineering in western cultures will be different from eastern cultures.

Figure 1 shows a framework representing the tension which may occur between the two forces of social aspects of requirements engineering and formal software development tools used in requirements engineering.

The diagram indicates that the project manager who controls the project environment will always be balancing these variables to produce the requirements for the information system being developed. Therefore it is impossible to move either of the sides of the triangle without impacting on the requirements. For example, if highly formal software development methods are chosen at the expense of social considerations the requirements will be affected, and vice versa. The onus will be on the project manager of the virtual team to create a balance between social processes and structured methods in order to gather adequately the needs of the users and keep the project on track.

CONCLUSION

Requirements engineering is a crucial stage in software development regardless of whether the development is local or global. During virtual software development previous research has recommended that more formal and structured methods of requirements gathering be employed to decrease the risk of misunderstanding or misinterpretation of the requirements. However, requirements engineering is a social process and formal, structured methods may impact on the social and cultural differences between virtual teams members.

Project managers therefore face the task of creating a project environment that is conducive to communication through electronic means and which takes into account the differences in cultural and social aspects of virtual team members as they communicate their requirements. A balance is required to satisfy the formal structured methods of requirements engineering which have been shown in the past to improve software development in project management terms of quality, cost and time, and the need to provide a project environment which encourages open communication and supports cultural differences in virtual software development. Then not only will the system be built right but the right system will be built. Further research is required to determine which requirements engineering processes and which project environment characteristics are more appropriate in helping to achieve this balance.

REFERENCES

Beger, G. (1995). Virtual Teams, *Training*, April, p. 36.

Boehm, B. (1981). *Software Engineering Economics*, NJ: Prentice-Hall.

Byrd, T. A., Cossick, K. L., and Zmud, R. W. (1992). A synthesis of research on requirements analysis and knowledge acquisition techniques, *MIS Quarterly* March, pp. 117-138.

Carmel, E. (1999). *Global software teams: collaborating across borders and time zones*, NJ: Prentice Hall.

Carroll, J. M., and Swatman, P. A. (1997). How can the requirements engineering process be improved?, in Sutton, D. J. (ed.), *Proceedings of the 8th Australasian Conference on Information Systems*, University of South Australia, Adelaide, South Australia.

Christel, M. G., and Kang, K. C. (1992). Issues in requirements elicitation, Technical Report CMU/SEI-92-TR-12, SEI Pennsylvania.

Damian, D. E. H., Shaw, M. L. G., and Gaines, B. R. (2000). A study in requirements negotiations in virtual project teams, *Proceedings of the 8th European Conference on Information Systems 2000*, Vienna Austria.

Darke, P., and Shanks, G. (1997). Managing user viewpoints in requirements definition, *Proceedings of the 8th Australasian Conference on Information Systems*, Adelaide, Australia.

Davis, A. M. (1990). *Software requirements analysis and specification*, NJ: Prentice Hall.

Drucker, P. (1988). The coming of the new organisation, *Harvard Business Review*, Jan-Feb, 47-53.

Goguen, J. A., and Linde, C. (1993). Techniques for requirements elicitation, *Proceedings of the IEEE International Symposium on Requirements Engineering*, IEEE Computer Society Press, USA, pp. 152-164.

Greenbaum, T. L. (1998). Avoiding a virtual disaster, *HR Focus* 75(2): 11-12.

Greenspan, S., Mylopoulos, J., and Borgida, A. (1994). On formal requirements modeling languages: RML revisited, In *Proceedings 16th International Conference on Software Engineering*, Sorrento, May

Grenier, R., and Metes, G. (1995). *Going Virtual: Moving your Organisation into the 21st Century*, NJ: Prentice Hall.

Hacker, M. E., and Kleiner, B. M. (1996). Identifying Critical Success Factors Impacting Virtual Group Performance, *Proceedings of IEMC 96. Managing Virtual Enterprises: A Convergence of Communications, Computing and Energy Technologies*. 18-20 August, Vancouver, BC, Canada. IEEE publication, 196-200.

Hartman, F., and Guss, C. (1996). Virtual Teams - Constrained by Technology or Culture, *Proceedings of IEMC 96. Managing Virtual Enterprises: A Convergence of Communications, Computing and Energy Technologies*. 18-20 August, Vancouver, BC, Canada. IEEE publication, 645-650.

Hocking, L. (1996). Systems analysis and early design as the negotiation of meaning and interest, *Proceedings of the 7th Australasian Conference on Information Systems*, Tasmania, Australia.

Jarvenpaa, S. L., and Ives, B. (1994). The Global network Organisation of the Future: Information Management Opportunities and Challenges, *Journal of Management Information System,* 10(4), 25-57.

Jarvenpaa, S. L., and Leidner, D. E. (1998). Communication and Trust in Global Virtual Teams, *Journal of Computer-Mediated Communication*, 3 (4), http://www.ascusc.org/jcmc/vol3/issue4/jarvenpaa.html.

Jirotka, M., and Goguen, J. (1994). *Requirements Engineering – Social and Technical Issues*, Academic Press, London, UK.

Jones, C. (1994). Globalisation of software supply and demand, *IEEE Software*, Nov, 11(6):17-24.

Kimball, L. (1997). *Managing virtual teams*, Teams Strategies Conference, Toronto Canada URL: http://www.tmn.com/~lisa/vteams-toronto.htm [on-line accessed 20 Sep 2000].

Kuiper, D. (1998). The art of defining computer system requirements: say what you need and need what you say, *Hospital Materiel Management Quarterly*, May pp 14-21.

Laudon, K. C., and Laudon, J. P. (2000). *Management information systems: organisation and technology in the networked enterprise* (6th ed.), NJ: Prentice Hall.

Liou, Y. I., and Chen, M. (1994). Using group support systems and joint application development for requirements specification, *Journal of Management Information Systems* 10(3): 25-41.

Lipnack, J., and Stamps, J. (1997). *Virtual Teams: Reaching Across Space, Time, and Organizations with Technology*. New York: John Wiley & Sons, Inc.

Loucopoulos, P., and Karakostas, V. (1995). *System Requirements Engineering*, Berkshire, UK: McGraw-Hill Book Company Europe.

Macaulay, L. A. (1996). *Requirements Engineering*, Springer-Verlag, London.

McLeod, G., and Smith, D. (1996). *Managing information technology projects*, Boyd & fraser, ITP Publishing Company: USA

Meadows, C. J. (1996). Globalising software development, *Journal of Global Information Management* 4(1):5-15

Melymuka, K. (1997). Virtual Realities, *Computerworld*, 28 April, 71-73.

Odedra, M. (1993). Enforcement of foreign technology on Africa: its effect on society, culture and utilisation of information technology, in Beardon, C. and Whitehouse, D. (eds.) *Computers and Society*, Intellect, UK

Park, S. H., and Kim (2000). Implementation of an efficient requirements-analysis supporting system using similarity measure techniques, *Information and Software Technology* 42: 429-438.

Prabhakar, B. K. (1999). Internet based collaboration software: a study of impacts on distributed collaborative work. Thesis Dissertation [on-line accessed 17 Jul 2000] URL: www.lib.com/dissertations/previe_all/9930342.

Saiden, H., and Dale, R. (2000). Requirements engineering: making the connection between the software developer and customer, *Information and Software Technology* 42: 419-428.

Sommerville, I., and Sawyer, P. (1997). *Requirements engineering – a good practice guide*, John Wiley & Sons, England.

Thanasankit, T. (1999). Social interpretation of evolving requirements – the influence of Thai culture, in Zowghi, D. (ed.), *Proceedings of The Fourth Australian Conference on Requirements Engineering*, Macquarie University, Australia, 29-30 September, pp. 87-102.

Thanasankit, T., and Corbitt, B. J. (1999). Towards understanding managing requirements engineering: a case study of a Thai software house, in Yoong, P. (ed), *Proceedings of 10th Australasian Conference on Information Systems,* Vol. 2, 1-3 December, Victoria University of Wellington, New Zealand, pp. 993-1013.

Urquhart, C. (1996). Tell me what you want: a tale of an analyst, a client and the search for solutions - a case study in requirements gathering, *Proceedings of the 7th Australasian Conference on Information Systems*, Tasmania.

Viller, S., Bowers, J., and Rodden, T. (1999). Human factors in requirements engineering: a survey of human sciences literature relevant to the improvement of dependable systems development processes, *Interacting with Computers* 11: 665-698.

Chapter 7

Virtual Organization as a Chance for Enterprise Development

Jerzy Kisielnicki
Warsaw University, Poland

The theory that enterprise has been developing along with the development of Information Technology and, especially thanks to the possibilities offered by Virtual Organisations (VO) has been presented and proven. This enterprise has both local and global effect. The enterprise development provides for an increase of both small and big organisation competitiveness and also for an opportunity for new organisational entities to enter the market. My own research on enterprise conducted in the group of economy and marketing department students have fully confirmed the conclusions resulting from D.Blanchflower's and A.Oswald's research on enterprise. A significant percentage of the population aim at becoming entrepreneurs (about 75% of the people with university education). The theory that VO is an effective way to become an entrepreneur and to overcome the obstacles listed in the research has been presented. The main obstacles are lack of financial resources and lack of business experience. VO not only helps in becoming an entrepreneur but also, through specially built enterprise labs, provides training opportunities and skill development for those who want to follow this particular career path.

INTRODUCTION

This chapter attempt at substantiating the theory that enterprise has been developing along with the development of Information Technology and, especially thanks to the possibilities offered by Virtual Organisations (VO). This enterprise has both local and global effect. The enterprise development provides for an increase of both small and big organisation competitiveness and also for an opportunity for new organisational entities to enter the market. Activities connected with the VO development allow for decreasing unemployment level, especially amongst the people with secondary and higher education. VO has a significant share in the training and skill development within the range of enterprise.

VO also brings significant economic effects. Certain economic, technical and social barriers have to be overcome in order to create VO. The basis for the decision to use VO is constituted by the analysis of the relation between cost and effect. In the paper, this relation will be presented from both macro and micro perspective.

The basis for the presentation will be both theoretical work and research on economic enterprise. The research has been conducted on the basis of the following:

* literature analysis with special emphasis on description of working VO,
* own opinion polling conducted amongst the students (both full-time and working) of management departments,
* interviews with managers of various enterprises.

The survey has been compared with research conducted by D.Blanchflower and A.Oswald (1999). On the basis of the conducted survey, we would like to show the connection of VO with the problem of unemployment, especially amongst the people with higher education. Further research on this particular problem will follow.

VIRTUAL ORGANISATION AND ENTERPRISE

The notion of VO can be understood in various aspects. Virtual organisation is a totally new type of organisation which has developed thanks to the development of Information Technology and, especially, the existence of global information networks and big data bases. It can also be treated as a response to free market requirements and the necessity to adjust to its competitiveness.

The notion of VO has not yet been given one, generally accepted definition. This definition must surely be associated with the possibilities provided by modern Information Technology. The first to use the notion of virtual organisation were W. Davidow and M. Malone (1992). However, this notion has not been commonly accepted. Thus P.Drucker (1998) defines the organisations described by us as "network organisations," while M. Hammer and J. Champy (1994) define them as "post-re-engineering organisations." Quite interesting and somehow surprising is T. Peters' (1994) definition, who calls such an organisation "a crazy institution." It seems however, that the term "intelligent organisations" suggested by J. B. Quinn (1992) best defines the core of VO functioning.

Virtual reality is usually defined by describing qualities and not the existing physical features. In literature, the following descriptions of virtual organisation can be found:

1. "A temporary network of independent enterprises - suppliers, customers and even previous competitors - connected - by information technology in order to share skills and cost of access to new markets" (Byrne and Brandt, 1993).

2. "An artificial entity which, due to maximum usefulness for customers, and based on individual base competence, introduces integration of independent enterprises in the (chain) processes of creating products and which does not require additional outlays for co-ordination and does not diminish the customer's importance through its virtual reality" (Scholzch, 1996).

The quoted definitions may be disputed. Doesn't the aim of VO specified in the first definition constrict the notion? Also the definition of temporarily independent organisations is highly disputable. If the organisations act together, their independence must be, to a certain extent, limited.

Also in the second definition, the statement that VO is an "Artificial entity" is slightly ambivalent and the statement that they not require additional outlays for co-ordination is not always true.

In this chapter, it was assumed that virtual organisation is an organisation created on the basis of voluntary participation and its participants enter various relations in order to achieve common objective. Participation in the organisation does not require any legal agreements. The duration of each relationship is defined for each participant who creates the organisation. The decision to liquidate or re-construct the organisation can be made by every participant who first decides that the existence of such relationship is not in his favour and who is first to quit. VO operates in the so-called cyberspace, which allows for a very short duration of the relationship similarly to a very short time required for performing tasks.

VO is constantly changing, entering alliance with other organisations. It is an extremely flexible organisation which, depending on the situation can change the form of functioning and interest. The organisation, as it was mentioned before, remains in the relationship with the entire VO for as long as it is beneficial for it. It means that operating within the organisation lasts for as long as the participants are convinced that it is more beneficial for them than it would be if they operated on their own. VO can operate everywhere where benefits are expected. The benefits in a very broad sense are the objective of this type of an organisation.

Throughout this paper, I use the term VO in a dual meaning: first, as an organisation which performs previously listed tasks and which has its objectives established, second, as a model which allows for managerial skills development and thus develops features determined as enterprise.

Enterprise, according to R. Griffin (1993), is a process of organising and conducting business activity and taking risks associated with it. The problem which we are interested in here concerns the answer to the following question: Would a person who wants to become an entrepreneur undertake activities associated with creating VO and it's functioning? According to J. Stoner and partners (Stoner, Freeman and Gilbert, 1996) the function which distinguishes entrepreneurs is their capability to utilise production and capital factors to produce new products and services. Enterprise has always been connected with risk. In this paper, we are investigating whether the people who are not entrepreneurs are inclined to become ones with VO assistance. An entrepreneur can choose from many possible paths of company development. Which one would he/she choose? In this paper, we would like to answer the following questions:

1. Do students completing a specialised course of studies in the field of management takes into account a possibility of organising and conducting, on their own, a business activity connected with VO possibilities?

2. Do studying managers who utilise possibilities provided by VO are inclined to change their professional status and become entrepreneur?

3. Are model solutions associated with VO a good tool for learning enterprise?

CONDITIONS FOR CREATING VO AS A PROBLEM OF CHOOSING ENTERPRISE DIRECTION

The influence of VO on enterprise is connected with the fact that to create such a type of organisation and to become an entrepreneur is very simple. According to W. Titz (1995), it is enough to "sit at home with six computers and

Picture 1: Investment outlays and operating expenses in VO. Investment outlays and operating expenses.

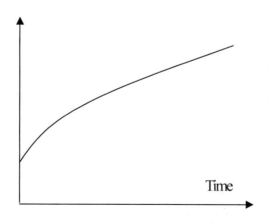

Time

Picture 2: Investment outlays and operating expenses in traditional organization.

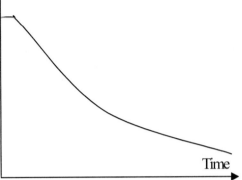

control a 10 billion dollar worth activity." It seems that the quoted specific amounts are disputable. The amounts are of symbolic meaning here. As practice shows, that to become an entrepreneur through using the path of performance with creating VO it is enough to:

* have a computer with access to Internet, have knowledge which your competitors do not have.

On the basis of the analysis of the investment outlays and operating expenses incurred in connection with VO creating and functioning and the comparative analysis of traditional organisations, their time characteristics may be presented in Pictures 1 and 2. Investment outlays and operating expenses.

The diagrams indicate that a break through point determined as the amount of the invested capital above which the organisation begins to exist and function on the market is much lower for the VO than for a traditional organisation. With time, the VO, in order to be competitive, must adjust to a quick progress in the field of Information Technology. However, the increase of financial outlays is not significantly rapid. It results from the fact, that the speed with which a computer operates increases according to the exponential function pattern while its price increases according to the linear function pattern. In a traditional organisation, significant outlays have to be made on activating production and start the activity. VO outlays do not depend so strongly on the field of activity as it is the case in traditional organisation.

A characteristic feature of the VO is a possibility to quickly generate profit. Theoretically, it is possible to generate income in a very short period of time after the organisation becomes to operate. In practice, the time required for generating profit is longer and it depends, like in traditional organisations, on coming into existence on the market. During a survey on various organisation types, on the basis of SWOT strategic analysis, the key factors which are important in the decision to create VO were determined.

It needs to be stressed that, in this particular situation, what is considered to be an opportunity may turn out to be trouble. For example, it is generally believed that the development of Internet may be a big opportunity for the development of virtual organisations. This way, the organisation does operate on a significantly big area. Special wide-spread reach is possible, i.e., Europe, Australia, New Zealand or Africa. However, there are more and more problems with utilising Internet. The most common problems are as follows:

* long waiting time for connection, especially during high traffic hours,

* matters connected with data protection which are not fully solved. Telecommunication organisations unanimously state that the majority of users causes high traffic on the lines which, in consequence blocks the telephone network. In order to improve this situation, additional high outlays need to be made to improve the infrastructure, which makes the VO possible to use. We shall come back to this problem further in the course of our analysis.

The decision to create a traditional organisation is connected with the optimum product size. Analysing unit cost of manufacturing products we can determine the optimum, i.e., such the production level where unit costs are minimal.

The decision to create a traditional organisation is connected with the optimum product size. Analysing unit cost of manufacturing products we can determine the optimum, i.e., such the production level where unit costs are minimal. In the case of analysing VO, the product size has no influence on the optimum production level. It depends solely on enterprise and the unit cost of manufacture may constantly decrease. This situation is illustrated by Pictures 3 and 4.

The simplicity of becoming an entrepreneur with the help of VO from the macro point of view is not always easy. Creating VO requires modern infrastructure countrywide or region-wise. A sample analysis of modern management infrastructure in Central and Eastern European countries shows how old-fashioned it is. Capacity and the speed of transferring information within the communication network fall short of the parameters achieved in Western European countries and in the United States and Japan. Also the cost of using the Internet is relatively high. These factors do not favour enterprise development on the path of creating VO. That is why the state policy and activity of telecommunication companies has significant impact on the development of VO creation.

ENTERPRISE AND VO; PROBLEMS OF CHOICE - SURVEY RESULTS

Survey on enterprise aimed at providing answers to two basic issues, namely:

* willingness of present and future management staff to become, in the nearest future, entrepreneurs, and

Table 1: SWOT analysis for the project of creating VO

Strengths – S		Weaknesses – W
1.	Big flexibility of operations, bigger than in traditional organisations.	❑ Necessity to have Information Technology which makes transactions possible to realise, including:
2.	Big speed of realising transactions in comparison with most traditional organisations.	a/ global network, b/ big databases.
3.	Common operating policy in the organisation.	❑ Necessity to trust all the organisations operating within virtual organisations.
4.	Reducing the cost of realising transactions in comparison with traditional organisation cost in this field.	❑ Possibility to join non-competent and not verified organisations. ❑ Lack of behaviour models.
5.	Reducing investment outlays on organisation development.	
6.	Minimising legal services associated with transactions	
Opportunities – O		Troubles – T
1.	Quick reaction to appearance of the so-called niches.	❑ Inefficiency of computer hardware mainly due to the fact that they are not adjusted to transmitting multi-media data.
2.	Realising transactions despite legal and organisational barriers.	❑ Lack of legal regulations for operating of organisations included in virtual organisation group and their responsibility towards each other and their clients.
3.	Introducing to common virtual organisation the best of each partner in the area where he is fully professional.	
4.	Possibility to use the most modern methods and management techniques.	❑ Lack of preparation of both clients and organisations to use virtual organisations.
5.	Possibility of co-operation of such partners who, in the organisational organisation model had not worked together.	❑ Lack of supervision and related to it lack of co-ordination in the field of realising transactions.
6.	Within informational links there are no state duty borders.	

Sources: own analysis

Picture 3: Unit costs in a traditional organisation.

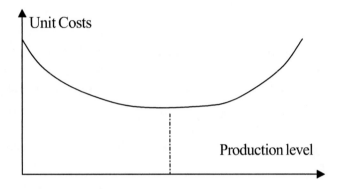

Picture 4: Unit costs in VO organisation (possible scenario).

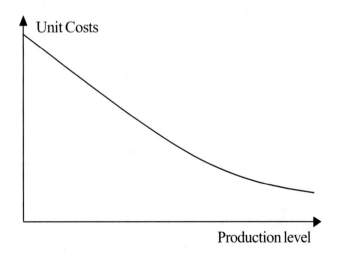

   *   obtaining information whether these people are willing to take into account the use of the possibilities given by VO in the process of building their professional careers.

   The basic question which has to be answered while analysing enterprise is how to define it. It was assumed in the survey that enterprise may be determined according to the standard which defines an employee's or future employee's (student's) attitude - would he prefer to be somebody's employee or self employed. This method is convergent with the method applied D.Blanchflower A.Oswald (1999) in their research on enterprise.

   The survey was conducted on the basis of a questionnaire distributed amongst the students of Economic Universities in Poland (Warsaw University, University of Commerce and Polish-Japanese Higher Institute for Information Technologies) in the period of February 1999 – June 1999. The questionnaire was anonymous.

   I have conducted survey on enterprise in three groups of potential entrepreneurs:

   1. students of economy and management departments who haven't worked in full-time employment but who have had some professional experience or who have worked on temporary contracts (the group constituted 650 people),

   2. working students of the same departments who study in order to change their status in the organisation or who are considering the decision to change their status from that of a paid employee to an entrepreneur (the group constituted 350 people),

   3. managers and executive staff who complement their knowledge in postgraduate courses, e.g. MBA. These people graduated from various types of universities and their education is very distant from the field of economy and management. For example, they hold the positions of directors or unit managers in hospitals (the group constituted 80 people),

   Results of the survey for the first group, i.e. students who have not worked in full-time employment.

   The following answers were given to the questionnaire questions relating to enterprise:

   1. Do you want to set up your own company immediately after graduation? Positive answers: 15%.

   2. Would you like to create your own organisation after getting appropriate experience?
   Positive answers: 85%.

   3. Will you work in an organisation owned by your parents or close relatives?
   Positive answers: 8 %.

   4. Do you plan, in the nearest future, to work in an organisation, which you do not own? Positive answers: 78%

Note: 18% of the respondents answered , It is difficult to say, I don't really know: the above questions.

The questionnaire also asked questions on the opinion on barriers in creating a self-owned organisation

The students think that the biggest barrier is:

*   lack of the knowledge needed to become an employer – positive answers: 38 %,
*   lack of sufficient funds - positive answers: 65 %,
*   lack of ideas to create an organisation - positive answers: 46 %,
*   fear of bankruptcy - positive answers: 47 %.

Results of the survey for the second and third group, i.e. managers and employees working for an organisation and the no- employed.

Here, the following answers were given. In brackets the answers given by the "non-employed" group were presented.

1. Do you want to become an entrepreneur in the nearest future? -   positive answers: 22% (30%).

2. If you had sufficient funds, would you want to become an entrepreneur ? -   positive answers- 66 % (75%).

3. Do you definitely not want to become an entrepreneur and choose a career in an organisation, which you do not own? - positive answers – 40% (65%).

Note: 23 % (15%) of the respondents answered: "I do not know, I'm thinking about it" to the above questions.

The questionnaire also asked questions on the respondents' opinion on barriers in creating their own organisation. There were four yes/no/ don't know format questions on this issue in the questionnaire. Both the managers and the employees think that the biggest barrier is:

*   lack of the knowledge needed to become an employer – positive answers: 15 % (8%),
*   lack of sufficient funds - positive answers: 80 % (77%),
*   lack of ideas to create an organisation - positive answers: 17 % (8%),
*   fear of bankruptcy and reluctance to take risks - positive answers: 43 % (56%),

Attention: the answers of the third group are given in brackets.

The questionnaire was supplemented with direct interviews which, in our opinion, enable us to learn more about the preferences and the mechanism of answering questions by the respondents. In the direct interviews, non-working and working students who wanted to become employers were asked if they consider VO to be the way to achieve their objective. The results are not so precise in this case. Very often the given answer suggested that the candidates are not really certain if they want to become entrepreneurs. Their fears were similar to those discussed in previously surveys presented in Hershey (Kisielnicki, 1999). It may be assumed that 20% of students of full-time studies consider the entrepreneur's career path with utilising possibilities given by VO. Amongst the working students, this percentage amounts to 5% and amongst the post-graduate and MBA students it amounted to 2-3 % only.

The obtained results suggest that the percentage of people interested in enterprise is quite significant and amounts to 66% up to 85% in the group of full-time students. The obstacles on the path of entrepreneur's career vary. In most cases it is determined as lack of sufficient funds. Most of the respondents consider this particular barrier crucial. The percentage of people who share this opinion amounts to 80%. It is difficult, for a beginning entrepreneur, to obtain a bank loan. That is why, those solutions which do not require big investment seem to be the most interesting ones. As it results from VO features presentation made in the previous point, it is this type of organisation, which seems to be most attractive. The barrier of having big financial resources at the beginning of business activity is not that strong in case of VO. To the contrary, as it was presented earlier, it is a good introduction to enterprise development.

Comparing the survey results in the group of full-time students with the results obtained from the group of working students it may be seen that the full-time students are more inclined towards taking risks. Young people in general are more inclined towards taking risks. The difference in the answers of full-time students and non-resident students to the question on their plan to become an employer amounts to 20%. The people who achieved high professional status are much more cautious. During the interviews, as it could have been expected, it turned out that it refers particularly to people who work in well known international organisations. Those people see their future career connected with the change of organisation and participation in competitions for higher positions rather than associating it with the career of an employer, especially in connection with VO.

Although the result analysis indicates how many people want to become entrepreneurs, the results should not be accepted without reservations. Every questionnaire which aims at learning about human behaviour has a significant error margin as it may never be known how the respondents would really behave when they had to make their choice in real life situations. The percentage of people declaring their willingness to become an entrepreneur is usually much higher than the real percentage of entrepreneurs in the group of professionally active people. The indicators of the entrepreneurs share in the number of professionally active people amounts to 12 – 15 %.

During the course of interviews, it turned out that a certain percentage of the respondents (about 1-2%) is interested in creating a small VO. These were especially young women taking care of small children at home. They would like to establish an enterprise at home. They also realise that getting employment in the existing organisation is very difficult. They see the VO as a chance to create an organisation, which enables people to be both a professionally active person and an entrepreneur.

VO AS A TOOL FOR TEACHING ENTERPRISE

The questionnaire results indicate that a significant percentage of students (both full-time and working) feel the need to learn about enterprise. The confrontation of attitudes: fear of an entrepreneur's career on one hand and the voiced willingness to become an entrepreneur on the other hand calls for some sort of a compromise. The obtained results were confirmed during the talks with full-time students who expressed their fear whether their studies may prepare them to become entrepreneurs. Also the working students, as well as those participating in MBA courses talked about their anxiety before the change of their position in the world of business. Their anxiety may be defined as fear of making a decision to change their stability of a manager to a risky position of an entrepreneur. That is why, I believe it is necessary to find a way of smooth transformation of a manager to an entrepreneur. For this, we need such a tool which makes learning and improving enterprise possible. This tool should also enable the person willing to become an employer to verify his/her skills.

I strongly believe that an enterprise laboratory may become such a tool. In such a lab, students could fulfil the following objectives:

*   improve their skills in the field of enterprise in a traditional sense, i.e., study the mechanisms operating on the market and also within the specific organisations such as a company, a bank or a supermarket.

*   Get acquainted with the rules for moving and making decisions in cyberspace where there are cybercorporations, virtual organisations, electronic money and electronic markets.

A new era of information society will most certainly require a change in the attitude towards enterprise. According to J. Martin (1996), the motto of modern organisations is "Small, Bright, Fast and Virtual." This is what a student should learn in the enterprise lab. The difficulties of creating such a lab result from the fact that reality should be presented in a perfect way. The applied models should also allow for projecting future.

Many universities undertake the attempt to build such labs. The forerunners in this field are computer labs in which both businesses games and simulation model software for making decisions in various types of organisations is used. The students learning about enterprise should feel as if they were in a real world where they have to make their decisions. Only then, they can see the results of their own decisions. Multi-media computers enable the student to see the real world and its digital description along with a graphic description. The lab should allow for work of a few teams who have various specific objectives to achieve. It is good to create such organisational solutions in which the teams have no visual contact (thus the teams should be placed in separate rooms). Communication between the teams should be made through data transmission networks.

The recommended technical conditions should allow each team to use, through the Internet, various databases and knowledge bases, in particular the data base of the stock exchange. A sample model of an enterprise lab operation is presented in Picture 5.

Picture 5: Enterprise lab structure.

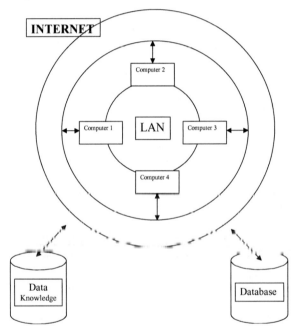

Technical equipment in the lab (computers and their peripheries) and the software should correspond to operational standards. I think, that for modelling an enterprise the following software is of great advantage: ERP (Enterprise Resource Planning), CRM (Customer Relationship Management), SCM (Supply Chain Management), teamwork systems of workflow type and specialised software enabling reality simulation and entering co-operation of each simulated organisation with other organisations. The weakness of enterprise teaching in a lab is that it will always be operating not in the real world but on a model. Even the best model does not fully reflect the reality. Also the decision making process is different in the case of spending your own money than in the case of spending unreal money.

Virtual reality and VO models allowed to create very useful tools for teaching enterprise. No such effective tools had existed before. The survey conducted in this field confirmed their usefulness and effectiveness. It is a solely philosophical question whether enterprise, unlike management, may be learnt or it is encoded in the genes. This undoubtedly interesting question is however not the subject of this paper.

CONCLUSIONS

VO is a very effective way to become an entrepreneur. The effects of applying VO are significant and universal. For the countries under transformation, the difficulties may be associated with lack of the appropriate infrastructure (network) and also relatively high cost of using the Internet. That is why, the countries which want to follow the path of enterprise increase should supplement their will with the appropriate policy.

My own research fully confirmed the conclusions resulting from D.Blanchflower's and A.Oswald's (1999) survey on the inclination to become en entrepreneur shared by a significant number of people (about 75% of the people with higher economic education). We believe, that VO is the best way to overcome obstacles and fear people face while creating their own institutions (i.e. lack of funds and experience). It seems that VO is the best method to overcome financial barriers and to learn enterprise as such. This organisation makes it possible to become an entrepreneur and also, through special enterprise labs provides possibilities for training and improvement for those people who want to choose this type of a career.

REFERENCES

Blanchlofer, D., and Oswald, A. (1999). Measuring Latent Entrepreneurship Across Nations, December, http://www:warwick.ac.uk/fac/soc/Economics/oswald/lague.pdf.

Byrne, J. A., and Brandt, R. (1993). The Virtual Corporation, *Business Week*, 8.02.

Davidow, W., and Malone, M. (1992). The Virtual Corporation, *HarperBusiness*, NY.

Drucker, P. (1998). The New Organisation, *Harvard Business Review*, no 1-2,1998.

Griffin, R. W. (1993). Management, Houghton Mifflin Company.

Hammer, M., and Champy, J. (1994). Reengineering the Corporation, *HarperBusiness*.

Kisielnicki, J. (1998). Virtual Organization as a Product of Information Society, *Informatica* 22, p. 3

Kisielnicki, J. (1999). Management Ethics in Virtual Organisation, *10-th International Conference of the Information Resources Management Association*, Hershey, Pennsylvania, May.

Martin, J. (1996). Cybercorp. The New Business Revolution , New York.

Peters, T. (1994). Crazy Times Call for Crazy Organisations, The Ton Peters Seminar; Vintage Books.

Quinn, J. B. (1992). The Intelligent Enterprise, The Free Press, NY.

Scholzch, Ch. (1996). Virtuelle Unternehmen - Organisatorische Revolution mit Strategischer Implikation, *Management & Computer*, 2.

Stoner, J. A. F., Freeman, R. E., and Gilbert, Jr., D. R. (1996). Management, Prentice Hall Inc.

Tapscott, D. (1998). The Digital Economy, Businessman Press, Warsaw.

Titze, W. (1995). Chairman von Gemini Consulting, uber das Ende der Konglomerate, in Hoffmann, W., Hanebeck, Ch., and Sheer, A.W. (Eds.), Kooperationsborse - Der Weg zum virtuellen Unternehmen , *Management & Computer* 4.

Chapter 8

The Development of Trust in Virtual Communities

Catherine Ridings
Lehigh University, Pennsylvania

David Gefen
Drexel University, Pennsylvania

This empirical study applies an existing scale to measure trust in the context of virtual communities on the Internet, and explores factors that build trust in this unique environment. The results show that trust is composed of two dimensions: trust in others' abilities and trust in benevolence/integrity. In addition, this research found that trust has relationships with perceived responsiveness, disposition to trust, and perceptions regarding the degree to which others confide personal information. Trust itself affected participants' desire to get and to provide information to others in the online community.

INTRODUCTION

The rapid growth of virtual communities on the Internet (Gross, 1999) and accompanying research expansion (Hiltz and Wellman, 1997; Wellman and Gulia, 1999) provides a fertile area of study. Virtual communities arise as a natural consequence of people coming together to discuss a common hobby, medical affliction, or other similar interest. Virtual communities can be defined as groups of people with common interests and practices that communicate regularly and for some duration in an organized way over the Internet through a common location or site.

Given that trust is among the most important antecedents of interpersonal interaction in general (Luhmann, 1979), and affects online behavior in particular

Previously Published in *Managing Information Technology in a Global Economy,* edited by Mehdi Khosrow-Pour, Copyright © 2001, Idea Group Publishing.

Figure 1

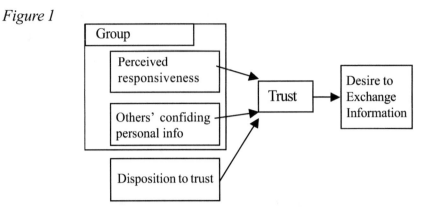

(Gefen, 1997; Gefen, 2000), this study examines the role of trust in virtual communities and how it affects the participants' desire to provide and receive information. The research also examined effects of group behavior and disposition to trust on the development of trust in other community members. The research model proposed by this study is presented in Figure 1.

THE CONCEPT OF TRUST

The definition of trust is dependent upon the situation in which it is being considered (Luhmann, 1979). Extending this logic, trust in virtual communities is likely to be better understood in the context of interpersonal relationships, i.e., trust between human beings (Rotter, 1971), or what Luhmann (1979) terms personal trust. His definition positions trust as a mechanism required to reduce social complexity and uncertainty, conditions that exist in virtual communities.

In this context, trust has been defined as the willingness to take a risk (Mayer, Davis and Schoorman, 1995). This definition has been also used in the study of trust in virtual teams (Jarvenpaa, Knoll and Leidner, 1998). Giffin (1967) has defined trust as "reliance upon the communication behavior of another person in order to achieve a desired but uncertain objective in a risky situation" (p. 105), further emphasizing that inherent in the notion of trust is some element of risk. Trust is thus a set of beliefs about others that will justify this risk (Giffin, 1967).

Trust is a pivotal and essential element in long-term social relationships (Blau, 1964; Luhmann, 1979). Individuals will often refrain from any interaction with others whom they do not trust (Luhmann, 1979). Trust is the confidence an individual has in that another person or persons will behave only as they are expected to and will do so in a socially acceptable and ethical manner (Lewis and Weigert, 1985; Luhmann, 1979; Mayer et al., 1995). This confidence is essential in long-term relationships because in the lack of a comprehensive set of rules to govern such relationships (Blau, 1964). Trust also reduces the fear that the trusted party will take unruly advantage or engage in otherwise opportunistic behavior (Fukuyama, 1995). Trust should be important in online communities for the same reasons. In an online community such opportunistic behaviors could include selling personal information that was provided with the understanding of confidentiality, using the community to deliberately and stealthily market products and services, making unfair practical jokes at members, and, in general, behaving in a dysfunctional manner that ruins the community. Such behavior applies also to any other type of community, except that in the case of an online community the anonymity provided by the Internet make such behavior much easier to perform by the perpetrator and much harder to notice by the victim.

HYPOTHESES

Trust is built through successful interpersonal interaction (Blau, 1964; Gefen, 2000; Luhmann, 1979). An individual who posts messages on a community most often expects some type of response. If there are no responses, trust in others will not develop, because of a lack of a successful interpersonal interaction. Conversely, if an individual posts a message and in a short period of time there are numerous replies, trust should be built. Thus it is hypothesized:

H1: Participants' perceptions of other members' responsiveness will be positively related to their trust in other community members.

An individual must have some cause for developing trust in others (Luhmann, 1979). In a virtual community trust is built by reading what others post. If others post personal information about themselves, they are making themselves appear to be more than just a stranger, and are showing that they trust others with sensitive information. By disclosing their gender, age, or perhaps a personal problem, they are less a stranger and more an acquaintance or friend. This personal information is intimately related to the development of trust.

Handling personal information with sensitivity has been suggested as building trust for e-commerce sites (Dayal, Landesberg and Zeisser, 1999). Just as trust is essential for consumers to divulge personal information for electronic commerce, it is proposed here that virtual community members will have increased trust in others when they see others confiding personal information on the virtual community. Thus it is hypothesized:

H2: Participants' perceptions of the degree to which others confide personal information will be positively related to their trust in other community members.

Disposition to trust is defined as a general willingness to depend on others (McKnight, Cummings and Chervany, 1998). This trait is stable across situations (Mayer et al., 1995). Disposition to trust may be especially effective when the parties are still unfamiliar with one another (Mayer et al., 1995; Rotter, 1971), as might be the case in a virtual community, where almost anyone can reply. Mayer et al. (1995) proposed that disposition to trust is positively related to trust. Disposition to trust has been empirically found to be directly related to trust in virtual settings (Gefen, 2000; Jarvenpaa et al., 1998). Therefore, it is hypothesized that:

H3: Participants' disposition to trust will be positively related to their trust in other community members.

Trust enables and determines the nature of interpersonal relationships (Blau, 1964; Gefen, 2000; Jarvenpaa et al., 1998). In a trusting environment, people are more inclined to help others and to request others' help, while in a less trusting environment, people tend to shun away from providing information or requesting it (Blau, 1964; Luhmann, 1979). It is thus hypothesized that when participants are trusting, that they will be more inclined to provide and request information:

H4.1: Participants' trust will be positively related to their willingness to provide information to others.

H4.2: Participants' trust will be positively related to their willingness to request information from others.

METHOD

The methodology used to test the hypotheses was a cross-sectional survey. Much of the past scholarly research in computer-mediated communication (CMC) has conducted experiments in laboratory settings (Sudweeks and Simoff, 1999). However, external validity in these cases is problematic since participants are a captive audience, sample size is small, and researchers usually contrast CMC with face-to-face interaction (Sudweeks et al., 1999). Experiments also have limita tions due to the difficulty in manipulating the experimental conditions (Potter, 1971) To maximize external validity, this research used field survey methodology as the most appropriate to test actual membership perception regarding trust in real virtual communities.

The population of interest was members of virtual communities on the Internet. It was highly desirable to use the technology of the Internet to both contact a subset of this population and to collect the data. Therefore, the survey was posted on the Internet as a Web page, and the request to participate was posted directly on the virtual communities.

MEASURES

Existing scales from the literature were reviewed and items were carefully adapted or developed for each construct. Both a pretest and pilot were conducted. All of the items (Appendix) were measured with 7 point Likert-type scales ranging from strongly disagree to strongly agree.

Trust

Trust is considered in this study as a belief. The measurement of the components of trust is taken from Jarvenpaa, Knoll, and Leidner (1998). The scales were altered slightly to fit the virtual community environment.

Responsiveness of Others

No existing scale could be found to measure the responsiveness of others in an environment such as a virtual community. Gefen and Keil (1998) developed a scale to measure the responsiveness of developers. While not directly applicable to this study, the notion of being responsive to requests (Gefen et al., 1998), was incorporated into the scale developed for this study. The items in this scale referred to the timeliness and quantity of responses.

Degree to Which Others Confide Personal Information

No existing scale could be found to measure the degree to which people confide personal information in an environment such as a virtual community. Thus a scale was developed specifically for this study. Consistent with the literature reviewed above (Dayal et al., 1999; Parks and Floyd, 1995), the items in the scale ask about the willingness of others to share personal information.

Disposition to Trust

The scale to measure disposition to trust was adapted from Gefen (2000). Gefen used the scale to measure disposition to trust in the environment of the Internet, which is similar to the environment in the present research.

Desire to Exchange Information

The most often cited reason for joining a virtual community is to exchange information (Hagel and Armstrong, 1997; Wellman et al., 1999). A scale to measure this desire was created specifically for this study. Drawing on the reasons from the literature, the items in the scale ask about coming to the community for information, facts, advice on carrying out tasks, and to share their knowledge. The first three items focus on getting information, the last two on giving information.

SAMPLING PROCEDURE

Researchers have developed criteria in order to include communities from study, such as minimal traffic volume and a minimum number of different posters (Witmer, Colman and Katzman, 1999). Therefore, rigorous criteria were developed regarding minimum number of postings and users. These criteria were chosen to make sure the communities were large and active. Communities using bulletin boards were targeted for this study since they could be easily observed.

In order to collect data from a wide variety of communities and to maintain randomness in the sample, a rigorous procedure was adopted in order to select communities for the study. A random number generator was used to pick communities from search engine results. Forty communities were selected, and the message requesting participation was posted on each of these directing respondents to the URL for the survey.

Data Collection and Response Rate

Community members were given 10 days to respond. A total of 696 responses were received from the 40 communities. Of this total, 663 responses from 36 communities were usable.

Self-selection is a limitation, which can be addressed by matching the demographics of the sample with the demographics of known population of Internet users, a procedure that has been used in similar Web-based survey research (Bellman, Lohse and Johnson, 1999). Unfortunately, there is virtually no public data available about the demographics of bulletin board users. However, several surveys of Internet users can be used to compare demographics (http:// cyberatlas.internet.com). The present sample is fairly similar to other surveys of Internet users.

Response rate calculation is difficult since it is impossible to know how many people viewed the post requesting participation. Several attempts at response rate calculation are reported here. One possible measure is the number of completed surveys per the number of unique visits to the survey. The rate of completions per visit was 60.66%, and the rate of usable surveys per visit was 57.71%.

A contact was made with one of the communities to gather information about community size to estimate response rate. This board averages about 875 visits per day. In the first 24 hours of the survey request, 44 surveys were received. If this was an average day, approximately 5% of visitors responded. Respondents from this community, according to survey responses, believe the core group of regular contributors is about 61 to 80 people. 87 of the 90 respondents are active posters. Therefore, it may be that most active community members did respond to the survey, yielding a response rate near 100%.

Response rate could be calculated by observing the community after the survey request was posted, and seeing how many people posted during this time period. This is problematic because as the request to survey moves farther down in the list of active threads it is unlikely that someone posting on the board five days after the researcher's post would even scroll that far down to read all posts. Nevertheless, to provide another possible way of ascertaining response rate, the number of unique posters on another board was counted for the 10-day period. There were 107 unique people who posted. There were 10 responses from this board, which is 9.3% of 107. This ignores any lurkers who might have read the post but declined to participate.

SAMPLE CHARACTERISTICS

The largest response from a single community was 90, (13.57%). There were 14 communities from which there were fewer than 10 respondents (n=78).

The majority (62%) was male, and 78% were between 18-49 years of age. The vast majority (91%) was Caucasian, and most (67%) had an education of at least some college. Most respondents were from the United States (93%) and were employed full time (70%). These demographics are consistent with most surveys of Internet users (www.cyberatlas.com). The respondents spent an average of 3-6 hours a week in the community and have been members, on average, for 9-12 months.

MEASUREMENT OF THE VARIABLES

A factor analysis using the Principal Components method with Varimax rotation was performed. Results suggested that several items be dropped from the scales in order to achieve a high level of reliability and validity. Specifically, an item was dropped if (a) it did not meet the threshold loading of 0.40 on any factor, (b) its highest loading on an expected factor was not above 0.60, or (c) it showed a significant variance across multiple factors (Hair, Anderson and Tatham, 1987).

Perceived responsiveness, desire to give information, and desire to get information loaded exactly as expected. Each had acceptable Cronbach alpha reliabilities: .85 for desire to get information, .89 for desire to give information, and .90 for responsiveness. Confiding personal information and disposition to trust also loaded on separate factors as expected after dropping the items, with resulting Cronbach alphas of .89 and .86 respectively.

The trust items loaded on two distinct factors. Other researchers (Blau, 1964; Jarvenpaa et al., 1998; Mayer et al., 1995) have suggested that trust is composed of trust in abilities, benevolence, and integrity. One factor emerged as the trust in abilities dimension (alpha=.91). Trust in benevolence and trust in integrity were merged together in the other factor. Other researchers (Gefen, 1997) have found similar results. Since very few of the integrity items remain in the factor analysis, it may be that integrity needs to be measured differently in the online environment. To maintain consistency, this factor was named trust in benevolence/integrity (alpha=.88).

TESTING THE HYPOTHESES

Linear regression was used to test the proposed relationships. The results are presented in Tables 1 and 2.

The perception of others' responsiveness was significant in the regressions, supporting H1. The degree to which others confide personal information was significant, supporting H2. Finally, disposition to trust was also significantly related

Table 1

Abilities Integrity Variables	Trust in	Trust in Benevolence/
Perception of Responsiveness	.317**	.371**
Others confide personal info	.196**	.152**
Disposition to trust	.157**	.168**
R^2	.214**	.241**

**p<.001

Table 2

Variables	Desire to Give Info. β	Desire to Get Info. β
Trust in Ability	.168**	.266**
Trust in Integrity/Benevolence	.191**	.302**
R^2	.101**	.253**

**p<.001

to trust, supporting H3. Trust itself affected both the desire to give and desire to get information, supporting H4.1 and H4.2.

DISCUSSION

Two dimensions of trust emerged in this study. Trust in abilities was distinct, but trust in benevolence and integrity combined into one dimension. It may be that conformance to socially acceptable behavior or standards (integrity) and a desire to do good (benevolent intentions) are synonymous in the virtual community environment. Jarvenpaa et al. (1998) applied the trust scale in a virtual team setting where the teams were composed of students working on a class project. This situation is distinctly different from the case of virtual communities where participants are drawn by a common interest.

This research sought to understand what mechanisms build trust in virtual communities. Investigate of trust antecedents revealed that perceptions of responsiveness, the degree to which others confide personal information, and one's own disposition to trust were all positively related to the dimensions of trust. This indicates that virtual community members will trust more when they perceive others are responsive with regard to personal, subjective perceptions of quantity and timeliness of responses. As expected, when others confide personal information, trust in others is higher. Thus when others show that they are willing to take a risk by giving information about themselves, higher trust in these others exists. This is significant because it shows that even though participants may come to talk about a particular topic (Honda motorcycles or real estate appraisal), they will trust others more if they know something personal about them. Disposition to trust is also positively related to trust in others, indicating that people who are generally trusting exhibit more trust in others.

As expected, trust plays a significant part in participants' desire to exchange information. People are more likely to have a desire to exchange information with others if they feel trust in others' abilities and benevolence/integrity.

The results of this study have limitations. There are thousands of communities on the Internet, and identification of the population of interest (virtual community users) is difficult at best. Response rate was virtually impossible to calculate. Finally, the cross-sectional design does not afford the opportunity to infer causality among the constructs.

IMPLICATIONS

The results of this study have many implications. Bulletin boards are beginning to be used frequently in education and organizational work in order to allow students or professionals to exchange information asynchronously. Work groups with these characteristics are certainly similar in many ways to virtual communities. Bulletin boards provide an appropriate to support this work. The primary reason why people join and use virtual communities is to exchange information. For the bulletin boards to be successful (i.e., for participants to exchange information) and foster the sense of community indicative of success, trust must be present. This research shows that it may be important to have team members that have a high disposition to trust, and it is important that the participants feel that others are responsive and willing to confide personal information. Communities will not achieve their goal, information exchange, without trust.

REFERENCES

Bellman, S., Lohse, G. L., & Johnson, E. J. (1999). Predictors of Online Buying Behavior. *Communications of the ACM, 42*(12), 32-38.

Blau, P.M. (1964). *Exchange and Power in Social Life*. New York: John Wiley & Sons.

Dayal, S., Landesberg, H., and Zeisser, M. (1999). How to build trust online. *Marketing Management*, 8(3): p. 64-73.

Fukuyama, F. (1995). *Trust: The Social Virtues & the Creation of Prosperity*. New York, NY: The Free Press.

Gefen, D. (1997). *Building Users' Trust in Freeware Providers and the Effects of This Trust on Users' Perceptions of Usefulness, Ease of Use and Intended Use of Freeware*, Doctoral Dissertation. Georgia State University: Atlanta.

Gefen, D. (2000). *E-commerce: The Role of Familiarity and Trust.* Omega: Forthcoming.

Gefen, D. and Keil, M. (1998). The Impact of Developer Responsiveness on Perceptions of Usefulness and Ease of Use: An Extension of the Technology Acceptance Model. *The DATABASE for Advances in Information Systems,* 29(2): p. 35-49.

Giffin, K. (1967). The Contribution of Studies of Source Credibility to a Theory of Interpersonal Trust in the Communication Process. *Psychological Bulletin,* 68(2): p. 104-120.

Gross, N. (1999). *Building Global Communities,* in *BusinessWeek Online.* Available at http://businessweek.com/datedtoc/1999/9912.htm

Hagel, J. and Armstrong, A. G. (1997). *Net Gain: Expanding Markets Through Virtual Communities.* Boston: Harvard Business School Press.

Hair, J.F., Anderson, R. E., and Tatham, R. L. (1987). *Multivariate Data Analysis with Readings.* New York: Macmillian.

Hiltz, S.R. and Wellman, B. (1997). Asynchronous Learning Networks as a Virtual Classroom. *Communications of the ACM,* 40(9): p. 44-49.

Jarvenpaa, S.L., Knoll, K., and Leidner, D. E. (1998). Is Anybody Out There? Antecedents of Trust in global Virtual Teams. *Journal of Management Information Systems,* 14(4): p. 29-64.

Lewis, J. D. and Weigert, A. (1985). Trust as a Social Reality, *Social Forces* (63) 4, pp. 967-985.

Luhmann, N. (1979). *Trust and Power.* Great Britain: John Wiley and Sons.

Mayer, R.C., Davis, J. H., and Schoorman, F. D. (1995). An Integrative Model of Organizational Trust. *Academy of Management Review,* 20(3): p. 709-734.

McKnight, D.H., Cummings, L. L., and Chervany, N. L. (1998). Initial trust formation in new organizational relationships. *Academy of Management Review,* 23(3): p. 473-490.

Parks, M.R. and Floyd, K. (1995). Making Friends in Cyberspace. *Journal of Computer Mediated Communication,* 1(4).

Rotter, J.B. (1971). Generalized Expectancies for Interpersonal Trust. *American Psychologist,* 26: p. 443-450.

Sudweeks, F. and Simoff, S. J. (1999). *Complementary Explorative Data Analysis: The Reconciliation of Quantitative and Qualitative Principles,* in S. Jones, (Ed.), *Doing Internet Research: Critical Issues and Methods for Examining the Net,* Sage Publications: Thousand Oaks. p. 29-55.

The Lifestyles of the Online Shoppers. http://cyberatlas.internet.com/big_picture/demographics/article/0,1323,5901_256591,00.html.

The World's Online Populations. http://cyberatlas.internet.com/big_picture/
geographics/article/0,1323,5911_151151,00.html.

Wellman, B. and Gulia, M. (1999). *Virtual communities as communities*, in M.
A. Smith and P. Kollock (Eds.), *Communities in Cyberspace*, New York:
Routledge, p. 167-194.

Witmer, D.F., Colman, R. W., and Katzman, S. L. (1999). *From Paper-and-
Pencil to Screen-and-Keyboard: Toward a Methodology for Survey Re-
search on the Internet*, in S. Jones (Ed.), *Doing Internet Research,* Sage
Publications: Thousand Oaks. p. 145-161.

Women Taking the Internet Lead. http://cyberatlas.internet.com/big_picture/de-
mographics/article/0,1323,5901_221541,00.html.

Chapter 9

Opportunities for Service-Learning Partnerships in the Information Systems Curriculum

Jonathan Lazar and Doris Lidtke
Towson University, USA

Service-learning partnerships involve students taking part in community service that relates to their academic course experience. Students who major in information systems are increasingly being provided with real-world experiences. These real-world experiences offer numerous benefits. Students can immediately apply their course knowledge to real-world situations. Students can get the experience of grappling with political, social, and ethical issues in a workplace setting. In addition, students can develop a sense of civic responsibility, by contributing their skills to their communities. This chapter presents the issues involved in implementing the service-learning paradigm in an information systems curriculum. Examples of successful service-learning courses are presented, and new possibilities for service-learning courses are discussed.

INTRODUCTION

Courses in the information systems curriculum are increasingly incorporating hands-on experiences for students. Student evaluation is no longer limited to exams and research papers. Projects are becoming an increasingly common part of

Previously Published in *Managing Information Technology in a Global Economy,* edited by Mehdi Khosrow-Pour, Copyright © 2001, Idea Group Publishing.

the Information Systems curriculum. It is one thing to describe to students how an information system is developed, modified, or maintained. It is a totally different experience for students to experience first-hand an information system being developed, modified, or maintained. If the students can work with real users in a real-world experience to develop an information system, this is a valuable experience. The question is how to place students in an appropriate real-world setting. An educational paradigm called service-learning would seem to be appropriate for forming a partnership. In service-learning, students take part in community service experiences relating to their coursework (Jacoby, 1996). This paper will discuss opportunities for implementing the service-learning paradigm in the information systems curriculum.

SERVICE-LEARNING

Service-learning is an educational paradigm in which students take part in community service (Jacoby, 1996). This community service is structured to relate to course material, with the goal of strengthening the course experience. The idea is that the service-learning projects offer an opportunity to immediately apply the material learned in the classroom. Instead of simply discussing the concepts in a classroom setting, students get a chance to use their knowledge to assist others (Jacoby, 1996). While gaining experience working in their community, students also strengthen their sense of civic responsibility. Service-learning can provide a strong educational experience for the students involved.

Community-based non-profit organizations are in need of assistance with technology. Non-profit organizations tend to have smaller budgets for technology, and therefore cannot afford to hire many people to work on their technology needs. For instance, schools frequently cannot afford to provide Internet training for their teachers (Lazar and Norcio, 2001). In some cases, schools might be required to spend their technology budgets on capital expenses such as hardware and software, instead of developing new resources or managing existing resources or providing training (General Accounting Office, 1998). Other non-profit organizations, such as parent groups, and support groups, usually are dependent on donations of money and time to effectively utilize technology. Groups of technology workers may come in on a Saturday to wire a school for the Internet. Professional user groups may take donations of old computer equipment, refurbish and upgrade the computers, and then donate the now-functional computers to non-profit organizations in the local community. Many community groups are dependent on the goodwill of their local citizens to effectively use technology.

Service-learning is a useful technique for incorporating real-world experiences into the curriculum. Local community groups are in need of assistance with technology. Students are in need of real-world experiences that relate to their course material, because they gain a better understanding of user issues only by working with real users (Lazar and Preece, 1999). By getting real-world experience, students can get a sampling of the ethical and political issues that can occur in a workplace (Lazar & Preece, 1999). Through their real-world projects, students may also make contacts, and develop professional networks that can help them in their careers (Shneiderman, 1998). In addition, students frequently assume that implementing an information system consists simply of programming. By going through the complete development lifecycle, working with users to gather requirements, develop a system, and then implement that system, students can see that there is much more than coding involved in information systems development.

Although service-learning is traditionally used in conjunction with classroom-based courses, service-learning could also be implemented as a co-op or internship program. Students can apply their knowledge from a number of different classes, to assist a non-profit organization with their technology needs. Of particular value are internships which allow students to be involved in the complete process of analyzing, designing, implementing, delivering, and maintaining a system. Alternatively, students can learn a great deal from in-depth immersion in one or more of these development phases.

There are many other advantages of service-learning. Students can "learn to learn," meaning that they learn new technologies, new techniques, and new programming languages in real-time, in the workplace. In a service-learning placement, students can learn the importance of documentation, an appreciation for which is not easily motivated in the classroom. By working with others in a real-world setting, students can develop the skills needed for successful teamwork. By seeing a variety of information technology positions available within an organization, students may have a better grasp of their area of interest, which can assist students in choosing elective courses to complete their degree program. Students gain valuable experience to help them prepare for their professional career. And when students have completed their degree requirements, their service-learning placements can be used as a "portfolio" of work, to show their level of competence (Lazar, 2000).

REQUIREMENTS FOR A SERVICE-LEARNING COURSE

An information systems course using the service-learning paradigm is appropriate for juniors or seniors who have a thorough understanding of the issues involved in the process of developing an information system. It is by no means appropriate for freshman or those new to the information systems major. Many new students tend to think that developing an information system begins with sitting down and coding. In reality, a long process of analysis and conceptual design first takes place. Because this understanding is necessary for a successful service-learning placement, a good prerequisite for a service-learning course would be either a basic **Systems Analysis and Design** and/or **Project Management** course. Both of these courses involve the process of developing an information system, as well as the issues (political, legal, user, financial) that can arise when building an information system. With this knowledge base, students are qualified to enter an organization and build an information system.

Good community partners are a requirement for a successful service-learning experience. Ideally, these partners should be non-profit organizations. Non-profit organizations, which generally have smaller technology budgets, are frequently unable to afford assistance with their technology needs. These non-profit organizations are ecstatic to have bright students to assist them, and the students are welcomed with open arms. The students feel that they are wanted, and that they can make a difference. This makes for a very positive experience for the students. In one service-learning placement, the non-profit organization was so happy to have the students there, that the contacts in the non-profit organization hugged the students every time that they came for a client meeting, and baked cookies for the students to thank them for all of their hard work. Good community partners are essential to the service-learning paradigm, because if the clients do not find the time to meet with the students, the service-learning project cannot be successful. At the same time, students must understand that they have made a commitment to the community partner, and students must live up to their end of the bargain. Feeling tired or partying the weekend before is not an excuse for late work in the workplace, and neither is it acceptable in a service-learning project. Service-learning mirrors the responsibilities that students will face when they enter the workplace after graduation.

SERVICE-LEARNING EXAMPLES

The following section will describe some of the possibilities for implementing service-learning in the information systems curriculum:

Web Design

As part of the requirements for a web design course, students can develop small web sites for non-profit organizations in the community (Lazar, 2000). In such a situation, the students must learn about both the web design process, as well as web programming, such as HTML and JavaScript. Alternatively, students could learn more about web design applications, such as FrontPage and Dreamweaver. For this service-learning approach to be successful, students must have both the tools to build web sites, as well as an understanding of the development process (Lazar, 2000). Students can go through the full lifecycle of analysis and design, by determining user requirements, developing a web site, and then testing and installing a web site. In addition, students can also re-design currently existing web sites, which can give students experience in maintaining information systems, a topic which is frequently left out of analysis and design courses.

Database Design

Students in database classes can apply their knowledge to help community-based organizations manage their data. Jimenez (1995) describes a class where students analyzed, designed, and implemented a database for a county department of health and human services. This relational database stored resources available related to child care (Jimenez, 1995). The students performed an analysis, developed entity-relationship diagrams, designed a relational database, and then implemented the database in Windows-based software database application. Users were involved in the development process, and functionality and usability testing were performed. Students also learned the importance of project documentation (Jimenez, 1995).

Computer Applications

Many universities offer courses dealing with computer applications such as word processing, spreadsheet, and database. These courses tend to be at the 100-level or 200-level. Although word processing is a popular tool, many employees in non-profit organizations are not as familiar with the powerful features of spreadsheet and database software. As part of their course requirements, students could assist non-profit organizations in developing databases of members or mailing lists, or in developing spreadsheets for tracking finances. Because students only receive very basic training in using these software tools, these projects might be relatively small, but they can give students a good introductory experience of working with users. These types of projects would also tie-in very well with business classes such as marketing and accounting. These courses typically enroll students of freshman and sophomore rank, so it is essential to make sure that the students are well-equipped to operate in a workplace, and understand the systems development life cycle, before sending the students out for a service-learning experience.

Online Communities

Online communities are network-based resources where people with common interests can go online to communicate (using listservers, bulletin boards, etc.) and share resources (Lazar and Preece, 1998). An online communities course is offered where students examine and develop online communities. In the service-learning approach, students talk to non-profit organizations and determine where there is a need for an online community. Students then build or re-design online communities for groups such as parent support groups, local schools, neighborhood associations, and others who want to utilize an online community (Lazar and Preece, 1999). The students become familiar not only with the software tools for building online communities, but also with the user considerations in building an online community (Lazar and Preece, 1999).

Business Process Redesign

A graduate course in business process redesign (BPR) included a community partnership, where students worked in a local organization to help redesign business processes. The course objective was to teach BPR concepts and techniques (Kock, 2000). The instructor decided that the most effective way for students to learn about BPR was to redesign business processes for a local company (Kock, 2000). The specific IT processes to be redesigned included help desk call response, new employee account set-up, and asset management (Kock, 2000). Although this partnership involved a for-profit company, this same course approach could be used for a non-profit organization. By the end of the course, students had created three deliverables, describing the analysis of the current processes, possible IT approaches for process redesign, and cost/benefit analyses of the different implementation plans (Kock, 2000).

Senior Capstone Course

Many information systems programs include a "capstone" course at the end of the program. These courses tend to synthesize the knowledge gained in other courses, and therefore, these courses are very appropriate for service-learning partnerships. Students can utilize skills gained in other courses, such as programming, database design, systems analysis and design, and networking. The type of service-learning project (database, programming, web design, etc.) may change, based on what the needs of the community-based organization are. The service-learning project could involve programming skills, software skills, networking skills, and/or database skills.

Networking

It is possible that students in networking courses could assist non-profit organizations in implementing local area networks. Frequently, non-profit organizations such as schools cannot afford many of the costs associated with implementing computer networks. Students could help in the network planning stages, the physical wiring, or the implementation of working networks.

THE EFFECT OF INFORMATION SYSTEMS ACCREDITATION

Accreditation has long been a strong component of Computer Science programs, through the Computer Science Accreditation Board (http://www.csab.org). Accreditation efforts in Information Systems have increased, and it is expected that accreditation will play a major part in information systems programs in the future. Accreditation teams are focusing on the goals and objectives of Information Systems programs, and then determining whether the programs are meeting their stated goals. Service-learning projects can be helpful in program assessment, by showing how well students are able to perform in real-life situations. Real-world projects completed by students can demonstrate that students, upon completing a program of study, have mastered the subject material and are able to apply their knowledge in a real-world setting to solve real-world problems. Successfully completed service-learning projects can be an additional outcome measure to evaluate the effectiveness of the curriculum in an IS program. More information about IS Accreditation is available at:(http://cis.bentley.edu/ISA/)

SUMMARY

Service-learning, when implemented appropriately, can be a good paradigm for information systems courses. Students can gain experience working in real-world settings with real users. These service experiences can help students determine which career path is most appropriate for them. At the same time, local community organizations get assistance with their technology needs, which they otherwise could not afford. Service-learning has successfully been used in courses such as web design and database design, and it could be appropriate for other courses, such as networking and senior capstone courses.

REFERENCES

Jacoby, B. (1996). *Service learning in higher education*. San Francisco: Jossey-Bass Publishers.

Jimenez, S. (1995). A computer science service project. *Proceedings of the CHI 95: Human Factors in Computing* (interactive posters),151-152.

Kock, N., Auspitz, C., & King, B. (2000). Using the web to enable industry-university collaboration: An action research study of a course partnership. *Informing Science,* 3(3), 157-166.

Lazar, J. (2000, in press). Teaching web design though community service projects. *Journal of Informatics Education and Research*, 2(2).

Lazar, J., & Norcio, A. (2001, in press). Service-Research: Community Partnerships for Research and Training. *Journal of Informatics Education and Research.*

Lazar, J., & Preece, J. (1998). Classification schema for online communities. *Proceedings of the 1998 Association for Information Systems Americas Conference*, 84-86.

Lazar, J., & Preece, J. (1999). Implementing service learning in an online communities course. *Proceedings of the International Academy for Information Management 1999 Conference*, 22-27.

Shneiderman, B. (1998). Relate-Create-Donate: a teaching/learning philosophy for the cyber-generation. *Computers & Education, 31,* 25-39.

United States General Accounting Office. (1998). *School technology: Five school districts' experiences in funding technology programs* (GAO/HEHS-98-35). Washington, D.C.: United States General Accounting Office.

Chapter 10

Information Security
for Libraries

Gregory B. Newby
University of North Carolina at Chapel Hill, USA

Libraries have made significant investments in computer-based resources, training and services. However, such investments need to be protected from misuse or mistake by taking an active role in information security.

INTRODUCTION

By most accounts, the proliferation of the Internet and other computer technologies has been highly beneficial to libraries. Investment in everything from online databases and computing equipment to personnel and training is significant. Libraries need to have policies, protection measures and trained staff in place in order to safeguard their investments in computer and computer-related technologies, personnel and services.

This chapter will address the topic of information security, making concrete recommendations for safeguarding information and information access tools. Instead of giving detailed instructions for security techniques, the emphasis here is on setting the agenda for the role of security in library environments.

Historically, formal training for librarians' use of information technology was in the relatively narrow specializations of library automation and online searching. Library automation training (e.g., Ross, 1984) was for library staff that would manage, evaluate, and sometimes design and implement technology systems in libraries. The OPAC (Online Public Access Catalog) was a centralized system based in the library or a regional office for circulation and holdings information, as well as other types of data (serials control, acquisitions, cataloging, etc.). Library automation training seldom mentioned any type of security for protection of data,

privacy or equipment. Even fairly recent books on the use of computers in libraries, such as Ogg (1997), make almost no mention of security issues.

Today, library environments are increasingly reliant on computer technology.
Many libraries of all sizes have discontinued use of card catalogs in favor of electronic versions – and many of the electronic versions previously accessible only
via terminals within library buildings are now Web-accessible. Online searching of
a plethora of databases and other information sources has become ubiquitous for
the end user, rather than being restricted to librarians trained in online searching.
Access to general-purpose microcomputers and software, as well as to the Internet,
is offered in nearly all libraries of significant size.

It is the position of this chapter that security training for librarians is extremely
weak, both on the job and in educational institutions. One result is that opportunities for problems related to information security in libraries are likely in many
library environments. Although some recent texts on library security address aspects of information and computer security (for example, Shuman, 1999), most
do not.

In this chapter, a pragmatic approach to addressing the information security
needs of libraries is presented. Effective information security must involve active
staff and active measures to minimize risk of damage, theft, subversion or sabotage. Following an overview of information security, sections discuss security personnel, privacy policy, the OPAC, public access workstations, and the library's
Internet connection. A concluding section addresses the emerging role of security
training for librarians.

OVERVIEW OF INFORMATION SECURITY

Information security is not simply computer security. Whereas computer security relates to securing computing systems against unwanted access and use, information security also includes issues such as information management, information
privacy and data integrity. For example, information security in a library would
include personnel security and policies, steps taken for effective backups, and the
physical integrity of computing facilities.

According to a recent survey of executive recruiters, computer security experts are among the six most sought-after professionals for the corporate world
(Radcliff, 1999). Yet, there are very few college courses addressing computer
security. Those that do mostly emphasize the mathematics of encryption rather
than hands-on information security and management.

Minimally, effective information security in libraries should include:
- Staff assigned to information security tasks
- Training all personnel in information security issues and procedures
- Specific policies dealing with information privacy, physical security of equip-
  ment, and computer security procedures

- Physical security plans
- Data integrity measures
- Levels of access to data or equipment, and monitoring for different types of access

These points are intended for all types of libraries – public, academic, corporate, and special libraries and collections. They are intended for libraries of all sizes, with all types of patrons, funding models and organizational structures. In a particular library, the investment in information services, computer equipment and personnel may be greater or smaller than in another library, but the need for effective information security exists in both.

WHO'S IN CHARGE OF SECURITY?

On November 2, 1988, a malicious and dangerous computer worm was released to the Internet by Robert T. Morris, causing thousands of computers to crash (Denning, 1990). One of the most important lessons learned in the aftermath of diagnosis, analysis and cleanup was that there was no easy way for computer network managers at one institution to find their counterparts at other institutions, even during an emergency. Furthermore, many institutions that were connected to the Internet (still in its infancy) had no person in charge of computer security, and little or no staff prepared to address security issues.

Today, most libraries are connected to the Internet, yet often without personnel specifically responsible for managing the security of the library network from intrusion or tampering. The estimated number of illegal intrusions into US government computers and networks exceeded 500,000 for 1998, with most intrusions originating from the Internet. By analogy, it may be assumed that attempts to infiltrate library computer systems and networks are frequent (even if they are not frequently detected). If a break-in occurred, would a library be in the same position as the Internet in 1988, with no clear plan for how to proceed, and nobody in charge?

The good news is that computers excel at record keeping. Network logs, firewalls, routers, packet sniffers and data integrity checkers are all capable of identifying illicit access to computer systems. However, even the most sophisticated automated system requires someone to identify that a security breach may have occurred and decide what action to take.

Recommendations for effective information security management include:

- All areas of information security risk must be assigned to specific personnel. For example, if there is a public-use computer workstation, someone needs to be responsible for its security. Similarly, someone needs to be responsible for the security of circulation data.

- Information security must occupy a non-zero amount of the personnel's time (e.g., a 5% or 10% allocation devoted to security might be appropriate for the person who manages a software loaning program in a library).
- Personnel responsible for security must actively seek information related to their areas. Reading vendor news releases, subscribing to security-related electronic mailing lists, or seeking security-related training may be appropriate. Alternatively, simply having regular intra-library information security discussion sessions may be sufficient.
- Develop an access level hierarchy for personnel. Insure that people with access to potentially sensitive data or systems are known, and that their access level will periodically be reviewed.

Information systems are like buildings: simply creating them is not enough. Ongoing maintenance is required in order to avoid inevitable decay due to interaction with the environment. To be diligent about the security of information systems, personnel with specific security-related job descriptions are a necessity.

WHAT IS YOUR PRIVACY GUARANTEE?

Libraries, especially public libraries, have an outstanding record of protecting the privacy of their patrons. The American Library Association's *Intellectual Freedom Manual* (ALA, 1996) assists librarians in defending the Library Bill of Rights. More recently, the ALA has taken a strong stand against the use of filtering software in libraries (see ALA, 1998), and specified guidelines for the freedom of computer and Internet use in libraries.

In spite of this record, there are two important security problems often not addressed in libraries. The first is the privacy offered for data that may be collected or collectable apart from circulation records. The second is the risk of penetration of library systems from outside parties who may access circulation or other data.

For the first case, consider Web browser software often found on library computers. Such software keeps a history list of sites visited, and keeps copies of recently visited Web pages in a directory on the computer. Effective information privacy would dictate a specific policy for such data: will it ever be analyzed? Should patrons take steps to erase the cache after they use a system? If a violation of library policy were suspected, would Web browsing history data be subject to search?

In some libraries, anonymity of access to computer tools may be guaranteed. In others, such as college libraries, display of a current identification card or signing out an access key may be required. Even if anonymity may be assumed, such as in a school library, a small user population might result in easy identification of individuals by library staff.

To turn to the second problem, consider that reasonable and prudent steps should be taken by libraries to insure that private data are kept private. The greatest risk might come from outside the library via an Internet connection, an unattended modem or from staff who abuse their access rights.

Recommendations are simple, but could be time consuming or difficult to implement:

- Maintain a comprehensive list of data that may be collected and the circumstances.
- For each type of data, what risks of misuse exist?
- Specify a policy for the collection of data and possible misuses.
- Identify personnel responsible for ensuring the policies are followed, and for remediation as needed.

For example, a library might require that patrons who wish to use a general-purpose computer first show their library card or ID. At that time, patrons should be informed what data will be kept from their session – will their use of the facility be logged? Will the amount of time be logged? Will different software packages, Internet sites or other records be kept, and if so will the data be linked to the patron's name? Finally, under what circumstances will any data collected be released, and to whom?

THE OPAC

Traditionally, the most sensitive data that libraries collect are circulation records. By necessity, these are linked to identifying information for individual patrons who borrow books or other materials. Online Public Access Catalogs (OPACs) are centralized systems that handle circulation and holdings information, as well as a variety of other data ranging from acquisitions budgets to cataloging modules.

OPACs are still with us. Two important changes to OPACs in the final decade of the 1900s have been consolidation in the OPAC industry and the expansion to Web- and Internet-based access models. For consolidation, the number of companies selling OPAC systems suitable for use in all but the smallest libraries has diminished rapidly. Fewer than a half-dozen companies would be suitable choices for, say, a large academic or public library.

Nearly all new OPAC systems are based on variants of the Unix operating system. Modern OPACs include functionality to make the holdings information searchable via a Web interface. Here lies the substantial security risk: Unix systems have many potential security flaws, and many well-known flaws have easy exploits available to any potential intruder.

Connecting a system with critical data to the Internet is a bad idea. On the Internet, tens of thousands of amateur (and professional) potential intruders may try to get access to the system. Even if the OPAC software itself is thought to be relatively free of security problems – a risky assumption to make – the underlying Unix operating system is almost definitely not.

Yet, this potential risk needs to be balanced by the desire to make OPAC services available to the outside world. Recommendations include:

- Only services needed should be running on the OPAC computer(s). Specifically, all Unix services (such as email, FTP, rlogin, telnet) that are not required for OPAC functions should be disabled.
- System logs must be kept, and analyzed regularly (daily or weekly) by staff. A logins record should be maintained; integrity checkers such as Tripwire should be used to spot illicit changes to the system software, and the system should be audited regularly for usernames, programs or data that are no longer used.
- Ideally, the OPAC should only communicate with authorized terminals. For example, computers located within library buildings. If outside (Internet) access is required, the ideal scenario is to have a duplicate of the holdings database (or other information, if needed) on a separate server. This way, if the duplicate server were compromised, the original data and services would be intact.
- Personnel must be specifically responsible for monitoring security updates from the OPAC vendor, as well as the underlying Unix system vendor.
- Regular attempts should be made to bypass OPAC security from both within the library (at computer stations) and outside the library via the Internet. Intrusion tools are widely publicized on resources such as the BUGTRAQ mailing list[1] and PacketStorm Security Web site[2].

Historically, OPAC security has relied on (a) obscurity, and (b) OPACs' relative inaccessibility. These factors have changed. The Unix systems that OPACs are based on have well-known security flaws, and flaws in the OPAC software are more likely to be found when the OPACs are accessible to the thousands of potential intruders on the Internet.

PUBLIC ACCESS WORKSTATIONS

Instead of "dumb" terminals that can only access OPAC services, libraries often use fully featured microcomputers. These PCs might use a Web browser as an interface to the OPAC's collection information, or they might use a telnet client. Additionally, the PCs could be used to run other software, or access Internet sites outside of the library.

There are several areas of possible risk, as well as various policy issues. Policies for what the computers may be used for, whether priority must be given to particular purposes (such as searching the OPAC), and what data may be gathered from the PCs users (mentioned above) must be developed.

Risks include illicit access to resources within the library, physical risk of theft or damage, and risk of illicit access to resources outside the library via the Internet. Policy issues have to do with equity of access (for which the ALA has specific guidelines, in both their *Intellectual Freedom Manual* and more recent 1996 "Bill of Rights in Cyberspace."), what services and facilities will be offered, and whether limitations on particular types of use will be made[3].

Computers within the library building might have elevated levels of access to information services. For example, a computer might be able to access a CD-ROM database or circulation records for a patron (e.g., to see what books you have charged out), or access an internal electronic message board for reference. Security problems for PCs connected to LANs are well known, and range from packet sniffing (by which usernames and passwords might be gathered) to weaknesses in the underlying PC operating system.

For theft or damage, the requirement is to consider any accessible item to be subject to tampering, theft, damage, sabotage or subversion. Loose Ethernet cables might be plugged into notebook computers brought to the library by potential intruders. Computer system units might be opened so that memory or other components may be stolen (especially in privacy-enhance computer use areas such as carrels). Floppy disk drives may be used to attempt to reboot a computer to a different operating system, or they may simply be used as a depository for chewing gum.

For libraries offering Internet access, an important risk is that this Internet access could be used for illicit purposes. Perhaps a disgruntled employee wants to send anonymous threatening email to her employer. Or a teenager steals a credit card to pay for access to pornography download sites. Or a computer expert uses his hacking skills to break into the FBI's computer network. In these cases, the library may be called on to try to catch the perpetrator. The goal for the librarian should be to make it difficult for the library computers to be utilized for criminal activities.

Recommendations span the range of possible misuses of library-based PCs:
- Perform a complete audit of software and hardware for each computer available. Insure there are no components that are not needed (e.g., additional software that might make illicit use easier).
- Secure wiring and the computer system itself. Assume that any possible illicit use will be attempted.
- To prevent packet sniffing (listening to data sent to other machines on the network), network *switches* should be used in place of network *hubs*. A switch provides a single network channel for each computer, removing the opportunity for sniffing.
- Assume that the software on the computers is subject to change, by either accident or malicious intent. One solution to this problem is to have the com-

puter software refreshed from a LAN server at every reboot. Another is to perform nightly backups to spot inconsistencies and flag problems. A third approach is to rely entirely on remote read-only servers for all software.
- Have personnel regularly attempt to bypass system security.
- Decide what level of external access to allow (see below), and what level of logging of access is appropriate.

For a medium-sized public library, expenditures for a public-use computer facility with Internet access could exceed tens of thousands of dollars annually, plus personnel costs. Taking steps to insure the equipment is secure is a sound policy.

YOUR INTERNET CONNECTION TO THE OUTSIDE WORLD

Connecting a library to the Internet means that the Internet can also connect to the library. Procedures for minimizing risk that potential intruders could steal, modify or delete information are well known, and focus on the use of Internet firewalls (e.g., Chapman and Zicky, 1995). A firewall can help insure that many exploits used to gain illicit access to data or systems will fail, such as IP spoofing attacks (where an outside computer masquerades as an inside computer to get elevated access privileges).

Libraries that host their own OPACs (versus those that use a regionally shared one) should consider an additional firewall for the OPAC itself, also perhaps for other particular resources such as cataloging workstations or circulation workstations. This would deliver a two-tiered approach to network security. At the first tier, a firewall system would help protect the library from unauthorized data. At the second tier, a separate firewall configuration would help protect particularly sensitive systems within the library from unauthorized use.

For example, it might be determined that many sorts of Internet data are allowed to go in and out of the library, but only data to particular ports would be allowed to reach the OPAC. The second level firewall would also prevent computers inside the library from sending illicit data to the OPAC.

Recommendations for the Internet connection include:
- Collect logging data from the firewall or router machines, and regularly examine the logs.
- Configure automatic notification (e.g., a pager message to the network administrator) in case of a network outage or serious break-in attempt.
- Physically or logically (via firewall) separate machines that are intended to be Internet-accessible from those that are not. For example, a dedicated CD-ROM searching station should not be able to access the Internet, even if it's next to a PC workstation that should.

- Treat any Internet connection as high risk. Personnel with any elevated systems access (e.g., the OPAC administrator) should not be permitted to access sensitive systems over the Internet – such as to login to the OPAC system and perform administrative functions. Minimally, if logins or other network traffic that might disclose internal messages (email), usernames or passwords are needed, the session should be encrypted. Encryption software for login sessions includes Secure Shell (ssh); encryption methods for email include S/MIME and PGP. Free or inexpensive solutions are available for such encryption.

The Internet is the greatest source of risk to information security in libraries. This is simply because there is a far greater number of potential intruders "out there" on the Internet then there ever could be within the library.

CONCLUSION

Information security includes personnel security, privacy, policy and computer security. Specific personnel must be assigned security-related tasks in order for any security system to be effective. Due to the continuing emergence of new security exploits, tools and techniques – coupled with the constant parade of software and hardware upgrades likely in most library environments – ongoing diligence is required to keep informed of security developments.

This paper has not attempted to cover every aspect of security-conscious systems administration and library management, only those issues that may be particularly under-appreciated or help lead to more rigorous thinking about security. For example, any information system should have good physical security, to prevent unauthorized access by both casual or planned attempt. Data backup and backup policies are a necessity for any data collection system, and hopefully are in place for all OPACs and related systems. More detailed treatment of security-conscious computer systems administration may be found in such sources as Garfinkle & Spafford (1996).

The traditional of areas focus for library security have had little to do with computer and information security. Disaster and contingency planning (George, 1994) should now include an emphasis on these systems as well.. A final notable issue omitted in the analysis above is the proper maintenance of non-computer based records, such as paper sign-in sheets for computer facilities, written library card applications, and the like. Clearly, such data need to be subject to appropriate policy and procedure.

Colleges and universities that train librarians have changed their emphasis from the relatively narrow world of OPACs and online searching to include the Internet, LAN and server administration, interface design, and programming. However, issues of security and privacy still tend to focus on issues such as risks from troubled patrons, book theft, and censorship (e.g., Chaney & MacDougall, 1992). When information security is addressed, it may be from the point of view of corporate information security management, rather than library environments (cf. Davies, 1992).

In the future, consideration of information security issues will likely be seen in basic courses in information ethics or technology. Currently, however, information security is often under-appreciated in libraries. It is recommended that steps be taken in all libraries to assess and minimize information security risks.

NOTES

[1] BUGTRAQ is a mailing list for discussion of security exploits and solutions. To subscribe, send "subscribe BUGTRAQ Your Full Name" to listserv@securityfocus.com.

[2] PacketStorm Security hosts a collection of security software. This resource is for people who want to test available methods of intrusion against a particular system. If library personnel are not using these types of programs regularly, a potential intruder may be! See http://packetstorm.securify.com/.

[3] The ALA has taken a firm stance against limiting computer-based activities. Minow (1997) analyzes Web content filters in libraries, suggesting a possible role for zoning certain types of content in particular areas of the library.

REFERENCES

ALA (American Library Association) (1996). *Intellectual Freedom Manual*. Chicago: American Library Association.

ALA (American Library Association) (1998). Access to Electronic Information, Services, and Networks: An Interpretation of the Library Bill of Rights. Chicago: American Library Association. Available online: http://www.ala.org/alaorg/oif/electacc.html.

Chaney, M. & MacDougall, A. F. (Eds.) (1992). *Security and Crime Prevention in Libraries*, Brookfield, VT: Ashgate Publishing Company.

Chapman, D. B. & Zwicky, E. (1995). *Building Internet Firewalls*. Sebastopol, CA: O'Reilly and Associates.

Davies, J. E. (1992). Computer Misuse. In Chapman & Zwicky, op cit.

Denning, P. J. (1990). *Computers Under Attack: Intruders, Worms, and Viruses*. New York: ACM Press.

Garfinkel, S. & Spafford, G. (1996). *Practical UNIX & Internet Security* (2nd ed.), Sebastopol, CA: O'Reilly and Associates.

George, S. C. (1994). Emergency Planning and Management in College Libraries. Chicago: Association of College and Research Libraries.

Minow, M. (1997). Filters and the Public Library: A Legal and Policy Analysis. *First Monday* 2:12. Chicago: University of Illinois at Chicago. Available online: http://www.firstmonday.dk/issues/issue2_12/minow/

Ogg, H. C. (1997). *Introduction to the use of computers in libraries*. Medford, New Jersey: Information Today, Inc.

Radcliff, D. (1999). Job Seekers' Best Bets. *Computer World*. September 13, pp. 50-51.

Shumann, B. A. (1999). *Library Security and Safety Handbook: Prevention, Policies, and Procedures*. Chicago: American Library Association.

Chapter 11

Faculty of Information Studies Knowledge Repository (FISKR)

M. Asim Qayyum, Gerry Oxford, Sungin Lee,
Laryssa Tyson, and Chun Wei Choo
University of Toronto, Canada

Knowledge repositories are increasingly being viewed as a special form of knowledge management (KM) in organizational memory information systems (OMIS). Presented in this chapter is the prototype of a knowledge repository which is envisaged to be an electronic repository of online pedagogical resources and is designed and implemented as a web-based software system, built to help foster a learning organization that works together to gather and share knowledge. This heterogeneous repository stores resources or pointers to resources of many different kinds including, but not limited to, electronic or printed material, courses, slide presentations, videos, or any other resource that is relevant to the subject matter. These resources can then be retrieved in a number of different ways such as subject taxonomies, reading or bibliographic list and can be viewed in a Web browser as simple web pages.

INTRODUCTION

"Only two percent of information gets written down-the rest is in people's mind", says David Owens, Vice President of knowledge management at Unisys Corporation and vice chair of The Conference Board's Learning and Knowledge Management Council (Hickins, 1999). So knowledge management (KM) places equal emphasis on capturing the tacit knowledge that is in people's heads, rather than targeting just the explicit knowledge that can be stored in a more shareable format. By managing its knowledge an organization would know more, and the

Previously Published in *Managing Information Technology in a Global Economy*, edited by Mehdi Khosrow-Pour, Copyright © 2001, Idea Group Publishing.

Figure 1: Breakdown of knowledge areas within an organization.

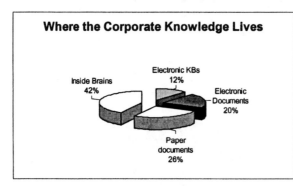

more it knows the more successful it will be. And this comes only after an understanding of what kind of information is available to the members of an organization, where it is and how it can be accessed (Hackbarth and Grover, 1999).

A similar viewpoint on the division of knowledge in an organization is shown in Figure 1. This figure shows the results of a study, carried out by the Delphi Group, of more than 700 US companies and serves to illustrate that only a portion of the corporate knowledge is in shareable format (Hickins, 1999). The majority (42%) of any one kind of knowledge resides inside people's head. And we have to realize that people leave organizations, taking away the knowledge that is stored in their heads, personal computers or in their possession in other formats.

Therefore, organizations must build knowledge management (KM) systems, such as knowledge repositories, to try to retain the maximum possible tacit knowledge and make it available to people who need it. This simple need for KM systems is supported by results from another survey, again by Delphi group, of 370 business professionals which shows that 28% had already begun or completed KM projects while 93% said that they will have undertaken such projects by 2000 (Anthes, 1998).

Data and information need to be integrated to arrive at knowledge, and knowledgeable people need to have the ability to integrate and frame the information at hand within the context of their experience, expertise and judgement (Hackbarth et al., 1999). What is data to some may be information for others, and knowledge is a higher order concept than either of these. In today's high paced technological environment, information is available in abundance as it piles up in the databases or streams into our desktop computers through the Internet. Knowledge is however information that has been edited and analyzed in such a manner so as to make it useful. And when knowledge from the past is brought to bear on present activities, thus affecting the level of organizational effectiveness, then that is called Organizational Memory (OM) (Stein, 1992).

Table 1: The types of information systems

Level	Name	Type of system/Focus
4	Knowledge Management	Organizational memory information systems (OMIS)
3	Information as a resource	Advanced database technologies
2	Data management	Data (base) architecture of the company
1	File and data organization	Data systems

This distinction between the handling of various systems concerned with data, information and knowledge is presented in Table 1 (Lehner, Mair and Klosa, 1998). We see that the projects requiring the use of OM information systems can be placed in a distinct category as compared to the other projects. This is because such efforts do not involve the simple development of a system, but require the incorporation of a concept of organizational development with a focus on enterprise wide knowledge sharing and learning. Dieng (Dieng, Corby, Giboin, and Ribiere, 1999) presents a useful discussion on the survey of methods, techniques, and tools aimed at managing corporate knowledge from a memory designer's perspective.

This development of OMIS is not technology driven but people driven (Hickins, 1999). And these systems can firmly be placed as organizational knowledge management systems as they adapt to the social dynamics of the workplace. These social dynamics may include factors such as the work habits, perceived benefits and knowledge sharing. In a nutshell, OM information systems contribute to the learning ability, flexibility and the mastering of organizational change (Lehner et al., 1998). For the purpose of this paper, we will use the terms OMIS and knowledge repository to point to the same type of knowledge management system. This is because the building up of a knowledge repository to cater to the various processes of an OMIS is essential as the organizations incorporate an OMIS as their mainline knowledge management system. And this in turn is because a knowledge repository embodies an OMIS's phases of acquisition, retention, maintenance and retrieval within its knowledge management framework (Hackbarth et al., 1999). This fact was also confirmed during a Web based survey (Maier and Klosa, 1999) conducted to classify existing OM systems which included knowledge agents, knowledge bases, expert systems and knowledge creation, structuring and communications integration platforms.

The objective of this paper is to present the design of the prototype of a knowledge repository, FISKR, that is in design phase at the Faculty of Information Studies (FIS) in University of Toronto. This repository is capable of storing resources or pointers to resources of many different kinds including, but not limited to, electronic or printed material, slide presentations, multimedia files, student papers, thesis, or any other resource that is relevant to the subject matter. In addition to this, support for the creation of course pages and reading lists is also provided for the faculty members.

We will start off by presenting in the next section, some of the related works done in the field of creating knowledge repositories for the management and sharing of organizational knowledge. Section 3 will introduce some of the features of our developed prototype and will also highlight the future design characteristics, which have not yet been implemented into the prototype. By incorporating the latter, we hope to transform the knowledge repository into a true organization wide knowledge-sharing tool, which could then be effectively utilized by the members of this Faculty.

RELATED WORK

In this section, we will highlight the working, functions and components of knowledge management systems and support using knowledge repositories as a tool for managing organizational knowledge. Some practical applications will also be introduced.

Organizational memory information systems (OMIS)

Stein (1992) presented the concept of OMIS as being the coherent integration of dispersed know-how from all over the organization. This system utilizes the concept of OM, which was also related to the term 'organizational knowledge base' because it retains knowledge. The OMIS then supports the organizational learning and enables continuous process improvement through knowledge conservation, distribution and reuse (Lehner et al., 1998). The relationships between the building blocks or different processes of an OMIS have been drawn in Figure 2.

The acquisition phase of OMIS gathers knowledge from all the available resources and caters for formal, semiformal and informal knowledge. An informal knowledge representation can include plain text documents whereas, semiformal knowledge would include documents with some structure such as the SGML/XML documents (Decker and Maurer, 1999). A high level of integration capability is required of the OMIS application to cater for all these different forms of knowledge representations that are present in the organization.

Figure 2: The OMIS processes

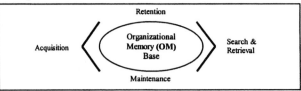

The retention phase would then require the underlying database to shape its storage formats so that it adapts to the various types of knowledge acquired during the acquisition phase, and thus retain it efficiently. Some of the mechanisms used to retain organizational information include schemas, scripts and systems (Hackbarth et al., 1999). Schemas can be groupings of people, places and things while scripts describe the sequence of events. Systems manage these schemas and scripts in a manner so as to facilitate a common objective. These can be databases, as utilized in the case of FISKR, distributed information systems or some other form of artificial intelligence systems.

The maintenance then comes as a by-product of the daily work of the users. The decision to update data, or to retain or delete it, must conform to the organizational objectives. The search and retrieval process could be facilitated through the use of meta-data i.e. a description of the knowledge item.

Practical use of OM information systems as knowledge repositories

What happens when a large organization does not have a knowledge management system in place? Canadian Imperial Bank of Commerce (CIBC) found that out the hard way *after* it developed a knowledge repository of external training programs and licenses that the bank owned (Tobin, 1998). It found that the bank owned 16 different training programs on a single word-processing system, and that three different groups within the bank had purchased nationwide licenses for the same management-training program. These costly duplications could have been avoided if the information had been placed in a single repository earlier on. This example certainly strengthens the case for developing an organization wide knowledge repository.

We can classify repository based KM projects in two ways. The top down approach looks at the knowledge present within a department and seeks to collect that within a KM system by a group of specialized personnel. Bottom up approach on the other hand would tend to create a repository first and then encourage the users to add their knowledge to it. We chose the latter category for implementing FISKR.

A notable example of building a bottom up knowledge repository as an OMIS is the *Eureka* project at Xerox (Hickins, 1999). This intranet communications initiative was part of Xerox's overall knowledge management (KM) strategy that seeks to create added value by capturing and leveraging organization wide knowledge. FISKR is designed to be similar to Eureka as it is also a web-based system and the knowledge in the repository is user contributed.

Xerox repositioned itself as a document company in 1990 (Year 2005 plan) and has gradually built up its reputation of being a leading knowledge company based on its strong knowledge-sharing culture. This culture has led to the development of knowledge-intensive products for the company. The company has some 23,000 technicians all over the world and some of the solutions exist only in an individual's mind. Thus, the experienced technicians can be expected to solve complex problems much more efficiently than a less experienced one. The database now houses more than 5000 tips, which are available to the Xerox employees via the World Wide Web right to their laptops.

This sharing of the tacit knowledge is aimed at gathering knowledge locked in people's heads, their notebook, or in their computers, things that we envisage FISKR to achieve. It is important to note that the knowledge sharing at Xerox comes out of the overall cooperative cultural developed there. Its Chairman Paul Allaire remarked that technology must support the distributed sharing of knowledge as the work has become much more cooperative in nature. Thus the system development has to work in parallel with the development of an organization wide sharing culture. The successful deployment of these two factors is expected to ultimately lead to an accelerated learning and innovative environment in an academic setting such as ours also.

Another Xerox product for knowledge sharing and management, which is perhaps more closely related to our research cum academic setting, is the *Docushare* that is targeted at its 500-plus employees in the research labs (Hickins, 1999). This tool is aimed at encouraging the normally closed-lipped scientists to share information with their colleagues while respecting their need for privacy.

Internet based knowledge repository to support customer service is also demonstrated by an Australian company which specializes in manufacture of CNC plate cutting machines and has customers all over the world (Mo and Christopher, 1998). The repository captures the knowledge of company's domain experts as well as information available from experienced users.

A noteworthy project in knowledge repository construction, using the top down approach, is the Optical Recorded Information Online Network (ORION) project which was developed at the Federal Express Corporation. The main objective was to cope with the massive employee documentation requirements of its ever-increasing worldwide workforce, estimated to be at over 90,000 employees (Candler, Palvia, Thompson and Zeltman, 1996). Although its architects did not conceive the ORION project as an OMIS project or a knowledge management project, we still tend to view the project as a good example of a knowledge repository. This is because like FISKR, this project takes inputs from various sources, disseminates, consolidates and stores the data into a repository from which the users can access it.

Another example of a top down approach is that of Ernst and Young of Canada, which manages a repository of information obtained from a variety of external resources that includes company information, industry analyses, financial benchmarks, news feeds etc. (Tobin, 1998). Butterball Turkey has developed an extensive knowledge base from its 40 years expertise in test kitchens and this is available to the consumers directly over the Internet or to its call center hotline operators, who handle almost 200,000 calls from the consumers per year.

A departure from the single repository idea is that of multiple repositories within an organization, a common practice at IBM (Tapscott, 1998). Each repository contains intellectual capital consisting of project proposals, work proposals, presentations, reports etc. Thus, an IBM consultant pursuing a new business opportunity anywhere in the world can mine the repositories for information, which leads to lesser time spent developing better proposals.

KM Success factors for FISKR

A challenge in the construction of an OMIS is to harness as much organizational memory into OMIS as is feasible and appropriate (Hackbarth et al., 1999). To achieve this and to ensure the success of FISKR as well as to blend it with the culture of FIS, it is essential that the students and faculty use the system without considering it as an additional burden imposed on top of their already overworked schedules. We realized that if our KM system is viewed as extra work then it may end up as a straight failure as people tend to ignore systems which require them to input data (Hickins, 1999). Thus the need is to make a system which would be useful to the users in supporting their class work and that they accept its usage as part of their routines. In a learning organization such as ours, the critical issue is how the individual learning is transferred to the organization and that is what we seek to implement through this project.

The above is to be ensured by developing a culture where the user is educated that this is to be a repository which is dependent upon them to contribute knowledge entries, and which will then serve as a searchable archive for researchers (users).

Other guidelines for developing a successful knowledge repository, which have been utilized by us in developing our repository, are (Tobin, 1998):
- In order to utilize the repository as a useful learning tool, it is to be well organized, kept up-to-date and easy to access and search. The users will tend to look for other sources if they find the repository complicated in use.
- The information in the repository is to be kept accurate. This is usually a drawback with most such systems because the data which is entered into a repository once can stay there forever even when it has been outdated or replaced by more accurate information. To implement this feature, our repository employs the concept of inclusion of subject specialists, who verify all user inputs as well as monitor the contents of the repository.

- All members of the organization are to be given direct access to the repository. While certain portions of our repository are password protected, no other approval is necessary for the majority.

The bottom line here would be that the information in the repository should be the information that the users need and that it may not be limited to knowledge generated within the organization. Both these conditions are satisfied as our repository grows through user submissions and therefore has the information that users require. It is envisaged to contain knowledge generated from inside as well as outside the organization.

DEVELOPED PROTOTYPE

The prototype of FISKR has been introduced to students in at least one course and during a couple of presentations and seminars. The interest has been encouraging so far and over time, we intend to move out of the prototyping phase to the actual system implementation phase soon.

The architectural representations

The 3-tier physical architecture of Faculty of Information Studies Repository (FISKR) is shown in Figure 3. This shows the various hardware and software

Figure 3: The FISKR physical architecture

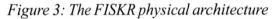
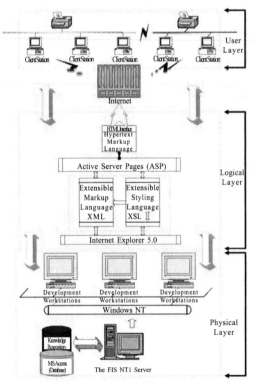

Figure 4: The FISKR logical architecture

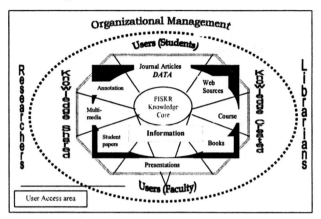

components that have been utilized in this prototype. Briefly, the system is web-based, built upon a Windows NT platform using the test server available at FIS. Microsoft's (MS) Active Server Pages (ASP) was chosen as the main script language to help in the creation of server side scripted templates that can generate dynamic and interactive web server applications. MS Access is the database at the back end, which acts as the main knowledge base. Extensible Markup Language (XML) is chosen to structure the data at the time of its retrieval from the database and this is then combined with extensible style sheet language (XSL) and converted to HTML for viewing on a standard browser. As Internet Explorer (IE 5.0) provides the best support for both ASP and XML therefore, we used that as a standard browser during the development.

A logical information architecture, which serves to demonstrate this goal and the user-oriented components within FISKR, is shown in Figure 4. This also shows the participants (users) along with their placement in this hierarchy with respect to the repository components as has been visualized for the usage of this repository.

Figure 5: FISKR search options

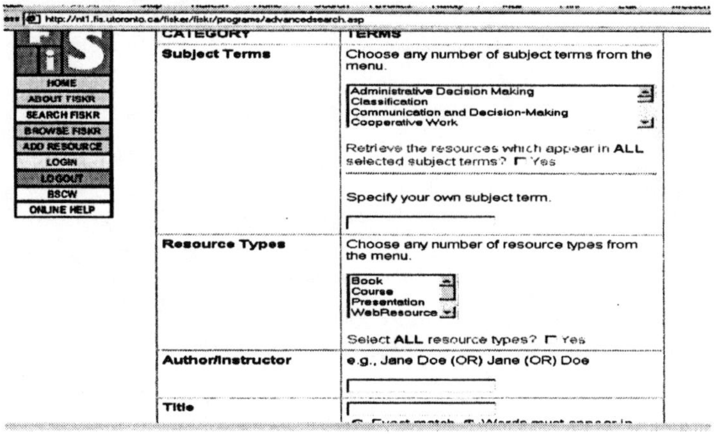

Operational features

The prototype of FISKR currently provides three options to the user;

1) Search FISKR allows an individual to search resources housed in FISKR by keyword, author name, title of the resource or type of resource i.e. whether it is a book, journal article, conference paper, research article etc.

2) Browse FISKR allows an individual to browse resources housed in FISKR by various predetermined classification schemes.

3) Add A Resource allows individuals to add resources to FISKR as well as annotations. FIS Faculty members are given the additional option of entering a 'Course' as a resource.

A typical search screen is shown in Figure 5. This is an advanced search screen where prior to this, the user is presented with a basic keyword search option also. The search can also be made by date or author information (Some options are not displayed in Figure 5).

When browsing resources according to some subject terms, a typical query result screen is displayed in Figure 6. On the top is a legend that is present in all search result screens so as to guide the user in identifying the type of the resource. In this Figure, the main topic being browsed is Information and its Social Contexts and the user is then presented with subtopics to choose the resources from. The user can then drill down to retrieve further information about the resource.

When adding a resource, the user is presented with an entry screen, which lists

Figure 6: Browsing results

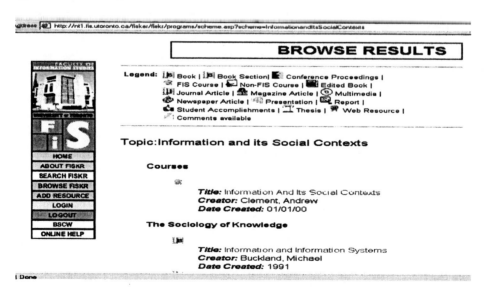

Figure 7: Adding resources to FISKR

fourteen possible resources that can be entered into the system. This is shown in Figure 7. Effort was made to identify as many possible resources as we could within the faculty and because of the modular nature of our system, any further type of resources could easily be added to the repository without incurring any major design changes.

We can divide the resources into two major virtual categories. One would be termed as that of containing explicit resources, or pointers to them, such as books and other published material. The implicit resource category would comprise of unpublished and little known personal work such as student papers, thesis, or multimedia files such as the audio and video of some lecture or presentation. These latter resources would be captured and placed in the repository 'physically' as the contributor would be required to upload the file to the server so that it is available to future knowledge seekers. Lastly, the user can also contribute a pointer to a useful web resource while identifying the relevant subject heading for it.

There are two main features of the resources' data entry in addition to entering the standard resource information like author name, resource name, type, publisher etc. One is that the user is asked to define subject category (or categories, up to a max. of three) under which the resource can be indexed in the repository. The other main feature is that the user is required to provide some annotation about the resource itself, a feature that will also contribute towards capturing some of the tacit knowledge flowing within the organization. This is because these comments by users will give more intellectual depth to the information contained within the repository. Annotations can also be added later by other users for any resource. Thus, multiple comments can be retained for individual resources.

Figure 8: Displaying detailed & structured data

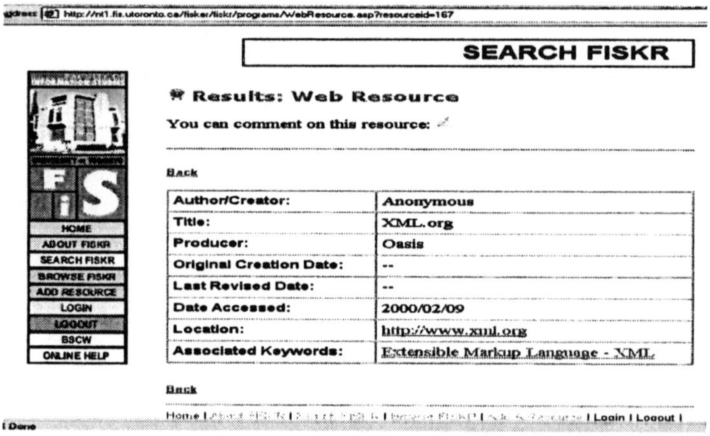

Preliminary entries into the database were made after interviewing some faculty members and through identifying the course-related resources in the one course in which the system was introduced to students. All entries into the repository by future users are to be placed in a temporary storage area and will be perused by a subject specialist who has the final authority in granting approval for addition of that resource into the main repository.

Potential FISKR Contributions (FISKR-II — The future)

FISKR has significant potential for the development and sharing of pedagogical resources within and between schools and departments in the University of Toronto as well as organizations outside the university. This is mainly because of the structure provided to the data through the use of XML, which facilitates data interchange. A typical structured output obtained through the use of XML and XSL is shown in Figure 8. Hyperlinks are provided to facilitate direct user access to web resources, as is the case in this figure also.

Commercially, the FISKR framework as well as its tools and applications would be of great interest to organizations designing and developing their own internal knowledge repositories. The use of XML and object-oriented methodologies to mark up and represent the content of resources permits great breadth and flexibility in the kinds of resources that FISKR can house. This usage will also provide structural support for a wide array of search, manipulation, print and display applications that will enrich students' learning experience and reduce an instructor's work.

Lindstaedt (Lindstaedt and Schneider, 1997) presents a method of storing e-mails in a knowledge repository and then categorizing them by scanning keywords in the subject line so that future retrieval could be made more structured. We intend to supplement our system's capability through a similar system, where the e-mails would become a part of the repository and will play an important role in capturing the elusive tacit knowledge flowing within the organization. For retrieving this (implicit) knowledge contained in embedded annotations from the knowledge base, the user will be provided options to look for annotations by Faculty members, or renowned researchers, which would lead to a more credible information about the resource. Other search on annotations such as by keywords, date, name etc. will further enhance their utility.

It is also intended to enhance the capability of acquisition of the web-based resources in future so that the data from it is extracted more efficiently. Ontology is to be developed for organized storage within the knowledge base that will be exploited by an automated acquisition of explicit resources through the use of web wrappers.

The browsing feature will be fully implemented through a Java based tree shaped structure of all the subject taxonomies present in the repository. Thus, the user adding a resource will be adding to a tree within the subject taxonomies, which have already been created by subject specialists. In a similar fashion, the resource entry would also be into a tree where the resource contributor would be able to choose the branch within the taxonomies where the resource best belongs.

CONCLUSIONS

We described our project, FISKR, in this paper. FISKR is envisioned to be a shared, collective resource; more the information to be shared through the FISKR repository, more valuable will the system become to its community of users. The faculty itself has a longstanding focus on managing information content and providing "smart, friendly" access to information content. FISKR is a direct application of these principles to our own organizational knowledge base, and will benefit from all the areas of expertise that the Faculty can bring to bear on it. The ultimate goal of this project is to support a learning organization. Thus the intent is to capture and share knowledge through faculty and student learning and to integrate the different know-how present within the faculty. We hope to also improve the information circulation and communication through the use of this system.

REFERENCES

Anthes, G. (1998). Defending knowledge. *Computerworld*, 32(7): 41-42, February.

Candler, J. W., Palvia, P. C., Thompson, J. D., and Zeltman, S. M. (1996). The Orion project staged business process reengineering at FEDEX. *Communications of the ACM*, 39(2): 99-107, February.

Decker, S., and Maurer, F. (1999). Editorial: Organizational memory and knowledge management. *International Journal of Human-Computer Studies*, 51: 511-516.

Dieng, R., Corby, O., Giboin, A., and Ribiere, M. (1999). Methods and tools for corporate knowledge management. *International Journal of Human-Computer Studies*, 51: 567-598.

Hackbarth, G., and Grover, V. (1999). The knowledge repository: Organizational memory information systems. *Information Systems Management*, 16(3): 21-30, Summer.

Hickins, M. (1999). Xerox shares its knowledge. *Management Review*, 88(2): 40-45, September.

Lehner, F., Mair, R. K., and Klosa, O. W. (1998). Organizational memory systems – Applications of advanced database and network technologies, *research paper no. 19*, University of Regensburg, Department of Business Informatics.

Lindstaedt, S. N. and Schneider, K. (1997). Bridging the gap between face-to-face communication and long term collaboration. *Proceedings of the International ACM SIGGROUP Conference on Supporting Group Work: The Integration Challenge*, Phoenix, AZ: 331-340, November 16 - 19.

Maier, R. K., and Klosa, O. W. (1999). Organizational memory systems to support organizational information processing. *Proceedings of the 1999 ACM SIGCPR Conference on Computer Personnel Research, New Orleans, LA*: 138-143. April 8 - 10.

Mo, J. P. T., and Christopher, M. (1998). An integrated process model knowledge based system for remote customer support. *Computers in Industry*. 37(3):171-183. November.

Stein, E. W. (1992). A method to identify candidates for knowledge acquisition. *Journal of Information systems*, 9(2): 161-178.

Tapscott. D. (1998). Make knowledge an asset for the whole company. *Computerworld, 17(11) 17, Dececmber.*

Tobin, D. R. (1998). Networking your knowledge. *Management Review*, 87(4): 46-48, April.

Chapter 12

From Lackey to Leader: The Evolution of the Librarian in the Age of the Internet

Jennifer Croud, Michael Manning and Janine Schmidt
The University of Queensland, Australia

Today hybrid libraries extend beyond physical walls. Librarians organise and facilitate access to information whether it is from print collections or new digital sources. To complement information management skills and technical expertise, they have developed strategies that lead their clients into effective access to, and use of, information.

Librarians are now teachers, research partners, and web designers. Through partnerships with faculty, and by fostering the integration of information skills into the curriculum, they are contributing to the teaching, learning and research processes.

Librarians in the digital age are people of intellectual flexibility, who embrace change and constantly update their knowledge and skills. They are people-oriented and able to interact closely with their clients.

This paper discusses the evolution of librarians in the age of the Internet, with specific reference to the roles of librarians at the University of Queensland Library.

INTRODUCTION

More information is available to scholars today, more quickly than ever before. A researcher can publish to a world-wide audience and at the push of a few keys a researcher on the other side of the world can retrieve the work. This work

Previously Published in *Challenges of Information Technology Management in the 21st Century,* edited by Mehdi Khosrow-Pour, Copyright © 2000, Idea Group Publishing.

may be in colour and include sound and video. Information available changes by the second and it may be accessed 24 hours a day regardless of location. Of course, it does not work perfectly all of the time - there are still various technical issues to consider but there is no doubt we are in the brave new world of the digital age.

Today's libraries are no longer mere collections of resources, or places to sit and study, or even places to ask questions. They extend beyond physical walls and librarians organise and facilitate access to the "right" information. Librarians have gone beyond the role of mere intermediaries to where they are teachers, research partners, and web designers.

This chapter discusses the evolution of librarians in the age of the Internet with specific reference to the roles of librarians at the University of Queensland Library.

THE LIBRARY IS HERE TO STAY

Despite what some writers have predicted there are numerous reasons why libraries as both physical and organisational units will continue. Not with old style facilities, but with ones designed to meet the new ways of accessing information.

int material may be housed and information sources of all formats accessed. Academics still value very highly publication in recognised (print) journals, housed in libraries. Discussions with academics and researchers at the University of Queensland have shown that they are not quite ready, yet, for the fully electronic library and want print resources retained. They want the best of both worlds but are moving very quickly and, depending on the disciplinary basis, are already at the cutting edge of information technology. However not everything is on the Internet and some things probably never will be. Print on paper, as opposed to words on the Web, in some cases is the most economical, efficient and effective way to distribute information. Students still need to access print materials and to work in appropriate study spaces. The physical concept of the library remains important. In 1999 the University of Queensland Library lent 1.5 million items from physical collections and shelved 3 million items.

In 1998 the University of Queensland Library completed a successful, award winning AUD$9.8 million refurbishment of its largest library. Spaces were created everywhere for computers (there are over 500), as well as group and individual study areas. Comments from clients, and increased usage, indicate the success of redesign. In 1999 the Library had 2.9 million people through its doors.

Organisationally, as Rowland (1998) notes, "libraries remain the appropriate structures through which to take decisions about the distribution of budgeted funds for the purchase of information resources." The University of Queensland Library subscribes to over 5,000 electronic journals. Contract negotiations to obtain appropriate access for clients to these is not easy. Some are available gratis with print versions, others in electronic form only. Still others are obtained at varying prices and on varying conditions in association with the print versions. Keeping track of the differing contract terms is problematic and extremely time consuming. Access requires careful management, sometimes by password, sometimes by IP address.

The Library is also the appropriate structure through which access to information resources is facilitated. Staff are experienced in information access and retrieval, new technologies and in negotiating with publishers. These tasks are beyond the ability of any individual researcher.

THE DIGITAL LIBRARY

The Internet has irrevocably changed the process of information generation, transmission and gathering. It is no longer just print on paper, but also words (and sound and video and real time interactions) on the Web. Links from within information sources connect to other sources. There are no boundaries, scholars and researchers communicate via email, electronic discussion lists, bulletin boards, video conferencing and chat.

Digital libraries are being developed world-wide. There are many definitions of **digital library.** The ARL definition is that

- the digital library is not a single entity
- the digital library requires technology to link the resources of many
- the linkages between the many digital libraries and information services are transparent to the end users
- universal access to digital libraries and information services is a goal
- digital library collections are not limited to document surrogate: they extend to digital artifacts that cannot be represented or distributed in printed formats.

The University of Queensland Library is currently undertaking several digital library projects including AVEL, a complement to Edinburgh's EEVL, and Agrigate. AVEL (Australian Virtual Engineering Library) will provide engineers and IT professionals in universities, research organisations and industry with rapid and efficient access to relevant (quality) Australian web based materials; and, an increased exposure of their work and R&D capacity worldwide. Agrigate, an Australian agricultural research gateway, will assist researchers in finding quality agricultural web sites that will benefit their research. It will identify Australian resources in the first instance and secondly link to overseas resources that relate to Australian projects or conditions.

As AVEL and Agrigate illustrate, the role of digital libraries is to provide an "alternative, supplement, or complement to the conventional printed and microfilm materials that currently dominate library collections" (Saffady, 1995 in Maxwell, 1998). Digital libraries extend the services of Libraries.

THE HYBRID LIBRAY - THE UNIVERSITY OF QUEENSLAND LIBRARY

Hybrid libraries integrate traditional and electronic library services - the University of Queensland Library is now a hybrid library.

The University of Queensland Library is the largest library in the state of Queensland, with over 2 million volumes, 20,000 journal titles and extensive video, microform and digital collections. The Library provides its services to almost 29,000 students, of whom 25% are postgraduates; 4,500 general, academic and research staff; and several thousand hospital staff, through a network of 14 branch libraries located on several campuses, in teaching hospitals and in a Dental School. Support services, including information technology, are centralised.

The Library uses the term cybrary (rather than hybrid library) to refer to its development of services in cyber, and physical, space. In 1998 it was joint winner in the institutional category of the prestigious Australian Awards for University Teaching for its description of the University of Queensland Cybrary. The awards are funded by the Commonwealth Government of Australia.

Through the Cybrary researchers are able to navigate their way to sources of information. The web site provides a single integrated interface to all library collections and services, including library opening hours, staff contacts, branch library layouts, and details of facilities and training programs. Researchers can search over 300 locally held databases, some full text, indexing thousands of journals. They can then either find the printed journals on the shelves, use available electronic versions, or obtain resources through the document delivery service. Access is provided to over 5,000 electronic journals. All are listed in the Library's web catalogue under title, and direct links are made to them.

The Cybrary provides access to many information services on the Internet. Some are licensed by the Library for direct use by students. Specialist assistance is also available to undergraduates who can find sub-sets of information in an electronic reserve collection. They can use electronic versions of examination papers, subject guides, subject and course notes, and reading lists. Also provided is easy access to various Internet search engines via direct links.

The Library assists researchers and students to use cybrary services through the provision of specially tailored information skills training programs. Programs focus on effective access to, and use of, information and are provided both in the classroom and also interactively via the Cybrary.

ROLE OF ACADEMIC LIBRARIANS

Since the advent of the digital age many scenarios have been proposed for the future of librarianship. These range from obsolescence to mastery. In the obsolescence view there will be no need for libraries and librarians as everything will be available on the Internet and users will be able to retrieve the information for themselves. In the mastery view libraries and librarians move to positions of prominence as information professionals in a world dependent on information (Hathorn, 1997). The University of Queensland Library experience is closer to the latter view than the former, though "mastery" may be too extreme a description. Librarians are a key component of the teaching, learning and research process at the university.

Roles are changing and expanding as libraries, and librarians, change to best serve their clients. The mission of the University of Queensland Library is: *we link people with information enabling the University of Queensland to achieve excellence in teaching, learning and research.* Existing services are constantly evaluated against the mission and new services developed with it in mind. Customer service is the focus of all activities.

Academic libraries are developing digital libraries of quality information and are offering services through hybrid libraries to support flexible learning. Librarians are facilitating the teaching, learning and research processes by developing Web sites and guides to information, and providing reference services. Libraries are partnering with computer centres to provide networked environments, and with faculty to assist them move through the multitude of information sources. Demand for reference services is increasing in the academic setting and more and more librarians are adopting a teaching role to assist clients to develop skills in information literacy. Tenopir and Ennis (1998) in their discussion of the impact of digital reference on librarians and library users, note a consequence of increasing numbers of electronic services is an increase in the need for user instruction. Librarians are moving from behind the desk to their clients' workplaces. They work with academic staff in departments, assisting researchers to find information, and to help them organise and present their teaching material.

Mediation and assistance

As Lipow (1999) notes, whether or not information seekers are successful in locating information depends on their selecting suitable resources to consult and successfully querying them. Users often require assistance in the process and the reference librarian provides this.

Librarians assist users to define and refine their queries, and then find information in sources appropriate to meeting their needs. This may be from print or electronic sources. The need for information assistance of this type has increased dramatically since the advent of the Internet. Finding relevant, quality information on the Internet is not easy. Search engines typically retrieve numerous hits and with no evaluation of "quality." Advanced searches on different engines require different search syntax. No engine covers the entire Internet, and a number of different engines must be used for a comprehensive search.

Librarians assist users at their point of need. Enquiries may be from someone coming to a physical desk in the library, but it may just as well be from a remote user via email. Reference librarians have long been contactable via email, and increasingly are moving to offer web based reference services. There are still technical constraints to be overcome with regard to offering fully developed, interactive services of this kind, for example video technology, such as CU-See Me.

The University of Queensland Library is currently developing a web based reference service to complement the traditional physical service-desk based enquiry service. Clients will be able to send an electronic enquiry from wherever they are, at any time, without restriction to library opening hours, and be assured of receiving a response within a given period of time. The Library is also exploring providing a 24 hour reference service in cooperation with overseas libraries. The intention is that from a web site it will be possible to access a service that will provide assistance with first-level queries.

Teaching and training

Users need training in how to best use the Internet in order to capitalise on its potential as an information resource. Librarians, with their knowledge of information resources and skills in online searching, have radically increased the amount of instruction and training they do.

The University of Queensland Library's range of information skills courses includes:

- effectively searching the Library's web site.
- general approaches to searching databases
- specific programs relating to the use of individual databases
- *Navigating the Internet*, which provides basic skills in the use of standard Internet tools, and *Research on the Internet*, which provides instruction in the use of search tools and indexes to locate relevant information on research topics.
- a ten hour course *Information Skills for Researchers and Postgraduates* offered to postgraduate students and researchers is a comprehensive program addressing all aspects of services provided via the ***Cybrary***.
- courses in *Endnote*, a bibliographic referencing tool.
- subject specific programs.

Attendance at courses is increasing. In 1997 over 12,600 people participated in information skills courses, in 1998 over 24,500, and in 1999 over 33,400.

The Library also provides a number of programs via the Web including "QUIK-IT", an interactive Internet training kit, and Webbook for Engineers which is an interactive information skills program using WebCT developed for first year Engineering students by library staff in conjunction with academic staff. WebCT is also being used for developing web based courses in other disciplines.

In September 1999 the Library conducted a series of focus groups to obtain customer input into the information skills program. Participants included both undergraduate and postgraduate students, and academic staff. Findings included:
- While over 24,500 students participated in the Information Skills Program in 1998, only a fraction of the need was met.
- Customers want flexible delivery of Information Skills training in a range of formats - print, electronic, online and self-paced, face to face.
- Customers are frustrated by their lack of computer skills and feel that this hinders their learning. They view the Library as an appropriate place to learn computer skills and consider that Library staff have the technical and pedagogical expertise to assist them.
- Lecturers' endorsement of program is crucial to acceptance and attendance by students. *Most students will not attend unless encouraged to do so by their lecturer*.
- Information Skills training incorporated into the curriculum of a subject was considered the most relevant, the most useful and most timely, regardless of whether it was for credit or not. Students who had previous experience of this endorsed it.

The Library is continuing to increase the number of courses it provides and constantly revises and updates courses to ensure their relevance. Material is delivered flexibly wherever possible. Some university courses have integrated information skills into their curriculum (Social Work, Law, Engineering) though this is not yet widespread. The incorporation of information skills instruction into the curriculum is being addressed as a priority. A Working Party of the Library Committee of the Academic Board is addressing policy issues and a taskforce of staff is addressing practical issues.

In 1998/99 University of Queensland Library staff reviewed the information technology requirements of one of the university faculties. As part of the review all staff and postgraduate students in departments of the faculty were surveyed. While findings cannot be extrapolated too far, being subject and location specific, they are interesting to note. Findings included:
- the majority of staff are interested in having further training in computer based technologies, particularly in using the web for accessing and delivering course materials.
- 63% of postgraduates would like to learn more about using the Web for research and 58% would like to know more about electronic databases related to their subjects.

Partnerships

Partnerships with faculty are increasing as librarians assist academic staff with teaching and research. Librarians provide advice to faculty on electronic information resources and access to them. This is particularly relevant in a networked environment where the emphasis is increasingly on flexible delivery. As information management competencies are integrated into the curriculum partnerships will increase even more.

At the University of Queensland librarians are being seen as experts with regard to delivering information across the Internet. Many active partnerships with faculty have developed, particularly with regard to the production of web based sources of information.

As there are some common issues for libraries and computing centres, partnerships between these units are developing in universities. In some cases the services are amalgamating. As Rapple (1997) notes, effective partnerships of this type eliminate duplication of effort and waste of resources and provide a more efficient provision of information technology service to clients.

At the University of Queensland the library and computing centre remain separate entities. However the Library provides access to computer facilities through its Electronic Information Centre (EIC) and a Help Desk, badged AskIT, was established at the beginning of 2000 to support students across the university in their use of IT.

AskIT provides general first line assistance facilities for Internet use and PC based software to all University of Queensland students. Its major interactive elements are a face to face enquiry service available at all campuses, telephone, email services, as well as a web site. Chat room and bulletin board facilities will be implemented at a later date. AskIT is located in, staffed and managed by the Library. The majority of queries (e.g., with regard to software applications, web browsers, file retrieval, dial-in access, printing requirements, and email) are handled by library staff. Queries of a complex, or technical nature (e.g., network access problems and password issues) are referred to the computing centre of the University.

The delivery of IT student training for the University is coordinated through AskIT.

Courses offered include IT Fundamentals, IT Intermediate, and IT Advanced. The recent Information Skills Focus Groups conducted by the Library validated this approach with findings indicating students view the Library as an appropriate place to obtain assistance with IT.

Design and production

Librarians are increasingly adopting roles as designers of web pages and digital libraries to facilitate access to information and meet the needs of clients. McNeely (1999) describes how the Richmond Public Library in British Columbia has created an award-winning community based Web site as part of its response to the digital environment.

Prior to 1997/98, when the University of Queensland Library restructured its web pages, the Library's web site was an array of ill-assorted data. This had arisen due to the incremental growth of electronic services. Focus groups with library users were conducted in 1997 to assist in the development of the web site. The aims of the focus groups were to determine the existing client needs in relation to the library web site; obtain client reaction to the model under construction; and, explore a number of existing library web pages to determine patterns of usage and reaction to layout.

The focus group findings were invaluable in redesigning the web site. The results of the research revealed that most peoples' approaches to the Library web site are task-oriented and frequently crisis-driven. Most students approach the Library in search of reference material for assignments, theses and papers. Hence, their primary need is direct access to the catalogue and databases. Whether experienced or not, they are interested in learning how to search more effectively. Level of experience and degree of confidence impact on the ability of people to explore a web site and experienced users are more likely than inexperienced ones to use search engines. Students want speed of access, instant comprehension of link words for efficient browsing, the ability to navigate/explore the site, help with searching, information on University courses and essential information on the Library.

In consideration of the findings, work began on a new presentation of the Library's web pages and the University of Queensland **Cybrary** was developed. Essential items of communication were placed at the first level of the web pages. Information categories were made as clear and concise as possible. Statements were designed to be immediately clear to the lowest level of user and details kept as brief as possible. Layout was standardised across all pages. Non-essential graphics were avoided to reduce the time taken in downloading

The success of the Cybrary is evidenced by levels of usage and feedback from clients. On one day in 1999 there were 20,000 uses of the first page of the Library's web site, 5,000 of these coming from within the library's branches and 15,000 external to the Library. Unsolicited comments from clients, such as that received through suggestion boxes, are consistently favourable and supports data obtained via surveys and evaluation forms.

The Cybrary is continually being evaluated for relevance and effectiveness. Links are constantly being updated. Redesign of the Cybrary is an ongoing process, new services are implemented and existing ones enhanced. The process is driven by client feedback. Quality and standards are monitored by library staff members of a Web Advisory Group (WAG).

CONCLUSION

Today hybrid libraries extend beyond physical walls. Librarians organise and facilitate access to information from print collections or new digital sources. To complement long held information management skills and technical expertise, they have developed strategies that lead their clients into effective access to, and use of information.

Librarians are also teachers and research partners. They are fostering the integration of information skills into the curriculum and increasingly partnering with faculty. They are contributing to the teaching, learning and research processes. Librarians are web designers and producers of information.

Librarians in the digital age are people-oriented, able to interact closely with their clients. They are intellectual flexibility, embrace change and are constantly updating their knowledge and skills.

In the past librarians provided the tools by which users accessed information. This tradition is continuing as they empower their clients to take control of new information tools for themselves. They are leading their clients into the new age of effective information use.

REFERENCES

Association of Research Libraries. (1999). Definition and purposes of a digital library. Retrieved from the World Wide Web October 7: http://sunsite.berkeley.edu/ARL/definition.html.

Hathorn, C. (1997). The librarian is dead, long live the librarian, *PreText Magazine* Retrieved from the World Wide Web October 7: http://www.pretext.com/oct97/features/story4.htm.

Lipow, A.G. (1999). Serving the remote user: reference service in the digital environment. *Proceedings of the Ninth Australasian Information Online & On Disc Conference and Exhibition, Sydney Convention and Exhibition Centre*, Sydney Australia, 19–21 January Retrieved from the World Wide Web October 7: http://www.csu.edu.au/special/online99/proceedings99/200.htm

Maxwell, V. (1998). Changing the game, *Australian Bookseller and Publisher* January/February, pp.28-9. Retrieved from the World Wide Web October 7: http://www.educause.edu/asp/doclib/abstract.asp?ID=CEM971A.

McNeely, C.V. (1999). Repositioning the Richmond Public Library for the Digital Age: one library's perspective, *Library and Information Science Research* 21(3) pp.391-406.

Rapple, B.A. (1997). The electronic library: New roles for librarians, *Cause/Effect* 20(1), 45-51 Retrieved from the World Wide Web October 7: http://www.educause.edu/asp/doclib/abstract.asp?ID=CEM971A.

Rowland, F. (1998). The librarian's role in the electronic information environment, *ICSU Press Workshop, Keble College, Oxford, UK, 31 March to 2 April* Retrieved from the World Wide Web October 7: http://www.bodley.ox.ac.uk/icsu/rowlandppr.htm.

Saffady, W. (1995). Digital library concepts and technologies for the management of library collections: an analysis of methods and costs, *Library Technology Reports 31*, May-June pp.221+.

Tenopir, C. & Ennis, L. (1998). The impact of digital reference on librarians and library users, *Online* 22(6) Nov/Dec pp.84-88.

BIBLIOGRAPHY

Bundy, A. (1999). A partner in learning and research: the Hybrid University Library of the 21st Century, *Academic libraries conference, Bandung Institute of Technology, Indonesia 26 February*. Retrieved from the World Wide Web October 7 1999: http://www.library.unisa.edu.au/papers/hybrid.htm.

England, M. & Shaffer, M. (1999). Librarians in the digital age. Retrieved from the World Wide Web October 7: http://abgen.cvm.tamu.edu/DL94/position/england.html

Matson, L.D. & Bonski, D.J. (1997). Do digital libraries need librarians? *Online* 21(6) Nov/Dec pp.87-92

Newton-Smith, C. (1995). A librarian without a library: the role of the librarian in an electronic age? Retrieved from the World Wide Web October 7: http://www.curtin.edu.au/curtin/library/publications/cnsswelectronicage.html.

Pinfield, S. (1998). With so much information out there, users often have difficulty finding what they want, *Ariadne* 18. Retrieved from the World Wide Web October 7 1999: http://www.ariadne.ac.uk/issue18/main/pinfield.html.

Rusbridge, C. (1998). Towards the hybrid library, *D-Lib Magazine* July/August. Retrieved from the World Wide Web October 7: http://mirrored.ukoln.ac.uk/lis-journals/dlib/dlib/dlib/july98/rusbridge/07rusbridge.html.

Schmidt, J. (1999). Coping with the change in scholarly communication at the University of Queensland Library, *Australian Academic and Research Libraries* 30(2) June pp.89-94

Steele, C. (1998). The digital full monty? Issues in global information access, *LASIE* December pp.16-26.

Tennant, R. (1997). Digital potential and pitfalls, *Library Journal Digital* November Retrieved from the World Wide Web October 7: http://ljdigital.com/articles/infotech/digitallibraries/19971115_2014.asp.

Wilson, T. (1995). The role of the librarian in the 21st century, *Library Association Northern Branch Conference, Longhirst, Northumberland, 17th November.* Retrieved from the World Wide Web October 7: http://www.shef.ac.uk/~is/wilson/publications/21stcent.html.

Chapter 13

Library Web Site Assessment

Ray White
Librarian, South East Metropolitan College of TAFE, Australia

S. P. Maj
Edith Cowan University, Western Australia

Libraries must increasingly compete as providers of information. Most, if not all, libraries now have a Web page that serves a variety of functions. Increasingly for some users the library web page may be their first introduction to a library. Furthermore, on-line use of library resources is becoming increasingly common. Accordingly an effective Web page design is essential. This chapter presents a Web page assessment tool, developed by the authors, based on a model used in the e-commerce sector. This tool was used to analyze the Web pages of libraries in the Australian Vocational Education & Training sector. The results clearly show both the strengths and weaknesses of Web pages. The lack of a standard method and guidelines for web page authoring is discussed.

INTRODUCTION

This chapter sets out to investigate the current state of Web site development within Vocational Education & Training (VET) sector libraries in Australia. The scope has been kept narrow to facilitate comparisons between Web sites. The different goals set for different types of Web sites would cloud issues and make direct comparisons difficult to achieve. In particular the paper aims to, develop a tool for comparing and assessing library Web sites, test the tool on selected library Web sites, identify strengths and weaknesses in the process of library Web site development and, finally, identify directions for future development.

Previously Published in *Managing Information Technology in a Global Economy,* edited by Mehdi Khosrow-Pour, Copyright © 2001, Idea Group Publishing.

Much is written on the application of the Internet to commerce. Here the potential for economic gain funds and fuels a frenetic pace of development. Libraries, on the other hand, have generally been required to meet the new demands and challenges presented by the growth of the Internet with little additional resources.

METHODOLOGY
Literature Research

McClue (1997) concluded that, from the library science perspective, most reports pertained "to the assessment of information content and its organization in the Web site." Smith (1997) proposed a set of criteria, which could be included in a librarian's "toolbox" when selecting sites to "be linked to a resource guide, library Web site or in judging the "appropriateness of information for a particular query or user." However, as suggested by McClure, none of this material considers the assessment of library Web sites.

McClure also indicated that, "Except for the field of computer graphics, most of the literature from the field of computer science does not deal directly with Web site design." He also, usefully observed that, "the literature from the business field focuses on designing Web sites for customer use."

As libraries increasingly regard their users as clients, it seemed reasonable that information produced for the development commercial Web sites could be used. Data on what is held to be good design could be turned into guides for assessment.

Abernathy (1999), for example develops some simple rules of what he refers to as Web site Wow. Windham (2000), concentrates on content. He states that "relevant and dynamic content…keeps the customers coming back."

Gomez.com is a commercial organization which measures the quality of e-commerce Web sites. The company produces a "scorecard" for each Web site it assesses. Up to one hundred and fifty criteria may be assessed on a scorecard for a particular class of web site. Criteria are gathered into five categories as follows:
- Ease of use
- Customer confidence
- On site resources
- Relationship services
- Overall cost

The chapter How to Manage a Library Website (2000) sets out a number strategies library Web site designers can employ to improve their Web sites.

In addition to these general ideas it also offers some specific suggestions, including:

- Keep the look and feel pleasant, consistent and functional
- Have the library catalog included on the site, preferably in a Web based format
- Provide a mechanism for communication with the library
- Establish a reference and information service either by e-mail or FAQ's

A different model was developed by Mich and Franch (2000) in the 2QCV2Q model. This model derives its name from the questions associated with the six loci, or sets of questions introduced by Cicero. The six questions are:

- Identity   Quis (Who)
- Content   Quid (What)
- Services   Cur (Why)
- Location   Ubi (Where)
- Management   Quando (When)
- Usability   Quomodo (How)

Web sites, even in their most simple forms, represent an expenditure of time and effort which, in accountable organizations such as libraries, has to be justified in some way. In order for a Web site to be assessed in terms of how well it fulfilled its purpose, its purpose needs to be clearly stated. Golding, Carter and Konia (2000) detailed the need for the development of Web site guidelines. In developing the guidelines they highlight the need for a thorough needs analysis.

As the literature research failed to produce an acceptable model for a library Web site assessment tool it was decided that one should be developed.

Assessment Tool

The 2QCV2Q model was selected as the starting point for the development of a suitable assessment tool. As developed by Mich and Franch (2000) the model was originally proposed for the evaluation of Web sites in the tourism sector. In modifying the model information was incorporated from all the other papers discovered in the literature research. This was combined with the personal experience of the author as the manager of a VET sector library Web site.

Particular emphasis was placed in expanding the content and services criteria. This was in response to a recurring theme in the literature that, content and interactivity are key factors in determining the usefulness of a library Web site. Each criteria requires a simple Yes or No response. Table 1 sets out the list of criteria developed.

As the only permitted responses are Yes or No the criteria had, in so far as possible, to be stated in a way which does not necessitate a value judgement to be made by the assessor. It proved to be impossible to avoid this in all cases. Forcing a Yes / No answer should, however, limit the confusion in the case of criteria which do not naturally produce a Yes / No answer.

Each of the selected library Web sites was examined by the first named author. Prior to this examination the author had not examined the site. This work aimed to validate the assessment tool. Further validation will require the application of the tool by a wider range of assessors.

Survey

To assist with the validation of the assessment tool and, provide information on the design, construction and management of library Web sites a survey of library managers was also undertaken.

The first section of the survey aimed to get a measure of the degree of importance library managers placed on their Web sites. Questions in this section required respondents to rank their responses to the following the statements:

Our Web site/page is:
* Very Important to the Operation of our Library
* Useful only for information about the Library (hours, locations, etc.)
* Used extensively by external students
* An important way of collecting information from the Internet
* An important way for our users to communicate with us

The second section asked for information relating to the planning process undertaken in the development of the library's Web site. The questions put were:
* Was your site planning included in the planning for your institution's site
* Was the planning for your site assisted by consultants or contractors hired by your institution
* Did you perform a Needs Analysis before designing or implementing your site/ pages
* Was the Needs Analysis formally documented
* Please list the main headings under which the analysis was documented
* Did you conduct any formal survey or research work in drafting the Needs Analysis

The next section looked at design and implementation. The questions in this section were:
* Was the design and implementation of your Web site included in the design of your institution's site
* Was the design for your site performed by:
    ~ Consultants or contractors hired by your institution
    ~ Specialist staff or computing staff working for your institution
    ~ Library staff
* What software tools were used in the creation of your Web site/pages

The following section looked at how the site gets updated. The questions in this section were:
* Have you documented a maintenance schedule for updating your web site/pages
* Is your Web site updated directly by Library staff
* Have you scheduled reviews of the design of your Website

The final section of the survey sought information about staffing issues in relation to the development and maintenance of the library's Web site. The questions put in this section were:

- Does your institution employ a Webmaster or a person responsible for the mainte-nance of its Web site
- Is there a member of the Library staff responsible for the maintenance of your Web site
- What level of formal training does this person(s) have in computer science or multi media
- What level of formal training does the Library manager have in computer sci-ence or multi media

The survey was prepared as a html form on the first author's Web site and the URL sent to selected library managers in an e-mail. Respondents were asked, in the e-mail, to complete the form on line.

Selection of Library Web Sites

The National Library of Australia's library gateway service (http://www.nla.gov.au/libraries) was used to select libraries for this survey.

RESULTS

Assessment Tool Results
Survey Results
Importance

The answers to the importance questions were given numerical values rang-ing from 1 for strong agreement that the site is important to 5 for strong disagree-ment that the site is important. As question two was phrased in the negative the scores were reversed for this question. The scores for each question were added and averaged to give a measure of the importance of the Web site to the library.

Important								Not Important	
1.4	1.4	1.8	2	2.4	2.8	3	3.2	3.4	4.2

Planning
Table 2 details the responses to the questions on planning

Criteria	Number of Positive Responses
Was your site planning included in the planning for your institution's site?	5
Was the planning for your site assisted by consultants or contractors hired by your institution?	1
Did you perform a Needs Analysis before designing or implementing your site/pages?	1
Was the Needs Analysis formally documented?	0
Did you conduct any formal survey or research work in drafting the Needs Analysis?	1

Table 1 shows the number and percentage of library Web sites, which obtained a Y against each of the criteria.
* To score a Y on this criteria a site had to list within two pages of results when searched for an the search engine.

Criteria	Number of Y's	Percentage of Y's
Identify		
Do the pages clearly identify the library service or library	31	91
Do the pages have a consistency of design with the pages of the parent organization	32	94
Do the pages provide a link back to the parent organization's home page	32	94
Do the pages include clear page identifiers	33	97
Do the pages include page footers or headers	22	65
Content		
Do the pages have more than one page	25	74
Do the pages have subject organized links to other web sites	18	53
Do the pages give details of library locations	32	94
Do the pages give details of library hours	31	91
Do the pages give details of collection strengths and weaknesses	4	12
Do the pages give details of library rules & conditions	21	62
Do the pages give details of library services	29	85
Do the pages give details of recent acquisitions	3	9
Do the pages provide an e-mail link	21	62
Do the pages provide an e-mail address	15	44
Do the pages provide a physical address	22	65
Do the pages provide a phone number	27	79
Do the pages provide a fax number	17	50
Do the pages include how to learn & study guides	6	18
Do the pages include referencing & citation guides	9	26
Do the pages include searching guides	13	38
Services		
Do the pages provide access to the library's catalog	18	53
Do the pages provide access to other library catalogs	17	50
Do the pages provide access to other on-line databases	1	3
Can users request, thru the use of forms, additional information	4	12
Can users request, thru the use of forms, reference information	0	0
Can users request, thru the use of forms, new items for purchase	3	9
Can users request, thru the use of forms, the loan of items from the collection	0	0
Can users request, thru the use of forms, inter library loans	2	6
Can users request, thru the use of forms, library membership	17	50
Do the pages provide access to search engines	11	32
Location		
Is the URL intuitive and easy to remember	25	74
Is the Web site easy to locate on Web Wombat (an Australian search engine)*	23	68
Is the Web site easy to locate on the alta Vista*	23	68
Are the pages linked from the parent institution's home page directly (one click required)	20	59
Management		
Is the information up to date	14	41
Do the pages include creation and modification dates	14	47
Do the pages use appropriate technology	33	97
Usability		
Can the pages be accessed with standard hardware and software	33	97
Do the pages support disabled access	0	0
Do the pages download quickly	33	97
Are the pages easy to navigate	34	100
Do the pages support languages other than English	0	0
Are the terms and symbols easy to understand	32	94
Does the site provide a site map or search facility	11	32

Design & Implementation

Table 3 details the responses to the questions on design and implementation

Criteria	Number of Positive Responses
Was the design and implementation of your Web site included in the design of your institution's site?	4
Was the design for your site performed by consultants or contractors?	0
Was the design for your site performed by specialist staff?	1
Was the design for your site performed by library staff?	6

Updating

Table 4 details the responses to the questions on design and implementation

Criteria	Number of Positive Responses
Have you documented a maintenance schedule for updating your Web site/pages?	0
Is your Web site updated directly by Library staff?	7
Have you scheduled reviews of the design of your Web site?	6

Staffing

Table 5 details the responses to the questions on staffing

Criteria	Number of Positive Responses
Does your institution employ a Webmaster or a person responsible for the maintenance of its Web site?	10
Is there a member of the Library staff responsible for the maintenance of your Web site?	7

Only one library reported that the person responsible for updating their Web site had any formal training . Two library managers reported some university training in an information technology related area,. Another library manager reported having attended an introduction to html course.

ANALYSIS

Assessment Tool Data
Web Site Ranking (All Assessment Tool Criteria)

Analysis of the data obtained from the Assessment Tool indicates a broad range of standards. Graphing the distribution of the number of Web sites against the number of positive responses to criteria (Y's) reveals a bi modal distribution. See Graph 1

Graph 1

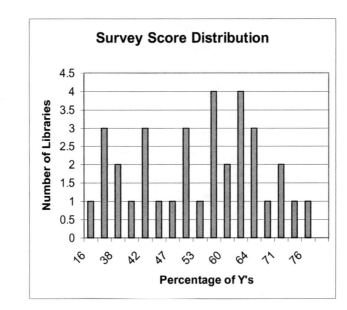

Clearly there is a cluster of Web sites which achieved positive results on approximately 40% of the criteria and, another cluster achieving around 65%.

This supports the observation that some library Web sites exist only because they are part of their parent institution's site. They often contain a minimum of information. Often the information is in a standard format for the site.

Other Web sites appear to demonstrate a strong commitment on the part of the library to use the Web to extend the services they provide. In many ways these Web sites appear to be following some of the patterns established in e-commerce.

Identity Criteria
Most library Web sites identify the library and the library pages well.

Content Criteria
Only 74% of the library Web sites surveyed had more than one page.

Location and contact information was generally well provided. Over 90% of Web sites provided location and hours information. 79% gave phone numbers and 62% gave an e-mail address.

Beyond this basic information, however, many sites failed to offer the user very much at all. Only 9% of sites provided information on recent additions to the library collection. Given the emphasis on currency in the e-commerce literature this represents a very poor result.

Another key content area found on a few library Web sites is study assistance information. In particular the assessment tool looked for three features commonly found on library Web sites in the academic domain; study and learning guides, searching guides and referencing guides. These appeared on only 18 – 38% of sites.

Services Criteria

Somewhat surprisingly only 53% of sites surveyed gave users access to the library's catalog. E-commerce literature stresses the need for Web sites to build a relationship with their users. One key way of doing this is by making the site useful in communicating with the provider and a means of conducting business. Frequently this is done with the use of forms, which allow the user to make their requirements known to suppliers. Less than 10% of the library Web sites surveyed provided any forms to request services or information.

Location Criteria

Most web sites were easy to locate using either an Australian (Web Wombat) or international (Alta Vista) search engine. Some URL's suffered as a result of the web page being hosted by a state level organization. This often made them long and not at all intuitive.

Management Criteria

Only 47% of library Web sites surveyed displayed addition and modification dates. Again this is contrary to the recommendations given to e-commerce sites which wish to ensure users revisit the site.

Usability Criteria

All the sites were simple to access and use. Only one of the sites surveyed required anything beyond a standard Web browser.

The lack of site searching software, or site maps (only 32% of sites had one or the other) was noted, but was not considered to be a significant problem given the relatively small number of pages on most sites.

Given that all the sites surveyed were owned by government funded institutions, it was surprising to note that none offered any assistance for handicapped users. Government policy clearly seeks to make access to government services available to all citizens.

Another apparent omission is lack of support for languages other than English. Australia is a very multi cultural country and, many students in the VET sector are migrants seeking to improve their language and other skills to prepare them to enter the workforce. In addition to resident, non English speakers the VET sector is increasingly seeking to market its courses to overseas students. However, the library Web sites surveyed make no effort to accommodate these users by providing even a minimum of non English support.

Survey Data
Needs Analysis

Only one library reported having done any needs analysis before designing its Web site. No sites reported having documented any analysis. Library managers provided comments such as:

"Most of the analysis process was done by the IT Centre. I searched the Internet for information about creating successful / useful Library web pages and passed on this information to the IT Centre staff."

Some libraries were required by their institutions to produce a Web site almost on the spot and were not given any time to do any analysis. For example:

"Development was on short notice and by library staff following the formation of TAFE ?????? from the 4 former ??????? TAFE institutes in 1998." (Author's note. Name omitted to maintain confidentiality)

Lack of a rigorous and well documented analysis appears to be a common feature in the development of library Web sites in the VET sector.

Training & Staffing

Training and staffing are major problems. VET sector libraries are often small and lack the depth of staff necessary to hold the expertise required to take full advantage of the possibilities offered by technology. As noted, only two library managers and one staff member were reported as having any formal training or skills in the information technology area.

CONCLUSIONS

This paper discussed the development of an assessment tool for library Web sites. The tool was based on a model proposed by Mich and Franch (2000) but, was customized for library application.

In the customization process considerable attention was paid to literature from the e-commerce field. While libraries have not traditionally been linked to the commercial world, they are increasingly being required to adopt more customer focussed, client centred methods of operation. In this environment it is entirely appropriate to borrow successful ideas from e-commerce.

The assessment tool was tested on a sample of VET sector libraries from across Australia. It produced a distribution of results, which had a close correlation with the subjective assessment of the first author. The results obtained could be logically explained and justified. It is felt, therefore, that the assessment tool is valid and could be applied effectively to other library situations.

In the process of testing and validating the assessment tool the strengths and weaknesses of VET sector library Web sites were examined. One particular problem is the lack of any formal needs analysis. Without a thorough understanding of the needs of the users and the purpose of a Web site it is arguably difficult for library managers to assess the efficiency and effectiveness of their web sites.

In many ways the situation may be analogous to the situation, which developed in the software industry before the introduction of systems analysis methodologies. The survey results indicate that Web sites are being developed on an ad hoc basis with bits being added as the need or inspiration arises. Experience with other software systems shows that it is almost inevitable this will eventually lead to the development of unmanageable Web sites.

Current systems analysis tools are not well suited to either Web site design or the library environment. A systems analysis methodology, which is suitable to both web site design and the library environment, is required if library Web sites are to progress.

In addition, institution management needs to clearly recognize the role of the library as a key provider of Web site content. Libraries will require additional staffing and training to enable them to take full advantage of the possibilities the technology is offering.

REFERENCES

Abernathy, D. J. (1999). The new rules of website wow. *Training and development*, 53(10), (Oct) p. 16.

About gomez, http://www.gomez.com/about.

Golding, J., Carter, A. and Koina, C. (2000). Library website management guidelines: what you need to know. *Australian Library Journal*, (Feb) pp. 51-56.

How to manage the library website (2000), http://www.wiredlibrarian.com/htmlw/htmls.htm.

McClure, C.R. (1997). User and system based quality criteria for evaluating information resources. http://ora.rsch.oclc.org/oclc/research/publications/review97/mcclure/chapter_1.htm.

Mich, L., and Franch, M. (2000). 2QCV2Q: a model for web sites design and evaluation, *IT management in the 21st century*. 2000 IRMA conference.

Smith, A. G. (1997). Testing the surf: criteria for evaluating internet information resources. *The public access computer systems review*, 8(3).

Smith, A. G. (2000). Evaluation of information sources, http://www.vuw.ac.nz/~agsmith/evaln.htm.

Szalay, M. and Datovech, J. J. (2000). Build your web identity. *E-business advisor*, May.

Windham, L. (2000). Create compelling web content. *E-business advisor*, Feb.

Chapter 14

The World Wide Web & Law Enforcement

Richard A. Halapin
Indiana University of Pennsylvania, USA

SUMMARY

The World Wide Web has exhibited the most explosive growth of any technology ever invented. Two events occurring in the 1992-93 period provided the foundation. First was the decision by Congress to open the Internet to commercial exploitation. The second was the adaptation of hypertext concepts to the Internet, which led to the Web.

Fueled by commercial exploitation, the Web grew in just 6 years, to over 40 million linked computers. Time to such maturity for older communication technologies was measured in decades. The growth has "left in the dust" the development of commercial, civil, and criminal law needed to secure the social benefits of Web technology. Similarly, "Law Enforcement" has been unable to adapt to the Web over such a short period.

While Congress struggles with a new "contract law" for Web commercial transactions, national awareness is growing about undesirable consequences of Web technology. Fraud, pornography, and violence, are exposing the threat potential of the Web. It is clear that "Law Enforcement" must plan for and take action to meet these potential threats.

Methods and procedures for countering threats require that law enforcement officials understand the mechanisms of the Web along all links from user to resource. These officials must also advise legislative bodies on their enforcement needs during "catch-up" with the Web.

Previously Published in *Managing Information Technology in a Global Economy,* edited by Mehdi Khosrow-Pour, Copyright © 2001, Idea Group Publishing.

Law enforcers may quickly acquire Web understanding through a Web Technology Laboratory (WTL). Such a laboratory would function as one of the 7000 Internet Service Providers (ISP) that are the interface between public users and the Web. Since communications between a public user and the Web flow through the ISP, law enforcement depends on understanding that interface.

Implementation of a WTL would require a modest investment of about $40,000. The social payoff in law enforcement officials' abilities to do what legislative bodies will ask of them, and to advise those same bodies on what is possible is unlimited.

WEB PROBLEMS

Commercialization of the Web has brought with it problems in a broad spectrum of public and private concern. National and international agreements are needed to keep the Internet as a relatively open and free medium. Areas of concern fall into groups of market access/control, legal, and financial.

Market Access/Control	Legal	Financial
telecommunications infrastructure	privacy	electronic payments
information technology	security	customs
technical standards	e-commerce Uniform Code	taxation
content	intellectual property protection	

Along with scramble for Web ownership and control, has come an empowerment of the individual as never envisioned. In an age when "freedom of the press" belongs to those that own a newspaper, "freedom of the Internet" belongs to those with Web access. The price of that access in many cases is close to zero, as libraries and schools rush to bring the benefits of Web access to the community. In the home, access begins with the price of a computer, already paid by over half the American families. While many are not connected, families paying the $15-20 monthly access fee are growing rapidly.

In the past, individual freedom has always been easy to champion since there was little chance for an individual to exercise that freedom in an influential manner. Web empowerment provides an individual the means to contact and influence on an individual and mass basis. Topic specific web sites, chat rooms, and mass email provide mechanisms for individuals to express their opinions and exert influence. The Web has even become a weapon of war with governments on both sides liberally spreading their propaganda.

A WIDE SPECTRUM OF THREATS

Many in society have or can obtain the necessary skills and resources to cause substantial disruption in Web services or destruction of Web equipment.

The diversity of people who might engage in such activity brings a broad scope of activity with potentially adverse consequences. Even national intelligence collection may not be distinguishable from threats such as industrial espionage, unintended errors, or curiosity driven hacking. The spectrum of threats includes:

- *Information warfare*: Cyber attacks on US military or economic warfare operations
- *Terrorism:* Disruptive tactics to influence US domestic or international policy
- *National intelligence:* Spying for a variety of economic, political, or military purposes
- *Criminal activity:* Individual or group manipulation of financial accounts or service theft
- *Industrial espionage:* Domestic or international spying on the activities of competitors
- *Recreational hacking:* Unauthorized access to information/communication systems
- *Blunders, errors, omissions:* Incompetent or accidental human actions or inaction
- *Natural events:* Quake and high wind or water driven destruction

WEB TECHNOLOGY

Accessing the Web – Access to the Web is through dedicated and dial-up access. Dedicated access is direct to the Web via a router, or the computer is part of a Web linked network. With dial-up access, connection is over a telephone line using a modem. Internet Service Providers (ISPs), provide dial-up access to the Web for about $20 per month. With a client base of about 500, an ISP gross annual income of about $100,000 adequately covers the cost of equipment, connectivity, and part-time help. Currently, as many as 7,000 small ISPs provide Web connectivity in the US.

Transmission Schemes – Transmission protocols for file transfer (FTP), email (SMTP) and remote computer control (Telnet) have been available for several decades. Telnet supports connection and utilization of a distant computer's resources. FTP is a fast process for transferring files from one computer to another. The transfer of Web pages is accomplished through the hypertext transfer protocol (HTTP) designed to transfer text and multimedia files.

Network Addressing – To attach to the Web, a computer must have a unique Internet Protocol (IP) network address. Packets can be correctly routed based on the four numbers making up the IP address. Each number ranges to a maximum of 255 and is separated by a period, e.g., 133.255.128.94. An IP address may also be assigned a unique name as part of the domain name system (DNS), e.g., mit.edu or microsoft.com.

Domain Name System – The domain name system makes it easier for humans to identify and remember the location of important resources. Because of this role in identifying resources, DNS addresses are also called Uniform Resource Locators (URL). A complete URL will also identify the transmission process used to access the Web resource. The translation of domain names to IP addresses is through services provided by special computers (domain name servers).

CLIENT TECHNOLOGY

Connection – Dial-up access to the Web is over telephone lines using a 33.6 or 56 Kbits/sec modem. Directly connected machines would use a 10 or 100 Mbits/sec network card. Either dial-up or direct access requires Web access permission provided by ISP or organizational network servers. Once Web access is granted, the client computer executes a Web client application or browser.

Process – The basic process consists of hypertext transfer protocol (HTTP) governed transmissions of text and multimedia files between a Web server computer and the client computer. The transferred files display on the client monitor according to Hypertext Markup Language (HTML) rules as interpreted by the browser.

Caching – When a user follows a link to a new Web server page, the browser requests the transfer of all files making up the page. If the page is being revisited, the browser may use files previously transferred to the client computer disk drive cache. Web page files are cached on the client computer for about 20 days and consist of several types, e.g., html, gif, mid, css, and js. Web sites may also transfer cookie files to the client cache. The cookies are retrieved during a later visit as visitor data.

SERVER TECHNOLOGY

Hardware – Web servers are more powerfully versions of desktop PCs. Servers also have a unique IP address and a domain name for Web use. Permanent access to the Web is via a router through a CSU/DSU (channel service unit/ data service unit) that connects to the local phone company or directly to a major ISP. Connections could be DDS (56 Kbits/sec digital data service), fractional T-1, or full T-1 (1.544 Mbits/sec). The servers run client logon, HTTP, FTP, Telnet, email, DNS or other services.

Web Page Access – Information on access may be stored on ISP or organization servers. User logs may be implemented as a management function of routers and name servers. The servers may also operate a shared cache to increase the speed of access for multiple users of the same site. Similarly, the email server may be configured to maintain a history of email transfers and a backup for restoration after unexpected disruptions of service.

Figure 1: Law Enforcement Web Technology Training Site

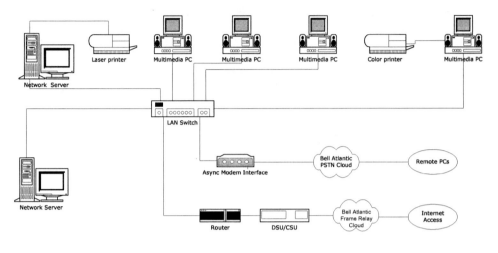

WEB TRAINING

Requirement – Web technology understanding is necessary for law enforcers to accomplish their tasks. That can be achieved through "hands-on" contact with hardware and software used on the Web. Officials should know Web components and procedures from the user interface to the Web server. Understanding evidence available from user Web footprints is the goal.

Officials will understand the evaluation of log and cache files, as they now understand the evaluation of telephone logs. They will experience the many available Web functions. Web experience will allow an understanding of the rationale for the legislation concerning Web activity. And finally, Web technology understanding will bring new tools and techniques to law enforcement.

Such "hands-on" can be provided to a stream of law enforcement officials through the creation of a WTL. The site would function as a small Internet Service Provider (ISP) for several hundred legitimate customers. While providing service, the site would encompass major Web activities for observation and study. Of particular interest would be user logs, caches, and computer email functions. An understanding would be developed of the functioning of chat, and web hosting services. Finally, the site would provide the ability to observe and examine the functions of electronic commerce on the Web.

Web Technology Lab Components – The WTL primary components will be 2 powerful servers, connectivity hardware, and four workstations. The workstations will support Web training and monitoring connectivity. The servers will support all network client/server and management services. The servers and workstations will be routed via fractional T1 and 56Kb/s connections. Web connectivity will be provided via a Hub/Router and a DDS/T1 CSU/DSU. Dial-up connectivity to the WTL will be via modem. Dial-up PPP remote connections accounts will be maintained for customer, officer, and staff remote access. The site goal is to network to the Web and provide accounts to officers, staff, and customers.

WEB TECHNOLOGY LAB COSTS

Equipment and Furnishings – Connectivity equipment, CSU/DSUs, routers, hubs, modems, and cabling ($12,700) account for about 32% of WTL costs. Servers and workstations ($17,000) account for another 42% of capital costs. Software, i.c., graphical operating systems, networks operating systems, and productivity software will be provided by hardware vendors through the hardware specification. About 12% of costs ($5,000) are associated with monitoring software and test equipment for use on-site or off-site. Other site requirements include office furnishings to support and house the equipment ($3,000). Such costs are about 7% of total.

Contractual – On-site communications installations will be the major contractual expense ($1,800). This category amounts to about 4% of costs. Costs to supply safe electrical power, adequate lighting, and cable-pulls are expected to be minimal.

Operating Cost – After installation, training operations will incur frame relay circuit costs (~$180-$460 per month), and internet tariffs (~$1200 per month). As customers increase at the site, revenues will gradually increase to about $4500 per month as capacity is reached. WTL staffing can be expected to be a six day, 12 hour operation, conducted by personnel in training.

Evaluation and Measurement The WTL will collect quantitative information concerning the numbers of officers and staff who participate in training and have active accounts. Evaluation will also be implemented by tracking Web, telnet, FTP and electronic mail usage.

Beyond quantitative measurements, a number of subject measures will be evaluated in determining site impact and success. Administration policy, planning, and resource commitment should reflect WTL support. Officers should be committed to self-training, active involvement with the Web, and excellence in innovation. Officer benefits should be evident from their ability to use computers and the Web in law enforcement.

Chapter 15

Citizen Access and Use of Government Data:
Understanding the Barriers

Richard Heeks
IDPM, University of Manchester, England

*Government data has a value to citizens. That value may be economic —
helping citizens improve their employment or income-generation potential –
or it can be personal/social – helping the citizen to improve their home or
community. Citizen access to government data can therefore be seen as an
important component of both economic and social development. Yet that
access can be a problematic process. This chapter, therefore, analyses the
barriers that need to be understood and addressed if citizen access to
government data is to become a more widespread reality.*

DATA AVAILABILITY

A pre-requisite for citizen access to government data is that the government
first makes that data available to citizens. On this, different governments have
taken different views, some of which create access barriers. These views can be
represented as lying anywhere within a triangle between three extremes, summarised
in Figure 1 (Heeks, 2001).

Previously Published in *Managing Information Technology in a Global Economy,* edited by Mehdi
Khosrow-Pour, Copyright © 2001, Idea Group Publishing.

Figure 1: Government Viewpoints on Public Sector Data

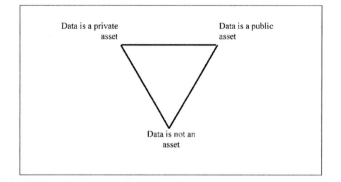

- *Data is a public asset.* Public sector data is owned by everyone since it has been gathered about and from everyone, often compulsorily. The view here is that data should, in general, be made freely available as it can assist both social and economic development. Data should either be made available freely or at a charge that merely reflects the cost of output and transmission. Citizens have a right to see the data held about them and other government data, with certain exceptions.
- *Data is a private asset.* Public sector data is owned by the department which owns the computer on which that data resides. The view here is that the public sector has invested money in producing data which often has considerable commercial value. Data should therefore be sold at the highest possible price to earn valuable revenue for the public sector. Citizens may see the data about themselves and some other items of data so long as they pay.
- *Data is not an asset.* Data is not seen as important enough to warrant open consideration of issues of ownership, value and charging. Where used, data is virtually a personal asset of particular public sector staff. Data is not generally made available and citizens do not have rights of access, except perhaps through 'under the counter' payments.

Different governments take different viewpoints. These different views will present differing hurdles to accessibility: very low barriers under a 'public asset' regime; much higher barriers under a 'private asset' regime. Growth of the Internet and its 'data must be free' philosophy may favour the 'public asset' view.

TECHNOLOGY AND OTHER ACCESS RESOURCES

If citizens can overcome the first hurdle – of having government data made available – they must then have the resources necessary to access that data. Some important access resources are rarely discussed. They include:

- *Money/time*: it costs money and time to access government data. Whilst people tend to have increasing amounts of the former, they have decreasing amounts of the latter.
- *Knowledge*: citizens can only access available data if they know the data exists, that it is available, and how it can be accessed. It would be fair to say that the vast majority of citizens in all countries do not possess this knowledge in relation to all public sector data. Vast swathes of government data remain untapped by huge numbers of citizens simply because they have no idea that it is there or how to get hold of it.
- *Motivation*: citizens must want to access public sector data. Public servants often assume a great thirst for government data exists among the general public, and they suppose that, if only those citizens were given access, they would drink down data by the gallon. In practice, many public information systems are marked less by the enthusiasm of a minority of citizens than by the apathy and disinterest of the majority. Most citizens of Western nations do not care what government is doing. Presented with the Internet, they will follow their main interests of sex, shopping and entertainment rather than details of the latest local government enterprise zone scheme.

The most-discussed aspect of data accessibility is IT. Why? Because, unlike the other resources, it is sexy and tangible. However, IT is very much a two-edged sword as regards access to government data. On the one hand it reduces barriers. Compare downloading a government report via the Internet with going out to buy a paper version. IT has made it far cheaper, quicker and easier to access that data. A wealth of data that, because of the barriers, was essentially inaccessible in paper form becomes accessible when it turns digital. Citizens can also re-use the data more easily because it arrives in electronic form. And a good search engine will reduce knowledge barriers though, as noted, motivational barriers are unlikely to be affected.

That represents the 'good news.' On the downside, IT raises barriers and has created a *digital divide* across which one group reaps the benefits of IT-enabled accessibility and one group cannot. The skills required for accessing manually-held information are little more than literacy. For IT-based data, computer literacy must also be added and not everyone has those skills. Just as important are the issues of cost and ownership. Accessing individual items may be cheaper with IT, but to get that far you need an IT infrastructure in place first – a computer, a network connection, software, and so on. That all costs money whereas, by comparison, actually reading paper-based materials costs nothing.

Governments are generally well aware of the dangers of IT strengthening the *social exclusion* that prevents some citizen groups from fulfilling their economic and social potential. A variety of initiatives are therefore in place that try to overcome ownership and use inequalities. These aim not just to increase access to government data but also to bring other perceived benefits of access to IT: access to IT-related skills, access to employment information, access to lower-cost online shopping, etc.

Some initiatives have focused on *increasing ownership*. For example, in 1997, the Israeli government set up a five-year social inclusion fund of c. US$50m which is purchasing home PCs for an estimated 30,000 poor families (Raab 1997). Other governments have used tax breaks or subsidies as ways to try to increase the numbers of those who actually own IT.

Ownership initiatives can only go so far and, for many, the costs of personal ownership will remain prohibitive. For these groups, governments may set up initiatives focused on *increasing access* to IT that is government- or community-owned IT. Such IT may be placed in a variety of locations:

- Public spaces, such as common areas within shopping malls.
- Semi-public spaces, such as libraries or sport facilities.
- Dedicated spaces, such as community telecentres housing a room-full of Internet-linked PCs.

Such placement of IT only addresses technology barriers, not skill barriers. For some, the skill barriers mean they require the assistance of an *IT intermediary* through whom the citizen indirectly accesses the new IT infrastructure, including electronic public data. Alternatively, they may require an *IT facilitator* who will train them or help them to gain access themselves. These roles may be informal, such as the public librarian who takes time to assist clients, or they may be formal, such as the telecentre worker whose job it is to bring community members online.

Despite all these measures, however, IT inequalities do and will remain. The watchword for government must therefore be 'supplement' not 'supplant.' Provision of public sector data and other services electronically should be seen as an additional weapon in the armoury that sits alongside paper-based or face-to-face methods. It should not be seen as way of replacing those more traditional methods. Unfortunately, cost-cutting pressures in government mean such principles can easily forgotten. As so often with technological change, it will then be the poor and disadvantaged who find they have gained last and gained least from the new technology.

FREEDOM OF INFORMATION LEGISLATION

Recognising some (though not all) of the barriers identified above, and in a bid to ensure access to data across the public sector (and beyond) some governments have introduced *freedom of information* (FOI) legislation. In the US, for example the Freedom of Information Act was introduced in 1966, amended in 1996 by the Electronic Freedom of Information Act, which guarantees public access to most federal government data electronically.

However, the overall impact of FOI for citizens seems limited:

"FOI is used mainly by business to obtain commercial information in Canada and the United States. In Norway and Denmark, it is used mainly by the press. ... In general, FOI does not appear to have been a very potent instrument in the hands of the public to promote greater transparency and participation. Indirectly, however, the threat of its use appears to have caused some greater degree of disclosure, though it has also led to greater use of oral discussion and decision-making, and in some cases the actual alteration or destruction of documents." (OECD 1998:42)

Thus, whilst legislation is a positive move in theory; in practice, it has not yet fulfilled its potential.

CONCLUSIONS: UNDERSTANDING ACCESS AND USE

Citizen access to government data is recognised to bring both economic and social benefits. Yet there are many roadblocks along the path to access. The very first requirement – availability of government data – can be problematic. Governments face the tension of new public management, torn between the public service ethos of providing data for free, and the neo-liberal ethos of charging what the market will bear. The former does not always win out. Nor, despite all the talk of 'egovernment' have public sector procedures yet caught up with the potential for electronic data provision.

In relation to access, a number of barriers exist. Freedom of information legislation has attempted to bring down some legislative barriers, but the self-preserving, sometimes self-serving instincts of many governments have neutered many such initiatives. Governments have been rather better at recognising technological access barriers, but the scale of the task means current projects are but drops in the ocean. And governments have been poor at recognising some of the less tangible access barriers, such as knowledge and motivation.

They seem to have been even worse at recognising that even if all the access barriers identified above could be overcome, they represent only the first step in the process since they merely present the data to the citizen. Many other resources are needed if that data is to be turned into information and if that information is then to be applied for citizen learning, decisions and actions:

- *Data into information.* Data remains data unless citizens have the skills and expertise to turn it into information. In particular, they need the knowledge: to assess whether the data is truth or lies, of value or not; and to apply that data by adapting it to their particular needs and circumstances. Many disadvantaged citizen groups lack such knowledge.
- *Information into action.* Information about new government tax rules is of no value if you cannot afford to pay tax. Information about a government decision that may damage your community is of no value if you lack the money, time, motivation or power to challenge that decision. Information about new employment opportunities is of no value if you lack the skills or knowledge to take up those opportunities.

A model is therefore needed, as shown in Figure 2, that takes understanding beyond just access issues to the whole chain of steps that turn government data into citizen action.

Figure 2: The Information Chain

The model is a reminder of the steps and barriers that citizens face in making use of government data. It is also a reminder that disadvantaged citizens will remain disadvantaged because of inequalities in a broad range of resource endowments – knowledge, skills, money, power and others – regardless of whether they can access data using IT. At best, then, access to data and access to IT are necessary but by no means sufficient conditions to address social exclusion.

REFERENCES

Heeks, R.B. (2001). *eGovernment: An International Text on Public Sector Information Systems*, London: Sage.

OECD (1998). *Impact of the Emerging Information Society on the Policy Development Process and Democratic Quality*, Organisation for Economic Co-operation and Development, Paris.

Raab, B. (1997). Israel, paper presented at *ICA Conference on Integrated Service Delivery: Changing the Role of Government*, 26-30 October, Sydney, Australia.

Chapter 16

The Practice of Information Resource Management in Australian Government Organisations

Richard Potger and Graham Pervan
Curtin University of Technology, Australia

The concept of Information Resource Management (IRM) was introduced in the mid-1970's by the United States federal government as part of its attempt to reduce the paperwork burden on the general public. Since then, the concept of IRM has evolved and taken on many meanings and diverse interpretations ranging from technical perspectives to purely "Information Management" perspectives. These diverse interpretations, at least in the Australian context, have held back the successful implementation of IRM in practice. As part of a larger program of research on IRM, a survey of IS/IT executives in some national and state public sector organisations was conducted. The survey revealed a lack of penetration of IRM in Australian public sector organisations, a pattern of mixed success and even a lack of awareness of IRM.

EVOLUTION OF IRM

IRM was first introduced as a concept in the mid-1970's by the United States federal government in an attempt to reduce the paperwork burden on the general public (Lytle, 1986; Owen, 1989). Although IRM was presented as a planning and control mechanism in the context of records management, the term itself was used to refer to information in a broader context than paper-based documents. The Paperwork Reduction Act (PRA) of 1980 established the framework for developing IRM programs in the United States federal government (Trauth, 1989). Subsequently, the Federal Information Resources Management Review Program was established in 1985 to provide policies and procedures for implementing IRM in federal agencies (Miller, 1988). The PRA of 1995 revises the PRA of 1980 as amended by the Paperwork Reduction Reauthorisation Act of 1986.

The concept of IRM has been significantly expanded since the late 1970's to include:

- the convergence of information technologies and top information executives to manage them (Holmes, 1977).
- the notion of IRM as a mechanism to convert business goals into strategic objectives (Poppel, 1978).
- the notion of information as a valuable corporate resource comparable to capital and labour (Diebold, 1979; Horton, 1979).
- the coupling of the management of the information resource to the overall goals of the organisation (Synnott and Gruber, 1981).
- the management of both information and information technologies (Horton, 1982).
- the function of coordination between the IS department and the user community (Sato and Horiuchi, 1988)
- the integration of the information planning process with the business strategy and the management of the information resource as a shared corporate asset (WAIPC, 1995)

The literature reveals a number of differing perspectives about IRM such as:

- The *information* perspective
- The *data administration* perspective
- The *technology* perspective
- The *management* perspective
- The *organisational* perspective
- Combinations of the *technology* and *data* perspectives

King and Kraemer (1988) noted that implementation of IRM suffers from ambiguities about what it is supposed to accomplish, the breadth of its intentions and the practical constraints of reform in complex organisations. Trauth (1989) noted that although IRM has taken on a variety of interpretations since its beginnings it has three main goals: to maintain a global view of corporate data, to position the CIO at a high level in the corporate hierarchy, and to integrate both information and information technologies.

Ryan, McClure and Wigand (1994) noted that IRM in the 1990s must deal with a fundamental shift in focus from efficient internal management of paper-based information delivery systems to effective management of an externally-targeted, digitally-networked, interactive, exchange of information and services with citizens.

IRM IN AUSTRALIAN GOVERNMENT

When we examine the Australian experience of IRM it is not difficult to understand why it has not progressed much beyond the publication of IRM policy documents and the creation of government Web sites and portals. Clearly, the existence of a state-wide IRM infrastructure dictated by legislation, the involvement of senior agency managers in information policy formulation and implementation, and the integration of IRM processes with other planning activities have been critical factors in the relative success of the IRM effort in America.

It is interesting to examine the development of information and technology policy by Australian federal and state governments (Middleton, 1997):

- 1982 – The State of Victoria is the first Australian state to introduce a Freedom of Information Act, in the same year as the federal Government. Several states now have FoI legislation.
- 1985 – The Federal Department of Science published a discussion document describing a public infrastructure of physical resources such as broadcasting, telecommunications and libraries, and an intellectual infrastructure of education supporting the development of an information economy.
- 1988 – The Federal Government, through the Information Exchange Steering Committee (IESC) of the Department of Finance developed the Government Open Systems Interconnection Protocol (GOSIP) to provide guidelines for public sector electronic information transfer.
- 1991 – The Jones Report identified 21 elements required for a national information policy. A Government response to this report 18 months later acknowledged that information was assuming an increasingly important role in society but avoided the adoption of a national information policy.
- 1992 – The State of Queensland published the Information Technology Industry Strategic Plan and created an Information Industries Board and an Information Policy Board within its Premier's Department. The State of Victoria published Information Technology Management guidelines and a policy promoting departmental use of the Internet.
- 1993 – The IESC published a document on Electronic Data Management giving guidance for electronic document management within the framework of an information management decision model, and a document management life cycle model.
- 1993 – The West Australian state government established the position of the Office of the Information Commissioner. The Commissioner is an independent

officer who is directly accountable to Parliament for the performance of statutory functions. The main function of the Information Commissioner is to deal with complaints made about decisions made by agencies in respect of applications to amend, or seek access to, personal information.

- 1994 – A Commonwealth State Internet Working Party was established by the joint Commonwealth/State Government Telecommunications and Technology Committee in September to facilitate the use of Internet by Commonwealth and State agencies by developing an official hierarchical information framework which, at its highest level, is based on the Australian Government Entry Point.
- 1995 – The Prime Minister established the National Information Services Council to discuss issues associated with the development of a national information infrastructure.
- 1995 – The Department of Social Security launches the Community Information Network pilot project to provide free access to a range of government and community information, and interactive communications facilities such as e-mail and bulletin boards.
- 1995 – The Ministerial Council on Employment, Education, Training and Youth Affairs agreed to a broad framework for the establishment of a national education network (EdNA) to provide a directory of educational services and an interactive massaging service.
- 1995 – The Information Technology Review Group (ITRG) recommended that the Federal Government adopt the concept of a Chief Information Officer (CIO) located in the portfolio of the Minister for Finance. The ITRG also made recommendations regarding various aspects of information management, a number of which would be the responsibility of the CIO.
- 1995 – The State Government of Western Australia in March released its draft document "Information Resource Management Strategies: A Best Practice Guide for Agencies". The document took an all-encompassing view of the information resource that should be managed and recommended the development of an Information Resource Plan through a series of planning activities that included:
  ~ Identifying the *information needs* of the agency from its Strategic Plan
  ~ Modelling how information is acquired, managed and stored within the agency (*information audit*)
  ~ Analysing how information is used (*information use*)
  ~ Displaying the relationship between sources, suppliers, and users of the information (*information mapping*)
  ~ Looking at communications, inter-relationships and movement of information throughout the agency (*information flows*)
  ~ Bringing these together with the needs of the users ad the organisation to analyse shortfalls (*information needs and gap analysis*), and
  ~ Identifying information that can be shared (*information verandahs*)

- 1997 – The Minister for Communications, the Information Economy and the Arts announced the appointment of the Chairman of the Advisory Board of the new National Office for the Information Economy.
- 1999 – The same ministry released the strategy document, "A Strategic Framework for the Information Economy - Identifying Priorities for Action." At its inaugural meeting in December 1998, the Australian Information Economy Advisory Council endorsed the strategic framework and agreed that it is essential for Australia to have a comprehensive national approach to these issues.
- April 1999 – The Western Australian Technology and Industry Advisory Council (TIAC) released a report, titled "Towards an Information Infrastructure Policy for Western Australia: The Business Aspect" (TIAC, 1999). The formal objective of the study, as defined by the TIAC, was:

"To identify Information Infrastructure policy options that will capture maximum economic benefit for all industries across the State."

So, while there have been numerous examples of government policy with regard to IT and related issues they have focussed largely on issues such as technical infrastructure, public rights to information (Freedom of Information Acts) and business opportunities. IRM principles may be found embedded in some of these government initiatives but none, except for the West Australian initiatives, have specifically addressed IRM as a discipline to be embraced by the organisation. The WAIPC guidelines are also the only government publication to specifically use the nomenclature 'Information Resource Management.' Even so, survey and anecdotal evidence suggests that the efforts of the Australian Federal and State governments with respect to IRM have not been entirely successful.

DESCRIPTION OF STUDY DESIGN

As part of a wider study of the practice of IRM in government and private sector organisations, a postal survey of 80 Australian government organisations (40 West Australian and 40 national) was conducted.

The aim of the government survey was to investigate:
1. The penetration of IRM in public sector organisations in Australia
2. The underlying reasons for success or failure in implementing IRM in government agencies
3. The opinion of senior IS/IT executives about the importance of IRM.

While it is acknowledged that an extensive series of case studies would provide greater depth of knowledge concerning IRM in particular organisations, it was felt that a focussed survey of a larger number of organisations would provide a broader picture and was likely to achieve the aim of the study in a shorter time. Follow-up case studies were planned.

To achieve the aims of the study a questionnaire was constructed to collect data in the areas of the respondent's personal profile, the organisational profile, the IS/IT departmental profile, technological factors, organisational factors and IRM factors. The initial version of the questionnaire was piloted tested on six IS/IT managers and suggestions for improvements were incorporated in the final version.

ANALYSIS OF RESULTS

A total of 31 questionnaires were received (response rate 38.75%) and a resampling mailout conducted a month later brought the total responses to 39 (48.75%).

Large regional organisations (>500 employees) were well represented in the sample (56%). With a median of $380M turnover, they spent an average of $5M on IS/IT. Hierarchical control along divisional/functional lines with formal procedures and rules dominated most organisational structures. The role of CIO existed in 15.4% of respondent organisations. Outsourcing of IS development was greater than in-house development.

A significant portion (31.6%) of respondent organisations reported that IRM had never been attempted. A few (5.3%) reported that IRM had been attempted without success, 60.5% reported that IRM had been attempted with some degree of success, while only one organisation reported a great deal of success.

Federal government organisation were more likely (76.9%) to have attempted IRM than their local counterparts (60.4%) with success rates being 69.2% and 64% respectively. This is a significant result considering the fact that the West Australian Government is the only government body in Australia to have published guidelines for the implementation of IRM.

A number of explanations, based on anecdotal evidence, for this situation may be offered. Firstly, individual government agencies are not compelled to comply with these guidelines. The desirability and feasibility of such legislation is debatable. Further, as a result of the lack of legislation, many public sector IS/IT managers have simply ignored these initiatives because of pressure of work from other areas. Secondly, the lack of a high-level Chief Information Officer at the state level to champion the implementation of IRM has meant that the management support so essential for its success has not been forthcoming.

Respondents were asked to comment on the reasons why IRM had never been considered or attempted with no, some, or a great degree of success in their organisations. A total of 19 comments (23.8% of all respondents) were received.

Inhibiting Factors

Seven respondents claimed that lack of management support or follow-through was a factor in either the situation where IRM had never been attempted or where its successful implementation in the organisation was limited.

One respondent, with limited success of IRM noted that the "focus of skill set was heavily technical (*sic*) oriented with low profile sponsor." Four respondents noted that a lack of awareness of the importance of the information resource was an inhibiting factor in the implementation of IRM, with comments such as "the information value is unrecognised," "starting to recognise that data does not necessarily equal information," and "information is a tool that they [management?] do not yet know how to use or exploit" and "not enough people have seen sufficient significance."

Four respondents indicated they had never heard of the term IRM or were unaware of it as a discipline. Other priorities or constraints were cited by three respondents citing reasons such as "other business issues are a higher priority," "lower business priorities than applications," "difficulty in estimating costs, priorities" and "constrained by lack of resources and constant change."

Another respondent with limited success noted that "many of the required disciplines are in place, however extension beyond computer-based data is limited."

Enabling Factors

The one respondent indicating that IRM had been implemented with great success cited the reason for this as being the fact that IRM was "a corporate approach, driven from the top, with strong endorsement and support from the CEO". This response was from one of the six (out of 39) organisations indicating the existence of the CIO role. Those organisations with CIOs were nine times more likely to have attempted IRM with either some, or a great deal of success than those organisations without CIOs. In a study of 110 American firms it was noted that lack of management support was the number one reason for the failure of the IRM effort (English and Green, 1991).

One respondent noted that the requirement for IRM has been recognised and that "a branch has been created to address it, but has been operational for a short time." Moody (1996) recommends the establishment of an IRM Group to coordinate IRM activities within the organisation. Another respondent noted that some success with IRM had been achieved in that "the last Corporate Data Model was part of the Information Architecture developed for the last 5 Year Strategic IT Plan."

A sample of other comments, categorised by answers to the question, are listed:

IRM has never been considered

"never heard of the term but have been doing some of it for years"

"discussions on IRM taking place, but no action yet"

"current data management practices considered satisfactory"

"seen as part of other activities"

"too expensive and difficult"

IRM has been attempted with no success

"difficulty in estimating costs, priorities"

"lack of commitment"

IRM has been attempted with some success

"has been in force for 2 years, generally successful and no sign that it will not proceed"

"not fully adopted in all departments"

"immature IM function in the organisation"

"being implemented. Too early to tell"

"in development stage. IM plan is being developed"

"in the initial phases through review and re-alignment of the IT function"

"formal project successful several years ago, but no follow-up"

IRM has been attempted with great success

"corporate approach driven from the top with strong endorsement and support by the CEO"

CHARACTERISTICS OF AN ORGANISATION THAT WAS SUCCESSFUL WITH IRM

The survey covers a great deal of interacting factors that will require more discussion than is possible for this paper. However, the following information obtained from the questionnaire of one particular respondent presents a profile of an organisation that was particularly successful in implementing IRM.

This was a relatively large national public sector organisation, with 800 employees overall and an IS/IT expenditure of M$14 in 1996. The organisation was characterised by having a hierarchical structure with formal procedures and rules.

It was reported that the organisation culture made it relatively easy to introduce change and innovation. This was achieved by targeted staff development programs and encouragement and support of innovation by individuals. Senior management was somewhat aware of the value of information resources, had a reasonably high level of IS/IT knowledge and a reasonably high perception of the strategic importance of IRM.

The IS/IT department, which had 62 staff, experienced growth over the previous three years and was headed by a CIO who reported directly to the CEO. The department had a federal structure with corporate organisation and control and with some input from other business units. Some system development was outsourced, while in-house development was conducted using multiple methodologies. The IS/IT department concentrated mainly on new applications of IT, standardising IT within the organisation, and assimilating new technologies into its base architecture. IS/IT was used mainly for cost reduction, competitive thrust, product differentiation and customer focus but less for management support or strategic planning.

The issues of coping with an increasing variety of information, reliance on information, client demand for more information, problems comparing consolidating or combining data across systems, and information shortfalls were reported as being somewhat problematic. In contrast, inaccurate or out-of-date information was not a problem at all, and the response was neutral for the issues of data administration difficulties, data access, duplication of data and inconsistency of data.

Both an Information Management Plan and a corporate-wide Strategic IS Plan, conducted after the Corporate Strategic Plan, were produced and these focussed mainly on integrating these plans with the business strategy and using IS/IT for competitive advantage. IS/IT planning was perceived as being interdependent, where development or modification of IS/IT was done in constant alignment within the strategic context. Information Resource Planning and Information Needs Analysis was conducted entirely in-house, but an Information Management Statement did not form part of project proposals. The organisation did report the existence of an Information Management Committee, but no performance indicators had been established. The role of Information Steward had been established within the organisation's business units.

Like many IT-mature organisations, the information resource was held in separate relational databases on different machines, with in-house standards for database design and implementation. A formalised Data Administration role existed within the organisation. Data integration was an objective for the organisation, but only to the extent that was feasible. Total data integration was not intended. A Corporate Data Model was not used. No data dictionary was available and users did not have access to ad-hoc query tools. Users found it reasonably difficult to combine information contained in different systems. Characteristics of organisational information such as timeliness, and completeness rated as very good, while accuracy, precision, conciseness and relevance were rated as quite good.

The most important driver for the implementation of IRM was the awareness of the strategic importance of information. This was followed by an increasing reliance on information, existing information shortfalls and problems comparing, consolidating or combining data across systems. Technical issues such as data administration difficulties, duplication and inconsistency of data were not seen as problematic. Critical Success Factors for the IRM implementation were, in order of importance, business buy-in and involvement, delivery of short-term results, early involvement in systems development and the measurement of results. The organisation was neutral on the issue of focussing on the most critical data. Although no formalised IRM group had been established, a performance measurement program for the IRM effort was planned.

The key message about IRM is perhaps best summarised by this respondent who noted that "Given the strategic importance of IS/IT to any sizeable organisation IRM is a MUST (respondent's emphasis). Efficiencies and competitive advantage will not be realised without a strong commitment to IRM, but the key to success of IRM is strong support and ownership by senior management. This requires significant effort by the IT group, but is absolutely essential".

CONCLUSION AND FURTHER WORK

This chapter has presented some results from a study of the practice of IRM in Australian government agencies. It is clear that implementation of IRM practices is not widespread and that even in the state of Western Australia, where government has been most active in publicising the benefits of IRM, the take-up of IRM practice is at best patchy and success rates are inconsistent. Many senior managers have commented that they were unaware of the concept of IRM.

A number of state agencies consider the methodology presented in the Guide to Information Resource Planning to be too time-consuming and, while they can see the eventual benefits of IRM, the commitment by top management to provide the resources necessary for such an effort is not always available.

The results of this study are limited to the public sector, but a comparative survey has also been conducted in the private sector (state and national) and a series of case studies have been carried out.

REFERENCES

Diebold, J. (1979). IRM: New Directions in Management, *Infosystems*, 26(10), November, pp. 41-42.

English, L.P. and Green, C.W. (1991). Results of the 1991 Advanced IRM Survey Part 1, *Database Newsletter*, 19(6), November/December.

Holmes, F. W. (1977). Information Resource Management, *Journal of Systems Management*, 28(9), September, pp. 6-9.

Horton, F. W. (1979). *Information Resources Management: Concept and Cases*, Association for Systems Management: Cleveland, OH.

Horton, F. W. (1982). *The Information Management Workbook: IRM Made Simple*, Washington, D.C.: Information Management Press.

King, J. L. and Kraemer, K. L. (1988). Information Resource Management: Is it Sensible and Can it Work? *Information and Management*, 15(1), August, pp. 7-14.

Lytle, R. H. (1986). Information Resource Management: 1981-1986, *Annual Review of Information Science and Technology*, 21, pp. 309-335.

Middleton, M. (1997). Information policy and infrastructure in Australia, *Journal of Government Information*, 24(1), pp.9-25

Miller, B. B. (1988). Managing Information as a Resource, *Handbook of Information Resource Management*, New York, NY: Marcel Dekker, pp. 3-33.

Moody, D. (1996).Critical Success Factors for Implementing Information Resource Management, *Proceedings of the 7th Australasian Conference on Information Systems*, pp. 485-495.

Owen, D. E. (1989). IRM Concepts: Building Blocks for the 1990s, *Information Management Review*, 5(2), Fall, pp. 19-28.

Poppel, H. (1978). Portfolio on Information Resource Management -The Process, *Data Processing Management* Auerbach Publishers.

Ryan, J., McClure, C. R. and Wigand, R. T. (1994). Federal Information Resource Management: New Challenges for the Nineties, *Government Information Quarterly*, 11(3).

Sato, O and Horiuchi, M. (1988). IRM as a Coordinating Mechanism: A Study in Large Japanese Firms, *Information and Management*, 15(2), September, pp. 93-103.

Synnott, W. R. and Gruber, W. II. (1981). *Information Resource Management*, New York, NY: John Wiley and Sons.

TIAC (1996). *Towards an Information Infrastructure Policy for Western Australia: The Business Aspect*, Western Australian Technology and Industry Advisory Council, April.

TIAC (1999). *From Mines to Minds: Western Australia in the Global Information Economy*, Western Australian Technology and Industry Advisory Council, February.

Trauth, E. M. (1989). The Evolution of Information Resource Management, *Information and Management*, 16(5), May, pp. 257-268.

WAIPC (1995). *Information Resource Planning*, Western Australian Information Policy Council, December.

Chapter 17

Business Process Reengineering Is Not Just for Businesses But Is Also for Governments: Lessons from Singapore's Reengineering Experience

K. Pelly Periasamy
Nanyang Technological University, Singapore

Business Process Reengineering (BPR) has been hailed as a cure for many of the woes in today's organizations. Many organizations have embarked on BPR but the results have been mixed. Failure is not uncommon but this does not appear to have affected the BPR drive to achieve dramatic improvements in organizational performance. The pragmatic goal-driven approaches adopted by corporations and other businesses position them advantageously in their BPR pursuits. But what about public bodies with their bureaucratic baggage? Is BPR relevant to them? If relevant, is it feasible in the public sector, particularly the public sector of developing nations which tend to have bigger baggage? This chapter draws on the experience of Singapore to suggest strategies for reengineering practice in the public sector of developing countries and other nations.

Previously Published in *Challenges of Information Technology Management in the 21st Century,* edited by Mehdi Khosrow-Pour, Copyright © 2000, Idea Group Publishing.

INTRODUCTION

That "change" is the only thing which does not change is a universal truth and organizations are no exception in spite of their inertia propensities. These changes in organizations tend to be either incremental ones or temporary "fixes" which become permanent in many cases ultimately. In numerous cases, the outcome of this approach is an organization which is ineffectively organized to cope with the demands of today's highly dynamic environment. This state of affairs is particularly evident in the public sectors of many countries, and more so in developing countries (Bartel and Harrison, 1999; Osborne and Gaebler, 1992; Libecap, 1992; McGill, 1999; Wescott, 1999).

People across the globe generally view the public sector as being inefficient in its deliveries (delayed and poor quality service) and ineffective in many of its activities (i.e. efforts do not reach the target group or do not produce the desired results). If a private corporation had had such characteristics, it would have ceased to exist. Public organizations have not been faced with the kinds of competitive pressures which private companies face. However, times are changing and public bodies worldwide are increasingly under pressure from within and without to deliver quality governance and public service. Media portrays a 21st century where governments will need to operate like businesses in serving their people and interacting with other governments and organizations. An inefficient government service would not only adversely affect the affairs of state and a country's position in the world but could also be a drag on its private sector which is increasingly being forced to play in a global field. Developing countries, in particular, need to take heed of this fact in their pursuit of higher level development and greater significance in a global economy.

What can be done to rectify such a situation in the public sector? Osborne and Gaebler (1992) call for "reinventing" it. How can it be reinvented? This paper contends that business process reengineering (BPR) offers an answer. It uses evidence from the BPR literature and data on Singapore's reengineering experience to suggest a reengineering approach for governments. The suggestion is particularly targeted at the public sector of developing nations.

Business Process Reengineering and its Relevance
to the Public Sector

BPR has been hailed by IT management gurus such as Davenport (1993) and Hammer and Champy (1993) as a cure for many of the woes in today's organizations. Numerous organizations have embarked on BPR but the results have been mixed. Failure is not uncommon but this does not appear to have affected the BPR drive to achieve dramatic improvements in organizational performance (Hammer, 1996a). Many companies, in their pursuit of business efficiency and effectiveness, are leveraging on their own experiences and that of others to creatively reengineer their business processes and operations. This task is being made more challenging by new business and technology developments such as the global economy and the Internet.

Differences Between Public Sector and Private Sector

In considering BPR as a prescription for public sector inefficiency and ineffectiveness, one needs to recognize that BPR is very much founded and practiced in the business world and that significant differences exist between the public and private sectors. The typical public body is subject to considerable political influences, strict rules and regulations, very high levels of accountability, and multiple conflicting goals (Robertson and Seneviratne, 1995). It neither has a competitor nor a market (in the conventional sense) to operate in and has a captive "customer" in the members of the public. Questions arise, therefore, as to whether these fundamental differences that exist between the business world and the public sector (Bozeman, 1988; Bretschneider, 1990) rule out the applicability of BPR to the public sector.

Is Reengineering Feasible in the Public Sector?

The public sector is often portrayed as being overly bureaucratic, overweight and averse to change (Claver et al., 1999). In fact, the terms "public sector" and "bureaucracy" are often used interchangeably. As noted by Ackoff (1991), bureaucracy calls for conformity to rules, regulations and procedures, and exceptions to rules, no matter how justified they may be, are viewed negatively. Amusing stories, such as the following, illustrate the consequence of such a state of the state:

• *The British created a civil service job in 1803 calling for a man to stand on the Cliffs of Dover. The man was supposed to ring a bell if he saw Napoleon coming. The job was abolished in 1945* (Townsend, 1971).

Even IT implementations, mainly targeted at improving operational efficiency, have not altered these general portrayal of the public sector, particularly of developing countries. Does this state of the public sector make it an ideal candidate for BPR or does it forebode potential failure for any BPR effort there? Osborne and Gaebler allude to an answer to this question:

"The fact that government cannot be run just like a business does not mean it cannot become more entrepreneurial. ..... There is a vast continuum between bureaucratic behavior and entrepreneurial behavior, and government can surely shift its position on that spectrum."

This chapter argues that reengineering is not only feasible but is also necessary for governments. Governments of developing countries, in particular, may find significant value in BPR for their national development agenda. In spite of significant differences between the two sectors, BPR lessons and best practices are also applicable to the public sector, as is evident from the literature (Grover et al., 1995; Huizing et al., 1997; Margetts and Willcocks, 1994; Neo, 1996c; Periasamy, 1996; Sia and Neo, 1998). Singapore's public sector experience not only supports this argument but also adds to the lessons for effective BPR practice.

SINGAPORE'S REENGINEERING EXPERIENCE

The extant literature on Singapore and annual reports and websites of various public bodies have provided ample data for developing this paper. Additional primary data was collected through interviews and examination of documents of selected organizations.

Singapore, an island city state at the tip of Peninsula Malaysia, was a developing country just a few decades ago. It is small in size, has a population of only 3 million people and has little natural resource. Its only natural asset is its geographic location. Today it is a developed economy which boasts of excellent infrastructure and world-class performance in a number of areas (Guan, 1997; Knoop et al, 1996; The Straits Times, 1998b). Its public as well as private sectors have consistently received top marks (The Straits Times, 1997). Much of the success has been attributed to the government's foresight and proactiveness. One such instance of foresight is the government's decision to position IT as a strategic resource and to progressively exploit it (Neo, 1996b).

Singapore's National Computer Board (now known as the Infocom Development Authority) launched the Civil Service Computerization Program in late 1981 to increase productivity and efficiency in the public sector and to serve as a model for the private sector (http://www.ida.gov.sg). Progressive reengineering on the back of IT has placed the civil service among the ranks of the best in the world (The Straits Times, 1998a). These reengineering achievements are evident and have been well documented (Guan, 1997; King and Konsynski, 1991;Neo, 1996a; Sia and Neo, 1998; http://www.gov.sg; http://www.ida.gov.sg). Information on some of these reengineering cases, the strategies employed and the principles followed are presented below within the context of relevant discussions.

STRATEGIES FOR REENGINEERING
IN THE PUBLIC SECTOR

Hammer's (1996b) key strategies for BPR implementation are as follows:
• Simplify Interface with Public

- Integrate Inter-linked Activities
- Exploit Natural Order of Steps
- Exploit Standardization but Recognize Diversity
- Leverage on Strategic Relationships

These strategies are discussed below with reference to relevant examples and Singapore's experience.

Simplify Interface with Public

The public's contact with a government department should be like that of a customer with a company. With progress in infrastructure and a more informed and educated public, the interface can be simplified or even be eliminated in some cases using new technologies and procedures. Some of the tasks could be relocated to where it makes most sense. The following examples illustrate the potential of this strategy:

- Banks have relocated their customers' most frequent banking transactions (cash withdrawal and enquiry on balance) to easy-to-use electronic cash points located at convenient locations available 24 hours.
- Most airlines today do not require reconfirmation of flight before departure.
- Insurance companies send completed renewal forms to their customers to verify, amend and renew their motorcar insurance policies.
- Payment of bills through GIRO arrangements eliminates customer-company interface and relocates work from the customer to the banks involved.
- Internet allows E-commerce transactions from homes and business sites.

    In addition to the above examples, there are also some cases from Singapore:

- A one-stop customer service is operated by the Housing Development Board[1], Singapore Telecom[2], Singapore Power[3], Inland Revenue Authority[4] and other organizations.
- Customer service over the phone or via the Internet at organizations such as Singapore Telecom and Singapore Power eliminates the need for direct customer contact to render service.
- Bills (e.g. for telephone and utilities), license fee (e.g. for motor vehicle driver and TV usage) and other such payments can be paid at post offices located throughout the country.

Integrate Inter-linked Activities

This strategy essentially involves an empowered employee, equipped with relevant technology, knowledge and information, carrying out a complete task in the process. Hammer and Champy (1993, p. 52) claim that an integrated process "operates ten times faster than the assembly line version it replaces". The one-stop customer service center which many utility companies (such as Singapore

Telecom) and banks (such as DBS Bank, Singapore) have implemented is a popular application of this strategy.

Singapore's Inland Revenue Authority (Sia and Neo, 1997; Sia and Neo, 1998) is a successful reengineering case in the public sector where inter-linked activities have been compressed and integrated. The whole process - from issue of income tax forms, completion of tax returns by tax payer, receipt and processing of forms, computation of income tax and collection of tax - has been integrated through careful structuring of tasks, activities and controls on the back of technologies such as automated document handling, imaging, AI and OCR. Images of tax returns rather than the actual tax return forms are processed. These images do not just speed up tax processing, they also contribute to achieving greater accuracy, more efficient tax collection and better response to queries from tax payers.

Exploit Natural Order of Steps

The natural precedence in a job, rather than artificial ones introduced by linearity or stipulated by outdated procedures, can be exploited in reengineering. Work is organized and sequenced in terms of the natural order of the constituent steps. This approach is widely practiced in the aerospace, automotive and other manufacturing industries (Hammer and Champy, 1993; Nolan, et al, 1995; Sethi and King, 1998).

Singapore's Tradenet (http://www.tradenet.com.sg/; King and Konsynski, 1991; Neo, 1996c) is a practical implementation of this strategy in the public sector for efficient trade operations. It is an integrated computer network through which trade documents and data are entered, processed and electronically communicated with minimum duplication from and to the various parties (the Port Authority, the Customs, importers/exporters, shipping companies, container hauliers, etc.) which play a role in the conduct of trade. Not only does this innovative reengineering dramatically compress trade-activity time through quick communication and parallel relay of documents, it has also significantly brought down costs and increased overall quality and capability of the trade infrastructure in Singapore.

Exploit Standardization but Recognize Diversity

A highly bureaucratic approach is inappropriate for the current world of fast changes and diversity; a more flexible approach is required. While a standard approach would be required for a government department to function, a clearly spelt out procedure for handling the exceptions also needs to be in place. In reengineering the process, the standard procedure is designed for the majority, the straight forward cases. The procedure for handling the exception is not allowed to impact the procedure for the majority. The "Green Lane" and "Red Lane" customs exits in many airport terminals is a practical implementation of this strategy.

The Singapore Inland Revenue Authority, in its goals to achieve maximum efficiency, has recently streamlined tax assessment forms in favor of wage-earners (the majority of tax payers) making it easy for them to complete the form. The wage-earner does not have to include normal wages and benefits, details of which are automatically provided by his employer directly to the Authority. Neither does he have to fill in details of dividends received from shares in listed companies. The next step in this reengineering is E-Filing, the submission of tax returns electronically through the Internet from anywhere in the world.

Leverage on Strategic Relationships

Businesses today are faced with the challenge of meeting changing customer needs and expectations, reducing costs, and being globally competitive. To meet this ongoing challenge, companies are implementing the notion of virtual corporation[5] as a corporate strategy. The 'virtual corporation' is a new kind of enterprise forged by trust and partnership arrangements with business partners and associates. The corporation is founded on IT and other technologies such that the enterprise delivering the goods and services is far more effective than what is permitted by its organization and physical structures. For example, in the retail industry, the retailer functioning as a virtual corporation shares information on sales and inventory with its suppliers via integrated information systems. The information sharing enables suppliers to make prompt deliveries and support low inventories in the stores.

The concept of virtual corporation is a reality and is beginning to extend beyond the business domain to the public sector. For example, the Singapore public sector has already embarked on creating an electronic public service which links various agencies together to deliver one-stop service to the public (Gilbert, Neo and Soh, 1996; Gurbaxani, et al, 1991; Neo, 1996a, 1996b; Neo and Soh, 1996; http://www.ida.gov.sg; http://www.gov.sg/). Creative use of IT in the realization of an efficient and effective "Electronic Government" has placed Singapore in a competitive position in the dynamic global arena. Singapore's Tradenet is a well-known virtual entity for conducting real import/export operations efficiently in Singapore. The "virtual corporation" strategy offers an opportunity for public bodies to deliver service far greater than what they are physically capable of individually. The virtual corporation concept, enabled by implementation of appropriate technologies, infrastructure, policies and procedures, will allow the dormant capability and potential of individual public bodies to be tapped in the interest of public service.

Figure 1: Key Reengineering Principles

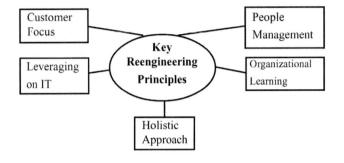

KEY REENGINEERING PRINCIPLES

Any reengineering effort, regardless of strategy employed, should adhere to a few key principles: customer focus, effective people management, leveraging on IT, functioning as a learning organization, and adopting a holistic approach (see figure 1). These principles embody lessons learnt by corporations and organizations in Singapore and across the globe in their reengineering successes and failures (Davenport, 1993; Earl, Sampler and Short, 1995; Guan, 1997; Hammer, 1996a; Hammer and Champy, 1993; Knoop, et al, 1996).

Customer Focus

Every organization, private or public, has a purpose. Its purpose can be defined it terms of how it serves its customers (public). Thus, without customers there would be no rationale for the organization to exist. What goes on inside the organization does not really matter to the customer. What matters is the deliverable and this must relate to the customer's (public's) needs, expectations and satisfaction.

Customer (public) focus is clearly evident in the many facets of Singapore's public sector – from the establishment of one-stop public service centers to the implementation of customer-focused quality procedures such as IS9000 and the implementation of IT:

> "IT systems need to be implemented with the public, the end user, as the focus and not the business functions of the individual government departments." - Ms. Wu Choy-Peng, Senior Director of Government Systems, Infocom Development Authority

People Management

Many organizations are jumping on the BPR bandwagon in the belief that if they get the technology right, their BPR efforts would bear the expected fruit.

However, research suggests that up to 70% of such BPR initiatives fail to achieve the desired goals (Hammer, 1996a; Hammer and Champy, 1993;1997 CSC/Index Survey). What, in spite of all the expenses and efforts, is plaguing BPR? Davenport (1993) offers an answer:

"The rock that reengineering has foundered on is simple: people"

According to senior executives from leading corporations such as Corning, Du Pont and Wal-Mart, people management is central to BPR (Lee, 1995). They maintain that most critical to reengineering are not mechanistic elements but rather organic issues like learning, change management, the creative tension between order and chaos, the continual pursuit of organizational self-awareness and people's values and expectations - in short, how stakeholders are managed during and after reengineering.

People affected by reengineering often resist when the change is not managed effectively. Reengineering must be sensitive to the people's feeling, views and aspirations via a proper change management program. As concluded by Sia and Neo (1998, p. 496, p. 513) in their study of Singapore's Inland Revenue Authority,

"the hard issues in BPR projects are often the soft issues. .... At the heart of change, it is the pool of people resources that matter. Organizations planning large-scale change should therefore not treat people issues lightly."

Successful BPR implementers point to careful planning and strong leadership as necessities for successful reengineering (Hammer, 1996a). They also contend that proper incentives must be in place for those affected by reengineering to support it: an employee is unlikely to contribute effectively to a reengineering effort when he feels that he may loose his job or be adversely affected. The incentives should be designed early as part of a holistic business process redesign.

Leveraging on IT

Davenport (1993, p. 17) argues that IT is indispensable to reengineering:
"By virtue of its power and popularity, no single resource is better positioned than information technology to bring radical improvement in business processes."

The real power of IT is not limited to just making old processes work better, i.e. merely automating tasks previously performed manually. It should enable organizations to break old rules, implement more-effective ways of working and create new business opportunities. It should enhance the capability of the human resource and make them effective knowledge workers who share information and knowledge with others. In short, IT should contribute to the transformation of an organization into a viable, if not a dominant, entity in the industry. Hammer and Champy (1993, p. 83) are uncompromising on this role of IT:

"A company that cannot change the way it thinks about IT cannot reengineer. A company that equates technology with automation cannot reengineer."

There is a realization not only in the private sector but also in the public sector that IT can and must play a key role in forcing down costs, increasing efficiency and enabling the organization to be more effective while still preserving its necessary functions. Singapore is a pioneer in this matter (Gurbaxani et al., 1991; Neo and Soh, 1996), and has positioned IT as a strategic resource to reengineer the state into an *Intelligent Island* (http://www.ida.gov.sg). Currently, the state is implementing Singapore-One, a broad-band wide-area network for linking homes, businesses, schools, public organizations and other entities together for efficient transactions, information access (anywhere, any time and no matter what) and E-commerce (http://www.s-one.gov.sg/mainmenu.html).

Building a Learning Organization

While a company's strategic initiative such as BPR may deliver immediate strategic advantage, the advantage is soon neutralized by similar efforts of its major competitors. Core competence is the more definite route to long-term organizational success and viability. At the root of competence is organizational learning[6] (Senge, 1992).

The viable organization of the future will be a "living" organization today, an evolving organization (via BPR and/or continuous improvement) where learning will be central; it will be a knowledge-based entity. Singapore is seeking to reinvent itself not just as another economically successful nation but also as a knowledge-based economy and a learning organization which can sustain the success and achieve new successes. In fact, continuous learning at all levels and the institutionalization of organizational learning is a fundamental principle in all major BPR efforts of the Singapore government (http://www.gov.sg).

Adopting a Holistic Approach

Reengineering calls for identifying of relevant resources, within and outside the organization, and organizing them such that they can collectively deliver optimal results. Organizations that seek to improve their performance by focusing on the pieces and not the whole are unlikely to succeed in reengineering:

".... tinkering with the individual process pieces is the best way we know to guarantee continued bad performance." (Hammer and Champy, 1993, p. 27)

While a company's reengineering effort may deliver immediate strategic advantage, the advantage could soon be neutralized by similar efforts of its major competitors. A holistic consideration of an organization's resources, including IT, and the fusion of these resources to deliver competence is the route taken by exemplars of corporate success such as Toyota and Xerox and the nation of Singapore (http://www.gov.sg/singapore21/). The *fusion* is a dynamic self-organizing arrangement which responds to and influences the ever-changing business environment via continuous learning about happenings in the environment and within the organization itself. Such a fusion founded on organizational learning is an essential principle for sustained reengineering success not only in the private sector but also in the public sector.

DISCUSSION

Many developing nations are undergoing metamorphosis or seeking to transform themselves on the basis of ambitious visions: becoming a developed nation, securing a place as a competitive player in the global economy, and commanding the respect of the other nations. But the state of some of these nations suggests that these visions are mere dreams. Irrelevant/obsolete practices, rules and procedures tend to gradually accumulate over the years, perhaps going as far back as the colonial era and independence days, and have left a baggage in the public sector. This baggage is causing a drag not only on the public sector but also tends to adversely affect the private sector in its global competitiveness. The ongoing efforts to improve parts of the service have not been sufficient to get rid of this baggage. While reengineering offers a means to decimate this baggage, some countries have chosen the privatization route.

Privatization

Privatization is viewed by some governments as the way to progress public service quickly. However, the results of privatization are mixed, many countries having taken this route on blind faith (Megginson et al., 1994). "It is now widely recognized that privatization, if implemented well, can have multiple direct and indirect benefits ..." (Heracleous, 1999, p. 442). At the core of the "if implemented well" condition are various critical success factors which includes process reengineering. In fact with appropriate reengineering, privatization may not even be necessary in some cases. Heracleous (1999, p. 442) lends support to this argument:"....the dominant view that state ownership leads to inefficiency should be reconsidered . .... it is possible to achieve world-class performance under state ownership, given certain contextual conditions." Reengineering is a useful tool for creating the necessary contextual conditions particularly in relation to organizational processes.

Implementing Reengineering

Successful reengineering is not achieved by merely adopting "best" BPR practices. It needs to be modified and structured to fit the target organization's characteristics and realities. It is also not just a technical task of process redesign, restructuring and technology implementation but is also a matter of political, cultural and social intervention. Hence it must be sensitive to prevailing organizational environment and culture (Bartel and Harrison, 1999; McGill, 1999). Public organizations in particular need to heed this fact in view of their unique characteristics and the significant differences that exist between them and private companies from where BPR practice has emerged. Singapore has been sensitive to these facts and has achieved success in its reengineering initiatives.

CONCLUSION

This chapter has argued that BPR, in spite of its business origin, is also applicable to governments and has offered evidence and suggestions in this regard. In particular, the chapter has advocated reengineering practice to developing nations as a way for them to progress. The chapter concludes by emphasizing that reengineering is more of an art than a science, in spite of its "engineering" label, and that this fact must be noted in any reengineering undertaking.

Reengineering practice is a complex matter requiring proper planning and execution. While adhering to key reengineering principles and deploying appropriate strategies, each reengineering initiative has to be separately planned, organized and executed on the basis of the target organization's heritage, culture, vision, structure, characteristics and environment. Copying a successful reengineering project from another organization, regardless of whether that organization is from the same sector or industry, is unlikely to deliver the desired results. This advice is particularly relevant to developing nations which are examining reengineering successes from nations, such as Singapore, for adoption. Singapore's reengineering achievement may be a model but is definitely not a blueprint for them.

REFERENCES

Ackoff, R.L. (1991). *Ackoff's Fables*, John Wiley & Sons, Inc.

Bartel, A.P and Harrison, A.E. (1999). Ownership versus Environment: Why are Public Sector Firms Inefficient? *NBER Working Paper No. 7043*, Graduate School of Business, Columbia University, March , JEL No. L33, D24.

Bozeman, B. (1988). Exploring the limits of public and private sectors: sector boundaries as maginot line, *Public Administration Review,* 48:2.

Bretschneider, S. (1990). Management information systems in public and private organizations: an empirical test, *Public Administration Review,* 50:5.

Claver, E., Llopis, J., Gascó, J.L., Molina, H. and Conca, F.J. (1999). Public administration: From bureaucratic culture to citizen-oriented culture, *The International Journal of Public Sector Management*, 12(5).

Davenport, T.H. (1993), *Process Innovation*, Harvard Business School Press,

Earl, M.J., Sampler, J.L., and Short, J.E. (1995). Strategies for business process reengineering: evidence from field studies, *Journal of Management Information Systems,* 12:1.

Gilbert, A.L., Neo, B.S. and Soh, C.W.L. (1996). Building National IT Infrastructure: Three Eras in the Convergence of Telecommunications and Computing in Singapore, in Neo, B.S. (editor) *Exploiting Information Technology for Business Competitiveness: Cases & Insights from Singapore-based Organizations*, Addison-Wesley Publishing Co., pp. 7-24.

Grover, V., Jeong, S.R., Kettinger, W.J., and Teng, I.T.C. (1995). The implementation of business process reengineering, *Journal of Management Information Systems*, 12:1.

Guan, L.S. (1997). Sustaining excellence in government: the Singapore experience, *Public Administration and Development*, 17, pp. 167-74.

Gurbaxani, V., Kraemer, K.L., King, J.L., Jarman, S., Dedrick, J.L., Raman, K.S., and Yap, C.S. (1991). Government as the driving force toward the information society: National computer policy in Singapore, *Information Society*,7.

Hammer, M. (1996a). *Beyond Reengineering*, Harper Collins, New York.

Hammer, M. (1996b). *Implementing Reengineering: Strategies and Techniques Workshop*, Center for Reengineering Leadership, Cambridge, MA, July 15-17.

Hammer, M., and Champy, J. (1993). *Reengineering the Corporation: A Manifesto for Business Revolution*, New York: Harper Business.

Heracleous, L. (1999). Privatisation Global trends and implications of the Singapore experience, *The International Journal of Public Sector Management*, 12(5), pp. 432-444.

Huizing, A., Koster, E., and Bournan, W. (1997). Balance in business reengineering: an empirical study of fit and performance, *Journal of Management Information Systems,* 14:1, Summer 1997, 93-118.

King, J. and Konsynski, B. (1991). *Singapore Tradenet (A & B): A Tale of One City*, HBS Case No. 9-192-071, Harvard Business School.

Knoop, C.I., Applegate, L.M., Neo, B.S. and King, J.L. (1996). Singapore unlimited: building the national information infrastructure, *Harvard Business School Case 9-196-012*.

Lee, T. (1995). Reengineering your Reengineering, *Datamation*, Dec. 1, pp. 15-16.

Libecap, G.D (1996). *Reinventing government and the problem of bureau-cracy* .JAI Press Inc, Greenwich, Conn.

Margetts, H., and Willcocks, L. (1994). Informatization in public sector organizations: distinctive or common risks? *Informatization and the Public Sector,* 3(1).

McGill, R. (1999). Civil service reform in Tanzania Organisation and efficiency through process consulting, *The International Journal of Public Sector Management*, 12(5).

Megginson, W.L., Nash, R.C. and van Randenborgh, M. (1994). The financial and operating performance of newly privatized firms: an international empirical analysis, *Journal of Finance*, 49, pp. 403-52.

Neo, B.S. (ed.) (1996a). *Exploiting Information Technology for Business Competitiveness: Cases & Insights from Singapore-based Organizations*, Addison-Wesley Publishing Co., Singapore.

Neo, B.S..(1996b). Introduction: IT and Business Competitiveness, in Neo, B.S. (ed.) *Exploiting Information Technology for Business Competitiveness: Cases & Insights from Singapore-based Organizations*, Addison-Wesley Publishing Co., pp. 1-6.

Neo, B.S. (1996c). Managing Risks in the Tradenet Project, in Neo, B.S. (ed.) *Exploiting Information Technology for Business Competitiveness: Cases & Insights from Singapore-based Organizations*, Addison-Wesley Publishing Co, pp. 193-214.

Neo, B.S. and Soh, C.W.L. (1996). IT2000: Planning for a New National Information Infrastructure, in Neo, B.S. (ed.) *Exploiting Information Technology for Business Competitiveness: Cases & Insights from Singapore based Organizations*, Addison-Wesley Publishing Co., pp. 25-50.

Nolan, R.L, Stoddard, D.B., Davenport, T.H. and Jarvenpaa, S. (1995). *Reengineering the Organization*, Harvard Business School Publishing

Osborne, D., and Gaebler, T. (1992). *Reinventing Government; How the Entrepreneurial Spirit is Transforming the Public Sector*, Addison-Wesley Publishing Company, Inc.

Periasamy, K.P. (1996). *Is Reengineering Feasible in the Public Sector?*, Malaysian Civil Service Conference, Intan, Kuala Lumpur, May.

Robertson, P.J., and Seneviratne, S.J. (1995). Outcomes of planned organizational change in the public sector: a meta-analytic comparison to the private sector, *Public Administration Review,* 55:6, 547-558.

Senge, P. M. (1992). *The Fifth Discipline: The Art and Practice of the Learning Organization*, New York: Doubleday.

Sethi, V. and King, W.R. (eds.) (1998). *Organizational Transformation Through Business Process Reengineering: Applying the Lessons Learned*, NJ: Prentice Hall.

Sia, S.K. and Neo, B.S. (1997). Reengineering Effectiveness and the Redesign of Organizational Control: A Case Study of the Inland Revenue Authority of Singapore, *Journal of Management Information Systems,* 14:1, Summer, 93-118.

Sia, S.K. and Neo, B.S. (1998*).* Transforming the tax collector: reengineering the Inland Revenue Authority of Singapore, *Journal of Organizational Change Management,* 11:61, p. 498-514.

The Straits Times (1997). *Singapore is tops for business...*, 22 August.

The Straits Times (1998a). *PS21 turns three: service best in Asia*, 25 May.

The Straits Times (1998b). *Singapore ranks third on Asia-Pac telecom index*, 13 June.

Townsend, R. (1971). *Up the Organization,* Coronet, London.

Wescott, C. (1999). Guiding principles on civil service reform in Africa: an empirical review, *The International Journal of Public Sector Management*, 12(2).

ENDNOTES

[1] Housing Development Board (HDB) - The public body responsible for providing and maintaining housing for the masses. (For details, visit: http://www.hdb.gov.sg).

[2] Singapore Telecom - recently privatized telecommunications company (For details, visit: http://www.singtel.com).

[3] /), Singapore Power - recently privatized utilities company (For details, visit: http://www.singaporepower.com.sg./)

[4] Inland Revenue Authority of Singapore (IRAS) - (For details, visit: http://www.iras.gov.sg/)

[5] A virtual corporation operates within soft boundaries defined in terms of its own resources and those available to it via its partnership arrangements with its business associates such as partners, suppliers and distributors. The corporation and its associates operate collectively to provide the products and services demanded by the corporation's eventual customers. They share each other's information and operate on a win-win formula whereby the parties achieve profitability and business effectiveness via cohesion

[6] Learning is at the individual level and may remain so unless it is transformed into organizational learning via documentation of what has been learnt or via interactions such as formal and informal meetings, group discussions, brain storming sessions, workshops, reviews and walkthroughs. Learning is about acquiring new knowledge, skills and perspectives in addition to information but is often confused with just receiving information. The informed can quote the information but his or her ability to act on the information is another matter. It is knowledge, the ability to exploit information, rather than information itself that delivers value - that ability is built up via learning.

Chapter 18

Intelligent Transport Systems for Electronic Commerce - A Preliminary Discussion in the Australian Context

Girija Krishnaswamy[1]
Edith Cowan University, Perth, Australia

Intelligent Transport Systems (ITS) refers to transportation systems which apply emerging hard and soft information systems technologies to enhance the overall performance of transport system, presenting a paradigm shift in transportation. Electronic commerce (e-commerce) with its ability to conduct business transactions through open networks and deliver products and services in a global market in which geographical boundaries and location lose their meaning, is creating a paradigm shift in commerce. Information and Communication Technologies (ICTs) is the unifying element in ITS and e-commerce. This chapter analyses the significance of ITS as an enabler to effective e-commerce by supporting logistics and improving supply chain management.

INTRODUCTION

Several studies have been done on different aspects of e-commerce. But an important component of e-commerce, 'transport logistics'[2] has not received the attention it deserves. Transportation of goods and the associated logistics play a key role in effective completion of e-commerce transactions. Again, despite the fact that there has been several studies on Intelligent Transport Systems, the relationship between e-commerce and ITS has not been explored. This paper analyses the significance of ITS as an enabler to effective e-commerce in the Australian context.

Previously Published in *Challenges of Information Technology Management in the 21st Century,* edited by Mehdi Khosrow-Pour, Copyright © 2000, Idea Group Publishing.

The chapter is organised into three sections. In the first section, the relationship between commerce and transportation has been discussed. The next section deals with ITS and provides a brief sketch of the economic benefits of ITS. The potential for integrating ITS and e-commerce is explored in the third section. The paper concludes by raising further research questions.

COMMERCE AND TRANSPORT INDUSTRY
Transport industry in Australia

Efficient transport system is important for any economy. More so for Australia since Australia is different in three distinct and interrelated factors from every developed nation with which it has trade and commerce links. The low density of population, geographic isolation from its international markets and the distances between domestic population centres make transport sector critical for Australia's international and domestic trade.

Transport Composite Index illustrates the significance of transport industry in Australia. It is an indicator of the overall transport activity levels using 12 components which cover transport and storage sector. The index shows progressive growth of transport sector in Australia (Figure 1).

Australia spends a significant part of its Gross National Product on transportation. If our transport system is underperforming in comparison with that of our major competitors, it clearly puts our enterprises and consequently our economies at a competitive disadvantage and puts jobs at risk. A one percent improvement in the efficiency of Australian transportation system would save the economy more than $1.4 billion over the next decade.

World Bank (1999) has identified the following issues in the transport sector.
• Globalization of trade: advances in international logistics (multi-modal transport technology, electronic documentation, and streamlined customs procedures) have greatly expanded the scope for international trade in goods and services.

Figure 1: Source*: Bureau of Transport Economics, March 1999.*

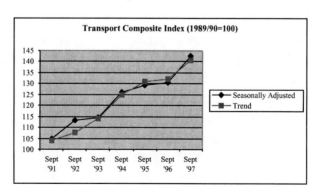

- Congestion and pollution.
- Transport sector deficits: Poorly managed public transport services impose heavy burden on public finance.
- Expenditure needs: large sums of money required maintaining and modernising existing transport infrastructure.
- Capital Flows: the current global financial crisis has sharply reduced private capital flows.

These issues are significant in the context of firms moving towards creating electronic markets and trying to gain competitive advantage through improvements in logistics and supply chain management.

INTELLIGENT TRANSPORT SYSTEMS

Intelligent Transport Systems (ITS) is defined as the application of information technology to the surface transportation system. This technology, which includes communications, sensors and computer hardware and software, allows both travellers and transportation providers to make more effective decisions. ITS which represents a paradigm shift in transportation is the collective name for a wide range of 'smart' technologies with roots in intelligent systems. ITS covers all modes - air, sea, road and rail and all components of each mode - vehicles, fixed infrastructure and control and operational systems. Like internet technologies, ITS also has its origin in United States. In 1991, US Congress authorised a program exploring the use of advanced computer, communications and sensor technologies to improve travel on highways and mass transit. Known as the Intelligent Vehicle-Highway Systems (IVHS) program, the effort was formally established under Intermodal Surface Transportation Efficiency Act of 1991. The initiative since then has been known as ITS program, to reflect its broader, more comprehensive scope as a test bed for developing technologies that enhance and improve the movement of people and goods and increase the capacity of existing roads and highways.

Rather than seeking to improve the transport system through the addition of physical capacity, ITS seeks to improve the operation of the existing transport system. ITS applies communications, advanced electronics and computer technology to improve safety, efficiency and environmental friendliness of transport systems. One of the critical areas of ITS intervention is reduction in congestion. Congestion has been recognised as one of the most significant transport related problems common to every country. In Australia it has been estimated that urban congestion already costs over \$5 billion[3] annually in travel time and vehicle operating costs, of which some 75% occurs in Sydney and Melbourne (ITS Australia[4], 1999). Costs of highway congestion include:

- Added travel time for persons and commercial movements;
- Speed-related effects on fuel use and other components of motor vehicle operating costs;
- Increased variability of travel time.

The congestion costs are borne by drivers in the frustration they are forced to endure and in higher insurance premiums due to senseless accidents, by industry in late deliveries that throw production line off schedule, and by the environment in smog-causing exhaust. Though the use of information technology to mitigate traffic congestion is not new[5], the paradigm shift in transportation occurs when there is a comprehensive solution to transportation problems, one that links the following components[6] into an integrated system.

Advanced Traffic Control
Electronic Toll Collection
Automated Cruise-Assist Highway Systems
Road Safety Enhancement
Incident Management
Driver Information
Route Guidance
Security and Emergency Services
Freight Management Systems
Automatic Vehicle Control Applications

E-commerce and ITS

Ever since internet based business took off in 1998 linking products and markets with a 24-hour ease never before imagined (World Bank, 1999), transport sector has been booming with high level of activity. Even before that, traditional commerce has had dramatic effects on transport requirements worldwide. Commerce has traditionally been a driver of transport industry, and globalization of business is transforming the landscapes of commerce. More firms from more countries now compete internationally as markets rapidly evolve into a single global market. Internet, compatible with, and facilitating globalisation, has the network potential to reform the landscapes of communication and trade.

E-commerce has opened an innovative way of doing business. It facilitates interactive processes such as intelligent collaboration, real-time management and intermediation, and on-demand service delivery. E-commerce has radically changed the way firms operate: on the one end, products and services are advertised and offered on the net. Buyers search and order the products on the net, and even effect payments through internet. On the other end, customers expect faster delivery of goods. This puts pressure on order fulfillment systems. Transport has become a more critical cost factor and integral component in the production and

delivery process. E-competition forces organisations to seek increasingly sophisticated logistics options to meet their inventory-production-delivery flow.

As early as in 1997, OECD[7] has identified delivery of physical goods as a
barrier to e-commerce.

> "... while online transactions are convenient, the immediate off-line de-
> livery of goods is often costly and inefficient. The high cost and inconve-
> nience of international parcel delivery are sufficient to limit the growth of
> international e-commerce to luxury goods" (OECD, 1997).

Organisations cannot afford to miss the economic rewards of e-commerce for
want of efficient supply chain management and order fulfillment systems. The industry estimates that the volume of global transactions on the Web climbed from
$8 billion to $80 billion in the past year, and by 2003 could reach $3.4 trillion,
changing traditional distribution channels forever (World Bank, 1999). As online
orders from consumers and businesses increase, internet sellers will have to sort
out the logistics chaos. Forrester's report 'Mastering Commerce Logistics' pre-
dicts that 'demand for order fulfillment solutions will reshape the existing landscape as logistics suppliers evolve to serve the small-package, individual oriented
needs of commerce site operators' (Forrester Research, 1999).

The role of transport systems in e-commerce cannot be undermined. Storing,
packing, shipping and tracking of hundreds of thousands of products from web-
based retailers have become a booming business for express shippers[8], transportation companies and even traditional postal departments[9]. Shipment tracking was
the first interactive internet application to find a market in freight transport. But
now this is just one of the several applications available on the internet, intranets
and extranets. Others include applications covering bookings, customs clearance,
insurance claims etc. A recent study[10] quantifying the usage for internet for business-to-business (B2B) applications revealed that for some carriers, half of their
interactions with customers are now carried out on the internet. In a survey[11] of
express mail and postal system officials; it was found that e-commerce will be the
primary driver of growth in their industry.

Here is the relevance of ITS to e-commerce. Products and services ordered
over the internet require more delivery trucks on the road to homes and businesses. ITS deployment streamlines the complex, large-scale freight handling and
service delivery systems and increases efficiencies in transportation infrastructure
maintenance. There could be potential gains from integrating ITS and e-commerce. This could apply to multi-modal transport; including port operations, rail/
road interfaces, as well as linehaul operations. The integration of ITS and e-commerce could improve supply chain management by providing useful tools for real
time scheduling of operations. Improving information flows over the internet about
movement of goods facilitate tracking of goods on its entire route. Organisations

could move towards virtual integration, where they create and compete through extended, integrated supply chains.

ITS could facilitate B2B integration, one of the huge strategic trends in the industry. More and more organisations are moving from internal application integration towards integration between business partners. B2B provides links between an organisation's key systems and the applications of its trading partners, suppliers and customers. This enables companies to work with their partners, outsource manufacturing, work with third-party logistics providers and link with their customers. Some analysts predict that B2B integration would give birth to the long-heralded notion of the virtual corporation.

CONCLUSION

E-commerce is redefining the scale and scope of retailing. In the rush to set up websites, organisations are ignoring the back-end fulfillment phase. Unguarded, this could lead to a situation where organisations might dread online success. More empirical work need to be done to look closely at the logistics of the entire process starting from ordering over the internet to delivery of the products/services. If just-in-time e-commerce is to become a reality, organisations need to manage their supply chain effectively. It is argued that effective supply chain management would lower purchasing, sales and marketing costs, reduce inventory, lower cycle times, improve customer service and offer new sales opportunities (National Office for the Information Economy, 1999). Empirical data pertaining to different industries, to identify possibilities for network of consortiums to take care of supply chain management is needed. To date, ITS activity has occurred almost exclusively in the transportation domain. We have to explore the possibilities of multidisciplinary research on the applications of modern information technologies to transportation systems.

NOTES

[1] The author gratefully acknowledges the financial support from Institute of Future Technology, Japan to attend the 3rd Asia Pacific Intelligent Transport Systems conference in Kuala Lumpur in July 1999.

[2] Integrated Logistics Network, Commonwealth of Australia defines transport logistics as all processes concerned with the movement and handling of goods from point of origin to point of consumption.

[3] This is approximately 35.5% of the Road Transport's share of GDP.

[4] ITS Australia is a joint endeavor between government, industry and universities to encourage development and application of these technologies in Australia.

[5] Many cities have installed traffic-management technologies like signal control system or electronic roadway signs that alert drivers to problems ahead and radio broadcasts of traffic conditions at peak commuting times.

6   There is increased demand for optimisation of the utility of existing roads, new ways of traffic coordination and better systems of traffic management. Intelligent Transport Systems holds the key to providing answers.

7   OECD also reports from a recent survey of on-line shoppers by a market research company, in which the most important criteria identified is the timely delivery of goods. 90% of those polled said that they are likely to buy from the same merchant if their goods arrive on time. The survey also found that repeat customers on average spend 50% more than first time buyers.

8   DHL Worldwide Express is projecting 40% annual growth for its online business.

9   Australia Post's Sprintpak service offers a logistic service that allows organisations to outsource their warehousing and fulfillment requirements.

10   Transport Technology Publishing's reference guide to quantify usage of the internet for business-to-business applications in the freight transport market.

11   DHL Worldwide Express survey at the World Express and Mail Conference in Brussels, 1999.

REFERENCES

Bureau of Transport Economics (1999). Government of Australia.

Forrester Research (1999). Mastering Commerce Logistics, Online, Available - http://www.forrester.com/ER/Press/Release/0,1769,160,FF.html.

Integrated Logistics Network (1999). Commonwealth of Australia, Department of Transport and Regional Services, Online, Available - http://www.dotc.gov.au/index.htm.

ITS Australia (1999). National Priority: ITS for Metropolitan Australia – Alleviation of Congestion and its major impacts, Online, Available - http://www.itsa.uts.edu.au/recommendations.html.

National Office for the Information Economy (1999). E-commerce and the Challenge for Australia, presentation at the Australian Institute of Management, Murray Valley Branch by Paul Twomey, Online, Available - http://www.noie.gov.au.

OECD (1997). Dismantling the Barriers to Global Electronic Commerce, Online, Available - http://www.oecd.org/dsti/sti/it/ec/prod/dismantl.htm.

Transport Technology Publishing (1999). Freight@Internet: The Impact of Internet Technologies in the Freight Transport Market, Online, Available - http://www.ttpnews.com/fir/fir.html.

World Bank (1999). The Net Effect on the Nation State, Online, Available - http://www.worldbank.org/ifc/publications/pubs/impwt99/effect/w9effect.html#electroniceconomy.

Chapter 19

Digitization as Adaptation: The Evolution of the Superfund Document Management System

Steven K. Wyman and Verne McFarland
U.S. Environmental Protection Agency, USA

In 1994, the U.S. Environmental Protection Agency's Superfund Program began to develop a paper imaging system known as the Superfund Document Management System (SDMS). SDMS came into being as an attempt to improve management of and access to Agency records. An Agency workgroup composed primarily of Superfund records managers developed functional criteria for the application, and elected an Agency regional office for implementation pilot. At the time of this writing all EPA Superfund regional offices have implemented SDMS. For reasons described in this chapter, even as SDMS achieved institutional acceptance it faced pressures to adapt to internal and external pressures. The emergence of the World Wide Web, the inevitability of electronic records, the rising costs of maintaining large paper collections all combined to produce a niche different in key aspects from that which the system was originally designed to occupy. This chapter discusses how the interactions of two life cycles — records and systems development — affected the fitness of the system to its environment.

Previously Published in *Challenges of Information Technology Management in the 21st Century,* edited by Mehdi Khosrow-Pour, Copyright © 2000, Idea Group Publishing.

DEFINITIONS: PHYLETIC GRADUALISM VS. PUNCTUATED EQUILIBRIUM

In 1972, Gould and Eldredge published a hypothesis that while macroevolution may normally unfold in a gradualistic manner, there was evidence to suggest that episodes of accelerated change occur, as well. The writers termed such accelerations "punctuated equilibria" and added the phrase to the lexicon of evolutionary theory.[1] Gould and Eldredge argued that fossil evidence showed that normal gradualistic background evolution was occasionally punctuated by episodes of relatively rapid change resulting in new species. In the gradualistic model, a species occupies a geographic niche and continuously adapts itself to incremental changes of climate and competition. In this model, the species is restricted by niche and by a localized (thus fairly homogeneous) breeding population from producing sudden and/or large changes in phenotype, which might reduce fitness to the environment. However, two scenarios sometimes occurred which removed those restrictions. The first scenario was a sudden change in the environment itself, such as dramatic climate change, or alteration of the landscape though tectonic or cosmic events, *etc.*, that changed the features of the niche to which a species had adapted. The species would have to undergo accelerated change to adapt to the new conditions, or else face extinction. The second scenario took place when a small group of the population migrated to another territory, such as beyond a mountain range. Differences in available niches and more rapid mutation rates permitted by a smaller breeding population might combine to allow this offshoot to transform into a new species. In the final step of Gould and Eldredge's argument, members of the newer species for whatever reason return to their ancestral range, where the new adaptations provide them advantages over the ancestral stock, which they quickly marginalize or eliminate as rivals for in common resources. Both scenarios describe external forces that pressure the original species to change or collapse. Information systems encounter similar adaptational pressures.

The remainder of this chapter considers in terms of a biological analogy, how the federal records' life cycle affected the Superfund Document Management System's system life cycle resulting in an episode of rapid change. We consider the genotype in our analogy to be the information (federal records) which created the need for SDMS. The SDMS system is treated as the phenotype, or structure designed to carry the genes (records) and interact directly with the environment. The environment is composed of anything, which can affect the niche that SDMS occupies, including organizational use and policies, new technological developments, or end user expectations. There is a deterministic element in this story, which cautions us not to take the biological analogy too literally: The SDMS Workgroup operates to assess internal and external pressures on the system and to direct how SDMS will respond.

GRADUAL CHANGE: PLANNING, DEVELOPMENT, IMPLEMENTATION AND MAINTENANCE

The Superfund Document Management System originated as a document imaging system intended to relieve the Agency of the burden of retaining large paper records collections onsite, and as a mechanism for improving access to records.[2] Two major obstacles stood in the way of a successful system, one a matter of production, the second one of acceptance. Digitization of a paper collection requires ensuring that the paper records are intact. The paper collection underwent intensive organization. The imaging teams indexed every document with over two dozen fields, scanned the paper, and performed painstaking quality assurance and control. For these reasons, there was a relatively long start-up time while the imaging teams built the online collections. Regional adoption of SDMS was voluntary, and during the first several years of implementation only a handful of regions so opted. At the present time, all ten EPA regional Superfund offices have implemented SDMS.

Records and Systems Life Cycles, and SDMS

We define the phases of the federal records life cycle as *creation or receipt, maintenance and use*, and *disposition* (archiving or destruction). There are many descriptions of an information system life cycle, but we will rely on a very simple version for the general level of this discussion. We define the phases of an information system life cycle as *planning / development, implementation, maintenance*, and *upgrading* or *replacement*. The relationship between an information system and the information it contains can be quite complex, and in many ways interactive. That relationship can force the analysis and design phases to overlap implementation, generating a feedback loop that forms an iterative process. This certainly has been the case with SDMS.

Before matching the life cycles we must state some common baseline assumptions held by members of the Agency workgroup responsible for SDMS:
1. Paper records will be imaged.
2. The images will replace paper in organizational use.
3. Paper records will be removed from the active collection to offsite archives.
4. The images will be legally acceptable surrogates of the paper originals.

Some assumptions are packed into these premises (corresponding to the numbers above):
1. There are always paper originals to which the imagers will have access.
2. Staff will use the system.
3. Staff will relinquish paper records.
4. The imaging system is developed to store and retrieve the records without altering them in any material fashion. The imaging system is in effect, an electronic version of the paper records collection, albeit with some value-added features.

Some additional expectations contributed to the decision to develop the imaging system:

- It can be more efficient to use online images than paper. The imaging system offers query capability allowing pinpoint retrieval, whereas paper restricts readers to browsing and physical bookmarks. Location of sought-after information on paper is also limited by infiling accuracy. Electronic bookmarking was designed into SDMS, as was the ability for the user to build special collections associated with their user ID. Optical character recognition (OCR) capability was included in the design, allowing full-text searchers within the limits of the OCR accuracy.
- Imaging records is cost effective. Paper records are subject to loss, misfiling, and deterioration. Each instance may result in high costs to search for or to replace.
- Records are entered into the system during the system implementation phase.

The reality of the implementation exceeded some expectations and fell short of others. A fundamental justification for the system - removing paper records to archives - often met with internal resistance. The transition to a paperless office progressed very slowly. Many potential users observed an extensive technology with relatively few complete records collection available for use. Indeed, the technology was slow to develop, implement and mature, and required a substantial investment of time, capital, and patience. All of these are normally scarce resources. Still, as the online collection grew incrementally larger, so too did the user population. The system did come together a piece at a time. SDMS users sometimes asked why some feature was lacking, only to be told (honestly) that it was planned or in development. Hearing such things over a period of years led some to become skeptical. Even so, the promised features would eventually be included in an upgrade. During its planning and implementation years, as the collections were being built, SDMS operated more as a mechanism for converting paper records to images than as an end-user product. The early years were akin to trying to get people to shop at a store as it was still being constructed. It may be possible to do, but it is inconvenient and the shelves often bare. The danger in this situation is that as system development went on over a period of several years, there were very few true users of SDMS. The development effort tended more towards providing a better imaging system than an end user system. The indexers and scanners involved in building the collections came to be perceived and known as SDMS "users." The virtue of this situation on the other hand, was that the SDMS technical teams managed a good deal of debugging and enhancement before a large group of users logged-on.

Decision Structure

Despite the initial implementation of SDMS in only three regions, from the very beginning the SDMS Workgroup was composed largely of Superfund records managers from all ten regions. Also involved in the Workgroup have been EPA Headquarters and a technical team from the National Computer Center at Research Triangle Park, North Carolina. The SDMS Workgroup is responsible for all decisions regarding SDMS form and function, and developed functional criteria along a approach. Decision making took a democratic 'majority rules' form. The Agency's IT Architecture Roadmap[3] placed parameters around the selection of hardware and software. Agency policy stipulated that whenever feasible, commercial off-the-shelf (COTS) software should be utilized, rather than to code applications in-house. SDMS was put together from commercial parts, but assembling those pieces and aligning the resulting application to changing Workgroup specifications resulted in a good deal of customization and coding.

Stakeholders: Internal vs. External

The SDMS Workgroup had to determine who would be the users of the images, as well as what special viewing equipment and training might be necessary. During the early years the primary targets for use of SDMS images were internal, i.e., EPA employees. To the extent that imaging large portions of the records collection was intended to enhance staff's abilities to perform their functions SDMS provided obvious benefits – once implementation and training reached effective levels. Others perceived the goal to be enhanced public access to Agency information. In fact there are few bright lines between perceptions of the application, while there are substantial overlaps of orientations, with differences of emphases. When different regions developed distinct views of what SDMS was created to accomplish, the stage was set for corresponding divergences in the system itself, as new features and modules were added. SDMS evolved over time: small variations in purpose at one time might produce larger differences in function later on. A constant challenge to the system's development and maintenance has always been keeping the regions aligned. This has gone rather well given the odds against it, and in 1998 the Workgroup met to select core and optional document sets, as well as standardize index field use, and create a formal charter and system management plan.

Aside from moving paper out of the regions, SDMS was initially designed to be an enterprise-wide system for Superfund records access. Linking together all the regional installations of SDMS so that a single point of access allows the user to query a single distributed system has not yet occurred, but is very likely over the next two years. Managers of the system have always walked a fine line between regional variations and maintaining a common orientation. We employ an analogy throughout this paper to help reveal how the interactions of the records and systems life cycles work. Drawing from the concepts and language of evolutionary ecology, we can view the information that populates SDMS as a "genotype." The information is contextualized as documentation of environmental work, and there are very structured processes and prescriptions for identifying, maintaining, using, and disposing of EPA records. Thus we suggest that EPA Superfund records form an "information species," or genotype. Because the records are being recreated in SDMS as images, with the purpose of preserving the genotype as well as manifesting its characteristics in a material form, we can consider the SDMS system itself as a phenotype. Obviously the same information could inhabit any number of other digital systems, meaning that the records / information is the primary material, while the system is secondary. Pursuing the analogy a step further, we assert that the evolution of SDMS as a means for increasing the survivability of information contained within individual Superfund records (genes) has been almost classically Darwinian. Progress has been steady and gradual, with each augmentation of the system being a natural extension of the basic architecture. For example, the addition of a CD-ROM mastering module dramatically increased the end user interest in the system, and made it possible to reach new audiences. However, that module is natural extension of the existing system. Similarly, the creation of a new indexing tool — the Consolidated Indexing Application — was a refinement of existing functionalities. The CIA module was developed with the option to plug in preferred viewers, making color imaging possible in SDMS. It provided tremendous improvements in efficiency and ease of use for the imaging teams. It transformed SDMS from a 16-bit to a 32-bit application, thus greatly expanding the options available to the Workgroup in deciding what SDMS can and should do. In fact, the additions of the CD-ROM mastering and Consolidated Indexing Application modules so improved input and output capabilities that it became more feasible to consider multiple purposes for the system. The synergies produced by these extensions of SDMS, along with a number of internal and external pressures led to a new way of thinking about the system.

In the early years of SDMS the design was a constant, meaning that even when a module or function of SDMS was completed and implemented, the discourse devoted to tuning and revising the system continued unabated. Various phases of the system life cycle, while perhaps discernable by operation, ran concurrently. Today it is fair to say that the original system design and implementation of that design are complete. The image and index databases are well populated and rapidly expanding. SDMS has achieved National System status and undergoes an intensive annual information technology investment review. In some regions imaging has moved beyond special projects, or imaging of targeted records only, to day-forward mode where every record that comes to the records center get imaged. The TIFF4 images populating SDMS are legally defensible in the courtroom, and nationally several certified records image collections have been provided to the Department of Justice on CD-ROM in lieu of paper.[4]

PUNCTUATIONAL CHANGE: UPGRADE OR REPLACE

At about the same time that SDMS was being constructed and piloted in two regions, the World Wide Web began its rise. Within five years it had taken the planet by storm. Its unprecedented ease of use and extension into practically every facet of increasingly ubiquitous information technologies made it a force that SDMS could not ignore. Computer users almost overnight came to expect intuitive graphical user interfaces, multimedia information, and linkage to whatever information they needed wherever it might be. SDMS faced rapid obsolescence even as it began to build critical mass of useful collections. It was just coming through its long developmental journey to full nationwide implementation when the Web volcanoes erupted altering climate and landscape forever. The SDMS phenotype suddenly found itself under severe external pressure. But that was only the beginning.

Costs and Benefits

Almost simultaneously two other sources of pressure came to bear. SDMS carried a steep price tag. Much of the software was developed in-house. The mass storage requirement led to the purchase of expensive CD-R jukeboxes. On the production side the level of indexing took substantial time and effort, translating into high contractor costs. The extensive QA/QC required to ensure the acceptability of the image as a certifiable legal record also inflated the total. Optical character recognition is no substitute at this time for structured indexing, although they do complement one another. Production of the data, maintenance of the system, and training for its use guaranteed that the costs would remain high for the foreseeable future. One benchmark used to measure costs was to track large sets of documents through the entire process. In one case that meant to the point of their delivery on CD-ROM to a federal courthouse in Little Rock, Arkansas for use by the Justice Department in a particular cost recovery action. For that set of 55,000 images the price-per-image to convert from paper to CD came to 85 cents. That is slightly higher than having contractors photocopy the same volume for trial use. However, the DOJ attorneys asked that 17 copies be provided to various parties. When the negligible CD-ROM duplication costs were weighed against the price for as much paper, the savings to the Agency exceeded $100,000.00. The system seemed perched to pay for itself over time, even though there remained questions of how to optimize processes and reduce production costs.

Electronic Records

One of the ways to reduce costs to produce images arose from the third source of pressure: electronic records. From every direction, including legislative, EPA clients such as state and municipal agencies, and the public, and more ... pressures built not only for the government to deliver public records to users electronically, but also provide for electronic records receipt. This is a major issue for federal records managers, and no one can really claim to have all the answer for how this should be accomplished. SDMS was conceived as an imaging system, and not as a repository for any digital format other than TIFF® images. If SDMS were to be the system for storing and retrieving electronic records, then they would have to be as TIFF images. In the configuration that existed less than a year ago, this meant that any records, electronic or otherwise, would have to be printed on paper, the paper scanned to produce TIFF images, and then both the paper and the images managed. Perhaps the paper would be sent to the archives as originally intended, but that approach seemed wasteful to everyone.

During the winter and spring months of 1999, the SDMS Workgroup began to reexamine its assumptions about SDMS. Everyone agreed the system should be reengineed into a Web application. TIFF images are not especially Web friendly, but a related image format — Portable Document Format®⁵ (PDF) — is in fact designed to be transmitted around the Web. Some experimentation revealed that it was possible to convert fax/printer drivers used by scanners to allow electronic production of TIFF or PDF images directly from the original electronic record. Additional research showed that this could be achieved with little or no loss of original formatting for as many as 250 file formats. The race was on.

As research progressed into using utilities to convert heterogeneous file types into a common electronic file format we found that a newer version of the Adobe PDF (4.0) technology even enabled the embedding of many different formats within a single PDF file. These could then be transmitted over the Internet and opened back up with an appropriate viewer with formatting intact. This capability made PDF especially attractive. From a records perspective it appeared possible to do two important things: preserve records content as virtually unalterable PDF images, or if necessary preserve the actual electronic records themselves inside of dynamic PDF "containers." An additional major benefit of the PDF format was immediately obvious: even if a file was converted to PDF and rendered an "image," this didn't necessarily mean a static image. We tested and found that webpages with links, visualization in the form of video, sound, some geographic information systems data, and much more could all be retained with some degree of executability in the PDF format. In February of 1999 the first true electronic record conversion into SDMS took place. One of the regions converted a WordPerfect® document that included tables of analytical data into TIFF images and then loaded the images into the production database without error. It should be noted that placing &/or converting electronic records into SDMS reduces the need for optical character recognition for digital originals. We tested OCR on digital records anyway and found that as one would expect, the results were extremely accurate OCR, although some special characters could cause false reads. With the knowledge gained from testing with conversion tools, advanced OCR packages, with new PDF capabilities, and from internal process reengineering, an electronic records operation began in the Superfund program in the fall of 1999. Several pilots are underway each representing a tremendous volume of records.

Expanding into the New Niche

SDMS is in the midst of a transformation. A large data migration began during 1999 to PDF format. Complex records, multimedia, hypertext, GIS, scientific visualization and modeling, analytical data, digital aerial photographs and much more will be input into the system as electronic records, replacing the paper stream a bit at a time. SDMS has already become a hybrid imaging / electronic records system. The Workgroup has always focused on preserving the integrity of the records and associated data over the form of the electronic record keeping system. That has proven the wiser course. Its progeny is rapidly replacing the ancestral system. As it evolves into a Web application with national system status, the standardization of data and indices allows ready linkage to other systems. SDMS is the scene of several convergences. It is at the nexus of social and technological change. It is on the verge of going from ten individual implementations to a single distributed system with official linkages to several other national Agency systems. The major stimuli for change have been threefold: the SDMS Workgroup listened to the system's users whose expectations rose along with the influence of the Web, standardization and integrity of the data were never compromised, and the genome itself - information on paper records - mutated into electronic records.

The completion of the original system's life cycle was forced by the life cycle of its contents. External events altered the environment for SDMS to a degree that the system must respond or face extinction from disuse. The records within the system, as well as all of the original and subsequent requirements for the system have undiminished value, on the other hand. The emergence of electronic records applied real pressure to adapt. Electronic records though, presented SDMS with a very different problem than paper ever did. Until the implementation of day-forward records scanning, records could be around and used for many years prior to being scanned. They may have gone through nearly their complete life cycle and be put into the scanning queue so that they could be shipped to the archives. Electronic records enter SDMS at a very early phase of their life cycle; just after creation in most instances. Successfully capturing electronic records into the electronic record keeping system greatly reduces the costs of managing records, while providing a more accurate representation of them. In essence, with faithfully preserved electronic records the originals populate the system. The restructured SDMS is both a new phenotype and a new genotype; it looks and feels very different than its predecessor and the information entering the system is coming in significantly more evolved forms. The synergies produced by the hybridization of a robust imaging system with more nimble electronic records features resulted in a new species better fit to a rapidly changing environment. If there is a single key to the successful transition from the old to new SDMS, it is that SDMS is not seen by the Workgroup simply as a technological system, SDMS is a collection of systematized concepts that transcend any particular medium or machinery. As long as that knowledge is preserved, then SDMS has a fair chance to survive further migrations and challenges.

ENDNOTES

[1]   Stephen Jay Gould and Niles Eldredge. *Punctuated Equilibria: An Alternative to Phyletic Gradualism*. In Thomas J. M. Shopf (ed.), Models in Paleobiology. San Francisco: Freeman, Cooper and Co., 1972. Pp. 82-115.

[2]   Verne McFarland and Steven Wyman. *Public Access to EPA Superfund Records — A Digital Alternative*. Digital Libraries '95: The Second Annual Conference on the Theory and Practice of Digital Libraries. June 11-13, 1995 - Austin, Texas. http://www.csdl.tamu.edu/DL95/papers/mcfarland/mcfarland.html>

[3]   The Roadmap is a web document on EPA intranet, and not publicly accessible via the Web.

[4]   Paper originals are rarely introduced into courtrooms in most EPA cases; the Federal Rules of Evidence provide for certified and verifiable reproductions to be presented instead. Images on CD-ROM are no less faithful to the originals than are very good photocopies. Title 28, U.S.C.A. 1732, Chapter 115 — Evidence; Documentary, Section 1732. *Record made in the regular course of business; photographic copies.* Kaki Schmidt, D.O.J.: Admissibility *of Electronically Filed Federal Records As Evidence*, October 1990, paper presented to "The Future of Superfund Information" conference, Dallas, TX, January 1997. John C. Montana: Admissibility *of Imaged Documents in Court*, November 1996, American Records Managers Association conference proceedings, and pp. 471-479.

[5]   Both TIFF (tagged image format files) and PDF (portable document format) formats are owned by Adobe Systems, Inc.

REFERENCES

Eldredge, N. (1999). *The Pattern of Evolution*. NY: W.H. Freeman & Co.

Gould, S. J. and Eldredge, N. (1972). *Punctuated Equilibria: An Alternative to Phyletic Gradualism*. In Thomas J. M. Shopf (ed.), Models in Paleobiology. San Francisco: Freeman, Cooper and Co.

McFarland, V. and Wyman. S.K. (1995). *Public Access to EPA Superfund Records – A Digital Alternative*. Digital Libraries '95: The Second Annual Conference on the Theory and Practice of Digital Libraries. June 11-13, Austin, Texas.

Montaña, J. C. (1996). *Admissibility of Imaged Documents in Court*, November, American Records Managers Association (ARMA) conference proceedings, pp. 471-479.

Schmidt, K. (1990). *Admissibility of Electronically Filed Federal Records As Evidence*, October 1990, paper presented at "The Future of Superfund Information" conference, Dallas, TX, January. Unpublished proceedings.

U.S. Congress. Title 28, U.S.C.A. 1732, Chapter 115 — Evidence; Documentary, Section 1732. *Federal Rules of Evidence.*

The views expressed in this chapter do not necessarily represent those of the U.S. EPA or the United States Government.

Chapter 20

The Implementation of Electronic Network Systems in Japanese Firms

Toshio Mitsufuji
Siebold University of Nagasaki, Japan

INTRODUCTION

This study aims at investigating the implementation process of electronic network systems in Japanese large firms, focusing on the innovativeness among industries to which firms belong. The electronic network systems such as Local Area Network (LAN) have spread rapidly during last several years. Accordingly, many firms in Japan have introduced them in their organizations. After the advent of the computer invention, computer and telecommunications technologies have merged into information technology, making a remarkable progress constantly for several decades.

The electronic network systems are a kind of information technology, going back to 1950s when data communications systems were first developed. In the beginning were these systems managed by professional people. However, due to the rapid progress of the information technology, even untrained people who have no specific knowledge about IT or do not belong to the IT section have been able to use the electronic network systems in business organizations since the late 1980s. In addition, especially with the appearance of multimedia systems and the expansion of the usage of Internet, many organizations have begun introducing electronic network systems since 1990s.

Previously Published in *Challenges of Information Technology Management in the 21st Century*, edited by Mehdi Khosrow-Pour, Copyright © 2000, Idea Group Publishing.

For this study, we sent questionnaires in 1996 to Japanese large firms in which they employed more than 1000 people. Based on the results and the interviews made in connection with this research work, we analyze first the state of the introduction of the electronic network systems, focusing on the innovativeness of firms. Next, we examine why the electronic network systems have come into wide use among Japanese large firms.

ELECTRONIC NETWORK SYSTEMS

Electronic network systems are a kind of information technology (IT) in the sense that IT is the technology into which computer and telecommunications technologies have merged and are no longer separable with each other. We examine mainly the business use of the electronic network systems. They can be classified as either the systems used in a firm (in-firm systems) or those used over a firm (over-firm systems). The "in-firm" network systems indicate these LAN systems in which information is transmitted between information terminals within a firm. The "over-firm" network systems indicate these telecommunications systems in which information is transmitted between the in-firm information terminals and those of the outside of the firm such as mobile systems, in-home devices and/or other firms' apparatuses, as well as between information terminals within a firm.

The electronic network systems originate from the invention of computers. In the early 1950s data communications systems were developed and installed first in the US. In Japan, soon after the introduction of computers, a business firm implemented a data communications system in 1959 after the several years' feasibility study. Since then, big organizations such as banks or railway companies introduced these data communications systems, while the implementations of these systems were limited to a few large companies. Moreover, specialists and engineering professionals, who would later come to form "fortresses" in firms, exclusively managed and operated these systems.

In the early 1980s, a craze for the information systems, so-called "new media" fever took place in Japan. The concept of new media was somewhat vague, but at least they were composed of by cable TV, fiber optics, Videotex, VAN (Value Added Network), LAN and so forth. Many Japanese firms began introducing LAN for their own information systems. LAN is a kind of the electronic network technology, while more often than not specialists and engineering professionals still exclusively operated them in the age of new media. However, around 1990, under the new craze for the information systems the multimedia replaced new media. The word "multimedia" is primarily an engineering term, which means the use of computers to present text, graphics, video, animation, and sound in an integrated way. With the progress of the multimedia boom, the functions of PCs have been greatly improved and much more efficient than before while the ratio of prices to functions have gone down utterly. The spread of multimedia PCs with the increase of Internet use has made the electronic network technology get off the ground. Not only the specialists and engineering professionals but also untrained people, who have no specific knowledge about IT or do not belong to the IT section, have begun using the electronic network systems.

INNOVATIVENESS OF FIRMS

Innovativeness is the degree to which an individual or other unit of adoption is relatively earlier in adopting new ideas than other members of a system (Rogers, 1995). The electronic network systems in the early 1990s are a kind of a new idea for firms, that is, an innovation. In this regard, the faster a firm introduces it, the more innovative it is in terms of their adoption. However, as this innovation has spread quite fast among firms and they adopted one after another almost in the same periods, it is not necessarily correct to determine that a firm is not innovative even if its adoption period is just a bit late. In addition, electronic network systems are too complex to determine the innovativeness of firms only in terms of the adoption period. It is more valid in this case to judge the innovativeness of a firm in terms of what kind of technological levels of innovations it introduces.

Accordingly, this study will compare the innovativeness among industries in terms of technological levels of electronic network systems implemented by firms (problem (1)). Some studies on innovations indicate that the fiercer the competition in the industry to which a firm belongs is and the more experienced a firm is in the innovation, the more innovative it is (for example, Pennings & Harianto (1992), and Attewell (1992)). In order to examine the validity of these arguments, we conduct the survey of innovativeness on Japanese large firms in which their employees are more than 1000. While many studies mention that a firm's scale affects its innovativeness (for example, Mansfield (1961)), this study does not consider the influence of the firm's scale on the innovativeness because we have chosen only large firms in this study [*1].

Secondly, we will investigate whether a firm may pay attention to the behavior of other firms in case of adopting electronic network systems (problem (2)). Bass (1969) states that while innovators adopt an innovation on their own terms, imitators implement it following the people or other units around them. We will examine the applicability of the innovator/imitator model on the implementation of the electronic network systems to the Japanese large firms of the 1990s.

A firm collects a lot of information using various communications channels, when it finds a gap between its result and expectation. Generally the planning and decision making will follow based on the analysis of the surrounding environment. It is usually thought that a firm would have some objectives in order to make a decision and to introduce an innovation. Therefore, in the third place, we will explore both the managerial and practical objectives, based on which it is thought a firm would implement the electronic network systems (problem (3)).

CARRYING OUT THE EMPIRICAL RESEARCH

We sent out questionnaires to 500 large firms in the autumn of 1996, getting answers from 160 firms. In order to examine the problem (1), we choose both the technological levels of the electronic network systems and the media types adopted in a firm. The technological levels of the electronic network systems in a firm are divided into four categories in terms of their usage (see Exhibit (1)). That is, (a) "in-firm and over-firm," (b) "in-firm," (c) "main division," and, (d) "specific division" levels are considered. The technological level of (a) is the highest as regards the innovativeness, while that of (d) is the lowest.

Media types adopted in a firm are divided into four categories in terms of the media usage; that is, (a) "figure and graphics," (b) "sound," (c) "still picture," and (d) "animation." Text media are excluded for the analysis because they must be used without doubt if firms introduced the innovation. We will infer that the more a firm adopts many media, the higher its innovative level is.

Second, in order to verify the problem (2), we classify a firm in terms of its awareness to other firms. That is, a firm introduces the innovation,
(a) without specific consideration of other firms,
(b) in order to obtain the competitive advantage over other firms in the same industry,
(c) in order to catch up with other firms in the same industry, and,
(d) looking for the behavior of firms in other industries.

Therefore, firms choosing the alternative of (a) would be innovators while those choosing (b), (c) or (d) imitators from the view point of the innovation and diffusion theory.

Third, in order to verify the problem (3), we explore both the managerial and practical objectives of a firm, based on which it would introduce electronic net-

Exhibit (1)

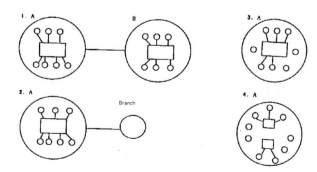

work systems. The managerial objectives of a firm are classified as (a) the effectiveness of the inner organization, (b) the restructuring of the divisions, and, (c) the improvement of the managerial indices such as ROE, ROI. The practical objectives of a firm are classified as (a) keeping the date of delivery strictly, (b) cutting down various costs, (c) improving the qualities, (d) realizing the paperless office, (e) cutting down the staff, and, (f) expanding the market share.

RESEARCH RESULTS

Based on the Japan Standard Industrial Classification, we classify the firms that answered to the questionnaires [*2] into "construction," "manufacturing," "transportation," "wholesale/ retail," and "financial/insurance" industries. The manufacturing industry is further divided into "raw material," "processing/assembly (with the exception of "electric machine/instrument")," and "electric machine/instrument" industries. We distinguish the electric machine/instrument industries from the processing/assembly industries, because as most of the former industries are the main suppliers of electronic network systems their attitudes toward this innovation might be different from those of other manufacturing industries. Exhibit (2) shows some of the research results of the questionnaires, from which we can get several findings as follows.

First of all, we compare the innovativeness among industries about the implementation of the electronic network systems (Problem (1)). The Exhibit (2) clearly shows that the technological levels introduced in the electric machine/instrument industries are relatively high. As is known well, firms that belong to these industries compete quite furiously with each other and have strong propensities toward the high technology, so that they are also considered to be highly innovative for the electronic network systems. This result gives support to the hypothesis which is ascertained by many empirical studies. In addition, because they not only develop a portion of the electronic network systems and/or whole systems in their own firms but also supply them, we can presume that the pro-innovation bias (Rogers, 1995) affects their behaviors of adopting this innovation.

On the other hand, construction and wholesale/retail industries introduce advanced media such as still picture and/or animation for the mid1990s. This tendency may represent the characteristics of the industries. Many figures and drawings are made for a design and used for a presentation in the construction industry, while animations are used for the layout of various goods in the wholesale/retail industries. The results also show that the technological levels of the electronic network systems introduced by industries vary considerably with each other, strongly suggesting the differences of innovativeness between industries.

Secondly, about 70 per cent of firms adopted electronic network systems without paying specific attention to the behavior of other firms (Exhibit (2)). Obviously

Exhibit (2)

(Figures represent per cent)

Industries	technological levels of electronic network systems (#)					media types (+)			
	over-firm	in-firm	main division	specific division	not adopted	figure & graphic	sound	still picture	animation
Construction	7	64	7	7	7	36	7	14	7
Raw material	42	35	19	3	0	58	0	6	0
Processing /assembly	26	55	15	4	0	57	4	19	0
Electric machine /instrument	63	25	13	0	0	50	13	25	13
Transportation	14	57	0	14	7	21	0	14	0
Wholesale/retail	15	54	15	0	8	31	0	23	8
Financial /insurance	0	30	30	30	0	40	0	10	0
Total	28	47	14	6	2	48	3	16	3

Industries	awareness to other firms (#)					managerial objectives (+)				
	by itself	com-petitive	catch up	looking around	others	effective-ness	restruct-uring	Improve-ment	not specific	others
Construction	71	0	7	7	0	79	0	0	7	0
Raw material	77	13	0	10	0	90	6	0	0	3
Processing /assembly	68	13	2	11	2	85	4	0	4	6
Electric machine /instrument	88	0	6	6	0	94	19	0	6	0
Transportation	71	0	0	14	0	79	14	7	7	0
Wholesale /retail	54	31	0	0	0	77	8	0	0	8
Financial /insurance	50	10	0	10	20	80	0	0	0	10
Total	70	10	2	9	2	85	7	1	3	4

Exhibit (2)

Industries	practical objectives (+)						
	delivery date	cost cutback	quality	paperless	staff cutback	market share	others
Construction	0	43	29	29	0	0	14
Raw material	6	39	23	35	26	0	35
Processing /assembly	17	43	26	53	30	2	21
Electric machine /instrument	25	56	31	50	25	13	38
Transportation	0	36	36	43	43	7	14
Wholesale /retail	15	31	31	38	15	8	15
Financial /insurance	10	20	30	20	10	0	10
Total	12	40	28	42	24	3	23

(#) The total does not reach 100 per cent because there are firms that do not answer.
(+) Multiple answers.

they should not be called innovators, because it must not be realistic that so many firms are innovators (Mahajan, Muller & Srivastava, 1990).

How can we explain this? Davies (1979) constructs the cost-benefit model of the adoption process of an innovation among firms assuming that they know the adoption result in advance and introduce the innovational technologies based on the economic rationality. On the other hand, Wildemuth (1992) states that based on the empirical research many firms in the US have introduced computer related appliances very opportunistically and in some cases there is no specific plan. In actuality, according to Wildemuth, they have adopted them not necessarily based on the rational judgement. On the analogy of the Japan's business culture in which a firm frequently looks around and is apt to follow suit, it is more plausible that many Japanese firms have introduced the electronic network systems opportunistically.

In addition, it is worthy of notice that many firms have adopted electronic network systems almost at the same periods. It should be said that they felt no need to pay specific attention to other firms, but judged it inevitable to install the systems. In this sense, a social basis on which the electronic network systems will come into wide use has been formed in Japan in the early 1990s, mainly owing to the emergence of multimedia personal computers, increasing usage of Internet and the expansion of the construction of fiber optic networks.

Thirdly, as far as the managerial objectives are concerned, 85 per cent of firms answer that they have introduced electronic network systems in order to improve the effectiveness of the inner organizations. Moreover, electric machine/instrument and construction industries point out the restructuring of the divisions and the improvement of the managerial indices such as ROE, ROI, as the objectives of implementing electronic network systems. Besides, many firms refer to the "cutback of various costs" and the "realization of paperless offices" as the practical objectives. In addition, we should take notice of the "keeping the date of delivery strictly" and "cutback of the staff" in Exhibit (2). Construction and transportation industries made no specific answer to the former. Of course it is not because they do not care of keeping the delivery period strictly but it must represent the characteristics of these industries. In the construction industry firms may think much more of the cutback of various costs. In the transportation industry they think much more of either realization of paperless offices or cutback of the staff. On the whole many firms seem to regard inner matters like cost cutback, paperless office and staff cutback as more important than outer ones like the market share in terms of the implementation of the electronic network systems.

Exhibit (3)

Year	firms adopting the electronic network systems	
	number of firms	% accumulated
Before 1990	27	16.9%
1991-1992	22	30.6%
1993-1994	39	55.0%
1995-1996	57	90.6%

(Total number of firms that answered to this questionnaire is 160.)

WHY DID FIRMS INTRODUCE ELECTRONIC NETWORK SYSTEMS ALMOST IN THE SAME PERIODS?

Many large firms in Japan introduced electronic network systems so rapidly since early 1990s. The implementation periods by firms are shown in Exhibit (3), which is obtained by totaling up the answers conducted in this research. We can clearly see from this Exhibit that firms, which have introduced electronic network systems in their offices, have increased steadily since 1990.

In this section, we will examine why many firms in Japan started to introduce electronic network systems so rapidly in the early 1990s. The origin of the electronic network systems can go back to the development of the data communications systems in the 1950s. Since then, the electronic network systems have shown the multi-generation and multi-phase development (Shimada, 1991). In the early 1980s, as the new media grew in popular among business people in Japan, many firms vied in introducing the LAN systems. However, the installations of the LAN systems were restricted within specific areas such as wholesale or distribution systems, and almost only professional people managed and operated them. In the early 1990s when the multimedia became in popular, several dominant technologies (Utterback, 1994) appeared almost simultaneously. Especially the multimedia personal computers for the network terminals and Internet and/or intranet for the network systems are the most important. Besides, we cannot overlook the appearance of the low price and high-speed hard disk, the low price and high definition printer, and above all the remarkable improvement of the word processing method for Japanese characters. As the technology clusters for the electronic network systems were finally formed in the early 1990s by a chain of technological developments, even the untrained business people of IT can use the electronic network systems.

In addition, innovations concerning the network or interactive technologies are apt to diffuse explosively, after their adoptions reach the critical mass (Rogers, 1989). With the development of the dominant technologies that hold the key to the success of the electronic network systems, the technology clusters were formed for the innovation, of which adoption reached the critical mass in the early 1990s, and they became implemented among firms at an accelerating rate.

Theoretical innovation diffusion models are broadly divided into two categories (Burt, 1987); that is, the contagion model in which innovations diffuse like an infectious disease, and the threshold model in which innovations diffuse when a member of a social system recognizes that a threshold value exceeds over a certain point (Granovetter, 1978). In addition, Burt proposes the structural equivalence model, in which innovations diffuse when a member of a social system, who recognizes socially equivalent members to adopt them, decides to do so.

According to the result of this research work and interviews with several practitioners in firms, the structural equivalence model is supposed to be the most appropriate to explain the introduction process of the electronic network systems. As the usage of information technology has been to a certain extent established in a firm, it acknowledges the importance of the IT innovations such as electronic network systems. Besides, it obtains all sorts of information from newspapers, technical journals or other mass media in which it is reported that many firms have become introducing the innovation. In consequence, knowing that structurally equivalent firms have introduced the electronic network systems, a firm also decided to introduce them without specific investigation such as cost-benefit analysis.

On one hand, the contagion model does not work out well for this case because about 70 per cent of firms have introduced the electronic network systems without the specific attention to other firms. It is incredible that 70 per cent of a social system are innovators. On the other hand, the threshold model would not explain well the implementation process of the electronic network systems, because, as is well known by IT professionals, it is quite difficult to estimate the benefit before introducing them or even after doing so. Many firms seem to introduce them opportunistically not necessarily based on the rational judgement. Therefore, we cannot apply the threshold or cost-benefit model for the implementation process of the electronic network systems among Japanese large firms at this period.

CONCLUSIONS

The dominant technologies emerged in the IT area such as multimedia PCs, Internet and so forth by the early 1990s, which laid the foundation of the development of electronic network systems. Many Japanese large firms implemented these innovative systems almost simultaneously at this period. This study empirically investigates the implementation process of this innovation, focusing on the differences of innovativeness among industries. The results are as follows. The implementation levels in terms of both technologies and media types among industries vary considerably, strongly suggesting the differences of innovativeness between them. This means that we should be careful enough to analyze in the aggregate the state of the implementation of the IT innovations such as electronic network systems.

Many firms introduce electronic network systems in order to improve the efficiency of their inner organizations rather than to obtain the competitive advantage over other firms. In detail, firms that introduced them refer to the cost cutback and the realization of paperless offices as the most important for the practical objectives. In spite of these generic tendencies, it goes without saying that we should recognize thoroughly the differences of characteristics between industries. In reality, we find some apparent differences of the implementation patterns between them.

Many firms do not pay specific attentions to other firms, when they introduce the electronic network systems. This does not necessarily mean they are all innovators. The structural equivalence model would be the most appropriate to explain the implementation process of the electronic network systems at this period in Japanese large firms. In addition, it is more plausible that many Japanese firms have introduced the electronic network systems opportunistically. It is sure that these findings depend mainly on the facts that the dominant technologies were established for the electronic network technology and that many Japanese firms had a certain amount of experiences to utilize the IT, by the early 1990s.

NOTES

[1] According to the research conducted by the Ministry of Labor (1996), the larger the firms' scales are in terms of the number of employees, the faster they introduce information technologies.

[2] The following analysis in this paper is made for these industries, due to the lack of the answers from other industries.

REFERENCES

Attewell, P. (1992). Technology diffusion and organizational learning: The case of business computing, *Organization Science*, 3(1): 1-19.

Bass, F. (1969). A new product growth for model consumer durables, *Management Science*, 15(5): 215-227.

Burt, R. S. (1987). Social contagion and innovation: Cohesion versus structural equivalence. *American Journal of Sociology*, 92, 1287-1335.

Davies, S. (1979). *The Diffusion of Process Innovations,* Cambridge University Press.

Granovetter, M. (1978). Threshold models of collective behavior, *American Journal of Sociology*, 83(6): 1420-1443.

Mahajan, V., Mullcr, E., and Bass, F. M. (1990). New product diffusion models in marketing: A review and directions for research. *Journal of Marketing*, 54(January), 1-26.

Mansfield, E. (1961). Technical change and the rate of imitation, *Econometrica*, 29(4): 741-766.

Ministry of Labor (1996). *The Informatization of Firms and the Works,* Tokyo: Ministry of Finance.

Mitsufuji, T. (1998). *Communications Technology and Society*. Tokyo: Hokuju-Shuppan.

Pennings, J. M., and Harianto, F. (1992). Technological networking and innovation implementation, *Organization Science*, 3(3), 356-382.

Rogers, E. M. (1989). The "critical mass" in the diffusion of interactive technologies in organizations, *The Proceedings of the Workshop on Survey Research in MIS*, Irvine, California.

Rogers, E. (1995). *Diffusion of Innovations (Fourth Edition)*, New York: Free Press.

Shimada, T. (1991). *The Information Technology and the Management Organization.* Tokyo: Nikkagiren.

Utterback, J. M. (1994). *Mastering the Dynamics of Innovation*, Boston: Harvard Business School Press.

Wildemuth, B. (1992). An empirically grounded model of the adoption of intellectual technologies, *Journal of the American Society for Information Science*, 43(3): 210-224.

Chapter 21

Outline of a Design Tool for Analysis and Visual Quality Control of Urban Environments

Predrag Sidjanin
Faculty of Architecture, DKS, The Netherlands

Waltraud Gerhardt
Faculty of Information Technology and Systems, DBS, The Netherlands

In this chapter, the main idea about a design tool and its object database system will be described. The design tool should improve design practice with respect to analysis and improving existing and planned urban environments. Preconditions for defining the design tool's purpose are the determination of the "well-situated" urban elements, their impact on cognitive mapping, and the exploitation of the knowledge on cognitive mapping for the improvement of urban environments. This leads to the conclusion that an urban environment design, which takes of the process of cognitive mapping into consideration, will be experienced by most of the people in the same way. Investigations of this process result in a conceptual model of the tool by using elements of urban environments, their relationships and their dependencies. The theoretical background of the tool is based on design theory, cognitive science and computer science. Design theory and cognitive science will be used to develop the conceptual model. This conceptual model together with computer science will be the basis platform for tool development. The tool uses a schematic representation of urban environment, based on Lynch's theory of "urban forms." Lynch's theory is crucial for the

Previously Published in *Challenges of Information Technology Management in the 21st Century,* edited by Mehdi Khosrow-Pour, Copyright © 2000, Idea Group Publishing.

tool development because it explains elements of urban environments. Systematic investigation of urban environments and their characteristics are also important for the object schema of the tool. The tool will use an object database system, which help to represent and to handle the urban elements with their properties and relationships, with their natural semantics. The information represented in the database will be used to analyze urban environment with the aim to improve and control their visual quality.

INTRODUCTION

The quality of urban environment has become important for present and future design and planning practice. Research presented in this paper focuses on developing a design tool for analysis and controlling of visual quality of urban environment, based on experience of cognitive mapping.

Planners, architects and urban designers have always been concerned with the relationship between people and the environment. The people-environment model is based on the hypothesis that a person responds to his environment as he perceives and interprets it in the light of his previous experience (Sprout & Sprout, 1965). Since the person's response in relation to the environment is assumed to depend on his perception of the environment, it becomes important to find out how this is perceived. This leads to the distinction between the 'real world,' which is called the objective or geographic environment, and the 'subjective world' or subjective environment; the construction of a mental map, which depends on what is perceived by the person.

The purpose of this chapter is to present the main idea of a design tool supported by an object database system. At first we explain the theoretical platform for cognitive mapping and how to use cognitive mapping in design of urban environments. In the second part we illustrate how to represent the needed information in object schemas and explain how to derive information using this schemas.

BACKGROUND

In architectural and urban practice, analysis of the urban environment plays a significant role. The need for certain analysis to contain precise characteristics of urban elements is in the context of the analysis of city sites. There has been a continuous effort by architect and urban planner to understand and express those needs and desires.

The architectural and urban planning process is a complex problem-solving activity. One of the ways of describing architectural or urban design is by means of graphical representation. The representation facilities must consider alternative options at particular levels of spatial organization. Graphical representation of city sites sometimes has limitations such as, differences in scales readability and details. These limitations can be a problem for correct analysis. The unification of representation is impossible for many reasons, but the characteristics to be analyzed, the criteria and finally the way (process) to do it, will be operational. This research formulates a typology of visual elements according to city sites focused on graphical representation. Typology is the main computational means for solving this problem.

Theoretical platform

The main focus of this research is analysis of visual quality of urban environment according to computational cognitive mapping. Learning about and understanding the urban environment for the purpose of cognitive perception, facilitates many methods which have been developed recently in different domains such as psychology, engineering and planning.

This research focuses on the analysis of urban elements as an integral part of large scale city sites. The results of the analysis are correlated to produce quality criteria for the city sites. In the domain of urban designing and planning, we examine the problem of urban quality analysis through the implementation of its elements in the cognitive perception process. Urban design and planning define the process of the research by means of existing theories of design and cognitive science. These two theories are a platform for creating a *conceptual model* of the tool.

Figure 1: Schematical outline of the urban theory

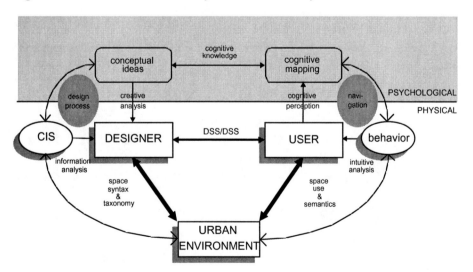

Design *tool* is based on the platform made by conceptual model and computational techniques, such as object database systems.

The research is employs developed theories in design, cognitive science and computer science. It addresses aspects of knowledge of cognitive perception associated with analysis of urban design elements and design evaluation by computational processing.

Outline of the urban theory

The simplified outline of the urban theory applied in this research is presented in Figure 1. The schema presents relationships between people and their environment. People are categorized in two groups: designers and users.

The schema presents the simplified model of the urban interaction process. The process of interaction started with real world information and the process of creativity, as a physical/psychological phenomena in the design domain. Real world information, here called *object database systems* (ODB), is sets of relevant information, which aids the process of creativity (the design process). This information is the data, which is transferred into the design process as *object-oriented database systems*. The result of using this design process is the improvement of existing environments. This process considers not only urban purposes, but also the people for whom the environment is designed and built.

Based on knowledge of the real world, and on the design process, urban designers can create a new final product realized in the urban environment. The new or improved urban environment has interactions with the users; people who pass through and use the facilities of the urban environment. People use the environment differently and their perception or familiarity with it is a called *cognitive mapping*.

Indirectly, the process of perceiving the urban environment interacts with urban designers and their process of creativity. Directly, through the process of decision making, ordinary people will be able to contribute more actively to the process of urban designing.

Theory of 'urban form'

Theory of 'urban form' defined by Kevin Lynch is located in the right-hand part of the schema. Lynch describes elements of urban environment and their interactions, and he defined the concept of *cognitive mapping* of how people behave within a particular urban environment.

Lynch defined things in his book "Image of the city" (1960), important for later explanation of the whole theory: first, physical elements of the city and second, psychological, perceptual senses. It is necessary to distinguish two forms of physical elements; natural i.e. air, sky, rivers, lakes, ponds, hills, etc. and man-made elements i.e. infrastructure, objects, vehicles, airplanes, etc. Natural and man-made elements, in fact, share some common characteristics, such as color, smell, noise, warmth, etc., which together help to build a perceptual form of the urban environment.

Lynch's theory defines two new important things for our knowledge about the urban environment. First, he defines a group of five elements of urban environment (physical characteristics of the real world) and secondly, he noticed the concept of *cognitive mapping* (the psychological or subjective world).

The perception generally is a product of the human mind and senses. People *recognize* a space and objects in it by the reflection of light, shape and depth. People *orient* in a space by identifying it's elements and patterns. Five elements of urban environment (paths, edges, districts, nodes and landmarks) come from Lynch's analysis of effects of physical, perceptible objects. In our research we concentrate on the main aspects of types and characteristics of physical forms and their elements. People perceive the elements in a hierarchical way. They make a '*mental interpretation of space*' by memorizing and retrieving elements of spaces and patterns in their brain. This process is known as 'cognitive mapping'.

Our research presents investigation of urban elements, as well as elements for cognitive mapping, and makes a precise systematization in a form understandable for *object-database* structuring and for computation processing.

DESIGN TOOL

The proposed design tool is capable of generating computer-based urban elements and cognitive mapping method, which identifies the problems and the information, required to solve the problems of particular city sites. A computational model of the device in which the real properties of the urban sites are defined precisely and the appropriateness of the model for the task in hand are demonstrated. This tool provides explicit representations of the patterns as well as the urban elements during qualitative analysis. The design tool aided by a multimedia object database system, which provides professionals with the means to achieve more efficiently, reliable solutions through qualitative analysis of urban sites.

Goals

The main goals of the design tool are: (1) to aid urban designers to analyze and test the visual quality of the urban environment by means of the cognitive mapping process, (2) to resolve visual-spatial conflicts and disfunctionality resulting from the increasing complexity and intensity of use of the urban environment, and (3) to help in the process of decision-making on the widest scale of interests.

The tool could help to find answers to the following:
• how to analyze the visual quality of the urban environment by using different multimedia representation sources

- how to find or predict which are 'well-situated' urban elements that will improve the cognitive mapping of the urban environment
- how to recognize 'what is what' in *confusing* urban patterns
- how to find and position landmarks in *dense* urban sites
  and some other questions similar to these.

Positioning in the design process

Our tool will be effective in analyzing visual qualities of existing urban environments and in the pre-testing of the new design or a re-designing for existing urban sites. We think, the tool will also be useful in the final design testing phase. The tool can be used in the process of decision-making by presenting different variables for a particular urban environment using different decision-making criteria.

Tool requirements

The functional requirements, the tool has to fulfil are:
- 'open' for different characteristics of *u.e.* such as geo-political, cultural, natural, social, physical, etc.
- 'open' for all types of *u.e.* such as small, large, dense, distributed, etc.
- open for all types of input and output multimedia data
- both global and detailed in analysis
- able to include the surroundings of even the smallest unit for analysis
- able to analyze in different spatial scales and measurement systems
- able to understand what is meant by analyzes of the static objects
- able to present the results of analysis in graphical, numerical and textual form
- able to do modeling/improvements in the existing data sources
- able to do modeling/improvements by various computer based techniques (such as: CAD, VR, www)
- open for 'self learning'
  The above requirements will be realized in different phases.

Operational criteria of the tool

The proposed tool has to satisfy certain basic operational criteria:
- The handling of visual data efficiently, which must be coded in each element and summarized then as *figural patterns*.
- The use of *typology* of visual elements has to be accessed by intelligent procedures such as recognition of similarity or by analogy to previously selected elements and examples. Such procedures can help in the case of visually incomplete information.
- The tool must provide user-controlled links between all elements in process which might help in (1) describing all elements in a detailed manner, (2) inter-

preting a group of elements as a figural pattern, and (3) representing additional resulting information of the entire analysis.

- The tool is *situated* in a complex of information, structured in terms of proto-typical conditions for the purpose of future analysis of other city sites. There-fore the system is self-learning and knowledge-based. The system is a prob-lem-solving by memorizing architectural needs and knowledge as a *look back* system.
- The system will, on the first level edit visual data, on a second level, analyze visual data and on the third level, (a) describe, (b) explain, and (c) modify the visual data which have been analyzed.
- The tool is able to identify conflicts in cases where the use of the system pro-duces contradictory results and can control them; identify results which dis-agree with common sense perceptions and modify in a restricted way assump-tions and presumptions of the system.

APPLYING OBJECT MODELLING CONCEPTS
The object model
An object model is a set of generic concepts to describe certain characteristics of real or imaginary objects. The object model is used to produce the definition of the object base. The result of the definition process is a set of object schemas. We use object model of Perspective-DB (Perspective-DB, 1997). Here we give a short introduction to main concepts, which are necessary to understand the object schema described in the paper. The object schema notations originates from (Essenius et.al., 1997,1998; Gerhardt and Simon, 1999).

The basic concept is the object type. An object type is a characterization of objects through the definition of its members. All objects that are characterized by the same types of members belong to the same object type. Members can be attributes (properties), operations and relations. Relations when applied together with connectors form relationships. An object type is represented graphically by a rectangle. Members are represented by rectangles attached to the object type they characterize. Connectors are lines between object types. The name of an object type is written on the rectangle's surface; the name of a member is written beside the rectangle. Operations can be specific for a certain object type (they are represented attached to the sides of the rectangle) or they can be generic, meaning that they can be applied to each object type (they are represented on the surface of the rectangle). If a generic member does not suite a certain object type, it will not be visible. Relationships may have attributes; they are represented attached to the connector.

A generalization object type is an abstraction of several specialization object types; it describes the common members of its specialization. Specialization inher-

Figure 2: Basic object types

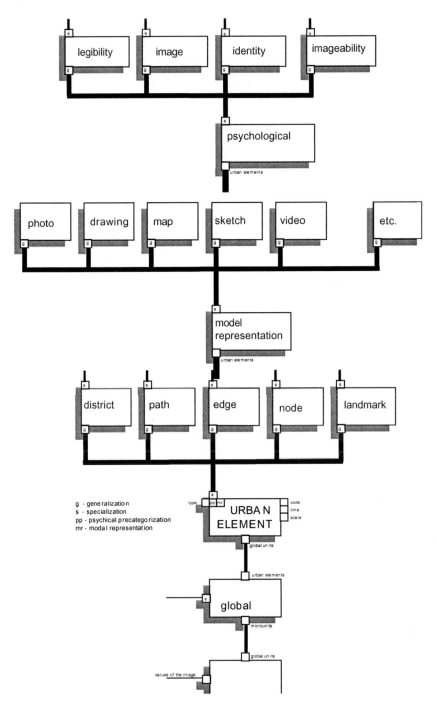

Figure 3: Specializations of "district" and "path"

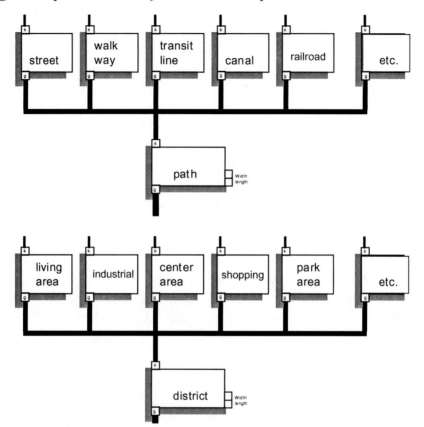

Figure 4: Schema of the object type "edge"

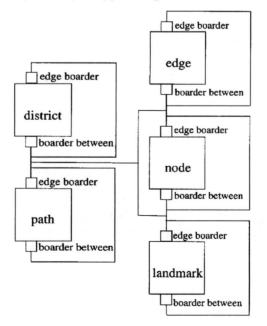

its members of their generalization. A specialization can choose not to use a member it inherits. Generalization and specialization object types form a hierarchy; the generalization is positioned beneath the specialization.

The structure of an object type is often hidden. However, when required it can be popped up and the user can zoom-in its structure. In this way, we can reach different levels of detail of a certain information with the same generic operations and features Perspective-DB offers, e.g. querying and navigation.

In this chapter, we only discuss and show those parts of the object schema used to describe the basic information necessary to "produce" and "use" conceptual urban design ideas during the design process. The examples give an impression how to describe physical information about urban environments, which support cognitive mapping. The following part of the paper is indicated in the left lower part of Figure 1.

The basic object schema

The basic object schema describes the generalization/specialization hierarchy of the object types needed to derive the information used to design taking cognitive mapping into consideration. We start with the object type "urban element" in Figure 2; it inherits its members from "virtual object" offered by Perspective-DB (is not represented here). "Urban element" has among other generic members: psychological precategorization of an urban element, and modal representation. "Modal representation" determine the media types that represent the urban element. An element can have several suitable media representations. Later we show how to work with such a member using "psychological precategorization" as an example.

Figure 3 shows a continuation of the generalization/specialization hierarchy of Figure 2. We choose "district" and "path" to give an idea. According to the inheritance rules, each of the shown specializations will inherit the members of its generalizations. They can add new members, which are in turn inherited from their specializations. In the example, all objects have a "code" as key, and "time" and "scale" as members. All districts as well as paths have "width" and "length" as members.

Example: Semantic categorization of "edge"

Edge:
Figure 4 shows a (reduced) description of "edge." The schema specifies that "edge" can form a border between each of the urban elements, including itself. It could be the border between objects of the same or different urban elements. For all the object types shown in this schema we have to imagine that a generalization can be overwritten by its specialization.

Comparable schemes specify also "node" and "landmark".

"Node", "edge" and "landmark" use the urban elements "district" and "path" to be explained and specified.

SUMMARY

In the chapter, the main concepts about a design tool are described which will improve architectural design by taking cognitive mapping into consideration. We discussed how Lynch's theory of "urban form" provides the basis of an object database system. The database system is the kernel of the design tool. The tool supports the designer by explicit representations of the patterns as well as the urban elements during the qualitative analysis process of a particular urban site. We sketched the functionality of the system. Furthermore, we have shown that the elements of urban form can be modeled as the basic objects of our database, and how they can be specialized. We sketched the structure of the database how it is presented to the urban designer. We have shown how to model "psychological" aspects of cognitive mapping and how to derive design information through several abstraction levels from an object database. Up to now, the object model of Perspective-DB supported us with all the needed modeling constructs.

REFERENCES

Essenius, E., Sim, M., Simon, N., Kist, P., and Gerhardt, W. (1998). A Working Generic Canonical Schematic UIMS for an ODBMS, in Ioannidis, Y., and Klas, W. (eds.), *Visual Database Systems* (VDB4), Chapman&Hall.

Essenius, E., Simon, N., Kist, P., Gerhardt, W., and Dankoor, M.(1997). *Reuse applied to be development of a GUI from ODBMS,* Technical report, Delft University of Technology, Delft.

Gerhardt, W., and Simon, N. (1999). Characteristics of an Object Model and Object Management to Support Decision Processes, to be published in Lasker, H. (ed); *Proceedings of the 11th Intern. Conference on Systems Research, Informatics and Cybernetics*, Baden-Baden, Germany.

Lynch, K. (1960). *The image of the city.* Cambridge, MA: MIT Press.

Perspective-DB (1997). *System documentation*, Bitbybit - Information Systems, Delft.

Sprout, H. & Sprout, M. (1965). *The ecological perspective on human affairs.* Princeton, NJ: Princeton University Press.

APPENDIX

Definition of terms

cognitive mapping - is a process of '*mental interpretation of space*' by memorizing and retrieving its elements and patterns in human brain *object oriented database* - is a system for collecting, storing and retrieving of interacting object that combine data and behavior created by an object-oriented programming language

Chapter 22

Nurturing Trust and Reactive Training: Essential Elements in ICT Diffusion Projects

David Tucker and Pascale de Berranger
Manchester Metropolitan University, United Kingdom

Small and medium sized enterprises (SMEs) make a substantial contribution to the economic and social wellbeing of many national economies. Consequently, the European Union (EU) is funding several initiatives aimed at stimulating growth within SMEs. In particular, there is concern that despite the potential benefits of information and communication technology (ICT), adoption rates in UK-based SMEs tend to be low. The aim of this paper is to identify important factors which contribute to successful diffusion projects. The main causes of low ICT adoption rates are identified. Using empirical data collected from a successful UK diffusion initiative, the paper reveals the importance of nurturing a trusting relationship with potential ICT adopters both before and during the diffusion project. It goes on to show that the provision of reactive training during the diffusion process is vital. Finally, the case study findings are compared with the literature and comparisons are drawn.

INTRODUCTION

In the United Kingdom SMEs are collectively responsible for 65% of employment and 57% of Gross Domestic Product (Madsing, 1997). Small businesses can gain competitive parity or even competitive advantage over large organisations by exploiting ICTs such as the Internet and e-commerce, yet many small business

Previously Published in *Challenges of Information Technology Management in the 21st Century,* edited by Mehdi Khosrow-Pour, Copyright © 2000, Idea Group Publishing.

managers remain dubious about the proclaimed benefits. This view is reinforced by the numerous newspaper reports which describe expensive ICT project failures. An important way to increase confidence in the business benefits of ICT is training and education Stair (1989). Unfortunately, many small business managers are compelled to expend the majority of available resources on meeting daily business needs and cannot give priority to education and training (Sargent, 1996). This situation could be alleviated by adopting an approach to training where employees can make immediate practical use of the knowledge gained (Curran, 1988; Kinni, 1994). Furthermore, SMEs tend operate in an ad-hoc manner (Doukidis et al., 1996), (Quelch and Klein, 1996). Hence training programmes are more likely to succeed if they are delivered in a similar manner. In many cases the smaller organisation needs more support to take advantage of information and communication technologies than their larger counterparts (Fariselli et al., 1999). If a diffusion project is going to succeed, training providers must possess interpersonal as well as technical skills and they need to be more sensitive to the specific needs of the smaller organisation (Allard, 1999).

Even those SMEs who would wish to adopt ICT often do not posses the full range of physical and intellectual resources with which to implement ICT to its full potential. The UK government has sought to address this problem in a range of diffusion projects. Unfortunately, there is a general mistrust of such initiatives. Reasons put forward for such an attitude are unclear aims and objectives, lack of support, poor value for money, and lack of understanding of the nature of, and constraints experienced by small businesses (Berranger, 1999). Moreover, there is little awareness of, or interest in, promotional schemes on the part of SME owners (Bannock, 1992). This situation has prompted the EU to finance the Northern Quarter Network (NQN) ICT diffusion project. The Northern Quarter (NQ) is a commercial region of Manchester - the third largest city in England. Historically the area was a manufacturing centre but is currently being regenerated and is home to numerous SMEs (Hill, 1995). It is this project which is discussed later in this paper.

ICT DIFFUSION

Most models and methodologies related to ICT diffusion and adoption are based on data collected in large organisations and may be inappropriate for SMEs (Doukidis et al., 1996). SMEs are often considered flexible enterprises (Levy and Powell, 1998) and some research suggests that such flexibility will make ICT adoption relatively simple to achieve (Montazemi, 1988) and that a greater speed of adoption than larger organisations might be expected (Storey and Cressy, 1995). These assertions appear to ignore the difficulties brought about by lack of time, cash flow issues, lack of expertise and limited knowledge of the technology, all of which typify SMEs. From the technology supply side, there are a bewildering variety of information sources. Furthermore the use of unfamiliar technical jargon by suppliers, coupled with the rapid pace of technological advancement, serve to increase the level of complexity and uncertainty faced by SMEs (Geisler, 1992; Fuller, 1993). Change agents can play a vital role in reducing uncertainty. Rogers (1983) has identified a number of factors in change agents' success including

1. Effort in contacting clients. Effort in the context of diffusion relates to the amount of interpersonal communication with potential ICT adopters.
2. Orientation. Client orientated change agents are inclined to have a close relationship and credibility with potential adopters.
3. Compatibility with clients' needs, knowledge of clients' attitudes, beliefs, social norms, and leadership structure.
4. Level of empathy with clients. Rogers hypothesised that although there is very little empirical support for this expectation, change agent success is positively related to empathy with clients.
5. Rogers (1983) also invoked the concept of information overload in relation to the large volume of information flow in the diffusion process, proposing that "… by understanding the needs and problems of his or her clients, a change agent can selectively transmit to them only information that is relevant ". Mass media communication channels were relatively more important prior to the commencement of a diffusion process, as opposed to later where personal communication would have a greater impact. The literature surveyed showed that mass media communication served to build awareness of an innovation (Rogers 1983; Attewell (1992) (Agarwal & Prasad 1998) but that it had also generated some uncertainty about it. To overcome this uncertainty and to foster trust, Charlton et al. (1997) suggest that it is necessary to identify and utilise existing informal communication networks and social networks.

The diffusion of innovation is frequently a social as well as a technical process (Rogers, 1983:4). Lee (1994) proposes that, "beyond the issue of competition, firms and organisations also have their own sense of the world around them, or culture, which inhibits (or promotes) the sharing of new knowledge and information". The cultural compatibility of the change agents and the potential adopters is therefore important.

In this paper it is proposed that cultural compatibility is a catalyst to forming highly trusting relationships and that it is this trust which underpins successful diffusion initiatives. Sako (1992) proposes that their are three distinct types of trust. The first is contractual trust in which both parties fulfil their contractual obligations; the second is competence trust where both parties perform their roles competently; and the third is goodwill trust which is characterised by a willingness to share information and a predisposition to do more than is actually required by the formal contract. Kanter (1994) likened successful business partnerships to human relationships as consisting of different stages including courtship and engagement. As the relationship progresses mutual trust becomes stronger. In Sako's analysis, competence and contractual trust are usually present in the early stages of a business relationship. If that relationship matures in the manner suggested by Kanter, then goodwill trust becomes dominant. As will be discussed later, it is goodwill trust that permeated the NQN project and led to successful diffusion of ICT.

FIELD STUDY

This chapter seeks to show how ICT was successfully diffused to the project participants. Both the geographical setting and the NQN network were instrumental in bounding the research. The Northern Quarter is a small geographical area in Manchester, which meant that access to the population under scrutiny was feasible. The project was carried out by a team from the Manchester Metropolitan University which facilitated entry. The NQN project involved a total of 15 companies with eight agreeing to be interviewed. This constituted a sufficient portion to be significant while being manageable from a practical point of view. In-depth, semi-structured interviews were chosen as a means of gathering data as they are a well-established tool for capture the essence of a phenomenon which a quantitative method such as survey would not do. All interviews were taped and transcribed. Although interviews followed an agenda they were left open so that comments and answers could open up the interview itself.

The sampling criteria were as follows:

1) interviewee had to work for an SME in the Northern Quarter
2) he/she had to have been instrumental in the decision to adopt or not to adopt the ICT
3) the organisation had to employ more than one person (i.e. sole proprietors and individuals trading as sole employee through limited organisations were not included as they were not considered to form a "company").

All interviewees reported the benefits of using ICT as being reduced paperwork, saving time and money (once set up), good for repetitive tasks and increased efficiency. None of the respondents used ICT for strategic purposes. One company manager explained that the problem with ICT adoption is "getting it all set out while working flat out at the same time". This issue was common to all interviews where respondents point to a lack of time as a problem. Some interviewees linked this predicament to the needs for 'diffusers' (i.e. change agents) to take account of it in training/support programs. Another respondent explained that the problems associated with ICT adoption stem from their lack of trust in ICT professionals. This concurs with Rogers' view that lack of knowledge and the resulting lack of trust is a major inhibitor of diffusion.

All interviewees expressed doubts, fears or uncertainties about ICT. These were based on either lack of knowledge of the actual technology and its use, or on a general mistrust of the information provided via mass media. Nonetheless, all respondents were aware of the potential benefits of using ICT and more particularly of the usefulness of establishing a presence on the world wide web (WWW).

The interviewees were asked to describe the specific characteristics of the NQN project which were instrumental in their decision to adopt ICT technology. The change agents were physically located in the Northern Quarter which enabled considerable face-to-face contact. This 'personal touch' was critical in building up the necessary trust between the change agents and the SMEs. The informal yet professional attitude of the agents was important as this was seen to be in alignment with the internal culture of the businesses themselves. Because of this, a mutual empathy emerged between the change agents and the businesses. Respondents rated care towards and understanding of their business, care and enthusiasm about the project itself, and general attitude, as highly important. Most respondents mentioned the need for flexibility in the training program to fit in with small business priorities.

It is interesting to note that all respondents but one saw the project as a joint effort between the change agents and themselves as opposed to a service, "it all came together as a community working for the same cultural end in the same area." Participants expressed how the change agents delivered training in the following terms:

- "they were able to guide us."
- "it was a real process of dialogue."
- "we looked at different companies' web sites where as before it was just talking about web sites. That helped us understand the capabilities of ICT ourselves and that obviously gave us idea on where to take our sites."
- "we said what we wanted and they explained the implications of our wants"
- "we'd come up with an idea and they would explain how to interpret in technical terms."

Once the participants had made the decision to adopt ICT technology they were asked what benefits they believed would accrue. These were reported as access to local and international markets, direct selling, improved company profile, the ability to train others and indirect financial benefits. These answers indicated that the respondents now had a good appreciation of ICT as a strategic resource. This was a major change in perception from the start of the project. Benefits were also related to a better knowledge of the technology. This is a function of the training being tailored to the needs of participants as opposed to being set as a rigid agenda. All participants expressed increased confidence with the technology.

Through mass media communications, the participants were aware that strategic benefits were generally attributed to ICT. However, a combination of the high uncertainty associated with mass media communications, a general mistrust of diffusion initiatives and a lack of organisational resources had previously inhibited the adoption process. The subtle manner in with the change agents infused themselves into the Northern Quarter played a significant part in engendering the atmosphere of goodwill trust which underpinned the project.

The change agents provided context-specific training to each SME and this served two important purposes. Firstly, the participants were better able to understand how ICT could have benefits for their specific businesses. This process was successful because of the goodwill trust which had already been cultivated between the change agents and the SMEs. This served to increase the confidence of the participants in ICT because they could see for themselves that there were real benefits to be gained. As one respondent stated: "Before it was just talking about it and not seeing it." The second purpose was the prevention of information overload. The participants were bombarded by so much information from the mass media that they were unable to absorb it or make rational judgements based upon it. The change agents overcame this by making context-specific information available. Furthermore, the information was released only at the time when it was needed. Thus each SME received a customised and flexible training program relevant to their specific business circumstances.

Just as critical was the agents' ability to provide information in an informal yet professional manner. The businesses themselves operated in a relaxed but efficient fashion. This is an example of the cultural compatibility which existed between the change agents and the participants. Knowledge of SMEs characteristics and their respective industrial sector were examples of client orientation in the context of this study and contributed to the change agents' success.

Prior to the commencement of the NQN project, the change agents had made a conscious decision to become gradually infused into the local social system. They then relied on dissemination of the project by word of mouth through informal communication networks and introductions by third parties. This approach had the dual advantage of saving money on advertising and, more importantly, fostering trust. Rogers (1983) highlighted how social systems could either hinder or improve the diffusion process. This unobtrusive approach used by the change agents was fundamental in allaying suspicions. Reliance on local communication networks was only possible because the change agents had been involved in local activities and attended industry-specific events and had so been accepted into the social system. The findings thus agrees with both Hackney et al 's (1996) and Charlton et al.'s (1997) view that, successful infiltration of the population of interest relies heavily on the identification and use of existing informal communication and social networks to foster trust.

Interview data suggests that empathy relates to a strong commitment to the project, commitment to the success of each organisation's ICT project, being involved in companies' problems and activities, and most importantly, being based in and having an understanding of the aspirations of the businesses in the Northern Quarter. The level of commitment, local presence and local involvement of the change agents increased the level of perceived empathy of the SMEs. Physical presence also facilitated ease of access to the change agents. This was compatible which the provision of a customised training program as described above.

DISCUSSION & CONCLUSIONS

The purpose of this research was to gain a better understanding of critical success factors in the ICT diffusion process. Clearly the change agent's approach to the NQN project was instrumental in fostering the goodwill trust which was an integral part of its success. The agents also displayed competence trust. Not only their technical understanding of ICT, but also there obvious knowledge of, and empathy with, the NQ businesses themselves. This appears to accelerated the development of an energetic relationship between the businesses and the change agents leading to successful ICT adoption. Contractual trust played little or no role in the project. The cultural compatibility between the changes agents and the SMEs was manifest in the similarity of attitude towards business practice. Both acted in a casual yet competent and professional manner and this undoubtedly had a beneficial effect on the project.

The second contributing factor identified in this paper was the provision of customised training programmes. There was a strong training element to the project, involving practices based on a reactive as opposed to prescribed training courses. Training programmes were customised to the needs of each participant and were designed to avoid the disruption of usual business.

It is hoped that this paper has given some useful guidance to those who are anticipating an involvement in future ICT diffusion projects. It is also hoped that the success of the NQN project will offer some encouragement to those who approach such ventures with trepidation. It should, however, be pointed out that there are two major characteristics of the NQ project which may limit the extent to which the research presented here could be more widely applied.

Cohesiveness of the Northern Quarter: This was due to a number of factors, the most important being the geographical co-location of the businesses and their small size. Cohesiveness was increased with the inception of the NQN project itself. It was a recognition that the importance of the Northern Quarter was understood by both the European Union and the UK government. This cohesiveness enabled a highly effective informal communication channel to develop. The change agents were able to use this channel very effectively to disseminate context-specific information about ICT to each participating business.

Table 1: Success factors in the NQ Innovation Diffusion Process

Unobtrusive infusion into the business district
Use of existing informal communication channels
Cultural compatibility
Ease of contact
Enthusiasm for the diffusion project
Enthusiasm for the business district
Knowledge of the general industry
Specific business knowledge
Delivery of context-specific information
Provision of experiential training
Timely delivery of information
Use language understandable to the participants

Homogeneity: All the businesses were in creative industries. This meant that hey had an inherent interest in exploring new technologies. They were also very conscious of their business image and saw ICT as a means of promoting it in a new way and to a wider audience.

There are numerous examples of other districts within the UK which possess similar distinguishing features and for which this research has direct relevance. Other countries within the European Community have similar districts, such as: Temple Bar in Dublin (Ireland), Poble Nou in Barcelona (Spain), and Veemarktkwaartier in Tillburg (Netherlands). Furthermore, many of the change agent characteristics identified here are not dependent upon the distinguishing features of the Northern Quarter and are applicable to any technology diffusion process. Hence the research reported here will have direct significance in other diffusion projects, particularly where they are similar in nature to the Northern Quarter. The main findings are summarised in Table I.

REFERENCES

Agarwal, R. and Prasad, J. (1998). The Antecedents and Consequences of User Perceptions in Information Technology Adoption. *Decision Support Systems*, 22, pp.15-29.

Allard, G. (1999). Entrepreneurs, Aesthetes and Electronic Markets: Researching Commodification in a Symbolic Space. Critical Management Studies Conference paper, Cultural Industry Stream, Hulme Hall, University of Manchester, Manchester, UK. July 14-16.

Attewell, P. (1992). Technology Diffusion and Organisational Learning: the case of business computing. *Organization Science*, 3(1), pp.1-19.

Bannock, G. (1992). Choking the Spirit of Enterprise. *International Management*, March, pp.30-33

Berranger (De), P. (1999). In Business Information Technology, Manchester Metropolitan University, Manchester, UK.

Charlton, C., Gittings, C., Leng, P., Little, J. and Neilson, I. (1997). Diffusion of the Internet: a Local Perspective on an International Issue. In T. McMaster, E. Mumford, E. B. Swanson, B Warboys and D. Wastell (Eds.), *Facilitating Technology Transfer Through Partnership, Learning from Practice and Research*, IFIP TC8 WG8.6, Chapman & Hall: London, pp.337-354.

Curran, J. (1988). Training and Research Strategies for Small Firms, *Journal of General Management*, 13.

Doukidis, G. I., Lybereas, P., and Galliers, R.D. (1996). Information System Planning in Small Business: A Stage of Growth Analysis. *Journal of Systems Software*, 33, pp.189-201.

European Union (1998). Culture, the Cultural Industries and Employment. Commission Staff Working Paper SEC(98)837, part 3 Conclusions, http://europa.eu.int/search97cgi/.

Fariselli, P., Oughton, C., Picory, C., and Sugden, R. (1999). Electronic Commerce and the Future for SMEs in the Global Market-Place: Networking and Public Policies, *Small Business Economics*, 12, pp. 261-275

Fuller, E. (1993). Business Development through IT Adoption - A Learning Agenda. *39th ICSB World Conference*, in Obrecht, J.J., and Bayad, M. (Eds.), *Business and its Contribution to Regional and International Development*, Robert Schuman University, Strasbourg, pp.95-104.

Geisler, E. (1992). Information Technology Department. *IEEE Transactions on Engineering Management*, 39(2), pp.112.

Hackney, R., Kawalek, J. and Dhillon, G. (1996). Information Technology & Communication Management Within SMEs: Opportunities for Partnership. *UKAIS Conference*, Southampton University, April 2nd-4th.

Hill, D. (1995). The northern quarter network. Institute for Popular Culture, Autumn, http://es-www.mmu.ac.uk:81/cgi-bin/betsie/parser2.pl www.mmu.ac.uk/h-ss/mipc/nqnrept1.htm, Part 1-4.

Kanter, R.M. (1994). Collaborative Advantage, *Harvard Business Review*, July/August, pp. 96-103.

Kinni, T. B. (1994). Train in the here and now, *Industry Week*, 243, 56-58.

Lee, A. S. (1994). Electronic Mail as a Medium for Rich Communication – an empirical investigation using hermeneutic interpretation. *MIS Quarlerly*, 18(2), pp.143-157

Lewis, P. (1994). *Information Systems Development*. Pitman, pp.139.

Madsing, D. (1997). NCC presentation on the Information Technology Initiative. Manchester Metropolitan University, December

Montazemi, A. R. (1988). Factors Affecting Information Satisfaction in the Small Business Environment. *MIS Quarterly*, June, pp. 239-256.

Quelch, J. A. and Klein, L. R. (1996). The Internet and International Marketing, *Sloan Management Review*, 37/3, pp. 60-75.

Rogers, E. M. (1983). *Diffusion of Innovation*. New York: The Free Press, pp.92.

Sako, M. (1992). Prices, Quality and Trust, Cambridge University Press, Cambs.

Sargeant, A. (1996). Training for growth; how can education providers assist in the development of small businesses? *Industrial and Commercial Training*, 28, pp 3-9.

Stair, R. M., Crittenden, W. F. and Crittenden, V. L. (1989). The use, operation and control of the small business computer, *Information Management*, 16, 125-130.

Storey, D. J. and Cressy, R. (1995). Small Business Risk: A Firm and Bank Perspective. Warwick Business School SME Centre, Working Paper. In Levy, M. and Powell, P. (1998). SME Flexibility and the Role of Information Systems. *Small Business Economics*, 11, pp.183.

Chapter 23

EMS Records and Information Management of Environmental Aspects and Their Associated Impacts with Metadata

Hans-Knud Arndt, Mario Christ and Oliver Günther
Humboldt University, Germany

Metadata in environmental management systems support searching and browsing operations. XML-based metadata systems can store metadata in a flexible manner that is suitable also for small and medium size organizations. Our EcoExplorer software package consists of three closely cooperating programs for the management of XML-based environmental metadata. It is implemented in Java and therefore platform-independent. The EcoExplorer is able to collaborate with online components of an environmental management system, as demonstrated by our eco-balancing and environmental accounting system ACCOUNT.

SCOPE

The European regulation on environmental management and audit scheme (EMAS regulation) and the International Standard 14001 on environmental management systems (specification with guidance for use) specify requirements for an environmental management system (EMS). ISO 14001 and amended EMAS II are applicable to any organization that wishes to[1] :

i) implement, maintain and improve an environmental management system;
ii) ensure its compliance with its stated environmental policy;
iii) demonstrate such compliance to others;

Previously Published in *Challenges of Information Technology Management in the 21st Century*, edited by Mehdi Khosrow-Pour, Copyright © 2000, Idea Group Publishing.

iv) seek certification/registration of its environmental management system by an external organization;

v) make a determination and declaration of compliance with the standard.

Organization in this context may be a company, corporation, firm, enterprise, authority or institution, or part or combination thereof, whether incorporated or not, public or private, that has its own function and administration[2].

Both standards require that organizations collect and compile data about environmental aspects and their associated environmental impact. Many organizations are reacting to these insights and developments by building or purchasing specialized information systems. These software systems may vary from stand-alone programs to systems providing an interface to the existing information infrastructure within the organization[3]. Software systems supporting more than one requirement of environmental management systems are called *Environmental Management Information Systems (EMIS)*.

EMIS are intended to provide the environmental management system of organizations with information that can be integrated with other information requirements to assist organizations to achieve environmental and economic goals. These systems facilitate the collection, aggregation and evaluation of environmental information for each element of an environmental management system. According to ISO 14001, an organization shall establish and maintain an environmental management system and therefore an EMIS that includes the following elements[4]:

i) Environmental Policy: An organization should define its environmental policy and ensure commitments to its EMS.

ii) Planning: An organization should formulate a plan to fulfill its environmental policy.

iii) Implementation: For the effective implementation, an organization should develop the capabilities and support mechanisms necessary to achieve its environmental policy, objectives and targets.

iv) Measurement and evaluation: An organization should measure, monitor and evaluate its environmental performance.

v) Review and improvement: An organization should review and continually improve its environmental management system, with the objective of improving its overall environmental performance.

In this article we will focus on the EMIS element EMS Documentation as a part of (iii) implementation and on the EMIS element EMS records and information management as part of (iv) measurement and evaluation.

EMS DOCUMENTATION: THE ECOEXPLORER
Integration of distributed environmental information

The ISO Standard 14004 (Environmental Management Systems - Guidelines on principles, systems and supporting techniques) contains the following practical help for the EMS documentation[5] :

Documents can be in any medium and should be useful and easily understood.

All documentation should be time-stamped (dates of revision), readily identifiable, organized, and retained for a specified period. The organization should ensure that

- documents can be identified with the appropriate organization, division, function, activity, and/or contact person;
- documents are periodically reviewed, revised as necessary, and approved by authorized personnel prior to issue;
- the current versions of relevant documents are available at all locations where operations essential to the effective functioning of the system are performed; and
- obsolete documents are promptly removed from all points of issue and points of use.

This information about the documents of the organization can be interpreted as *metadata*, i.e., data about data. In practice, relevant environmental information and documentation can often be found in various departments, that is, in their data processing systems. They may be spread all over the organization. Cost-intensive measurements and evaluations to obtain information specifically for the EMIS can be avoided by locating any suitable existing data sets and merging them into an integrated system. This integration, however, can be seriously obstructed by the incompatibility of data stemming from various sources. Different hardware platforms, operating systems, and data management and communication software entail an incompatibility of data formats which is commonly termed as *syntactic heterogeneity*. Even more important, though, is often the *semantic* heterogeneity of data. This denotes the incompatibility of data due to their different purpose and context. In most cases these data have been collected for other reasons than environmental protection and, moreover, they are probably not intended for use outside their original systems. Hence, they often lack important additional information concerning their organizational, temporal, and technical context.

For environmental information to be reproducible, exact information regarding the purpose and methods of their acquisition, limitations of these methods as well as the general frame of investigation has to be available[6] . The integration of distributed data therefore necessitates the acquisition of metadata and its maintenance in connection with the core data. This metadata has to be accessible for users of the environmental management information system.

First, parameters of the data acquisition are to be determined and maintained as metadata. The parameters have to reflect a reasonable compromise between benefits and costs of acquired data. Parameters can be classified into three groups:

- *Organizational parameters*: These parameters not only denote which departments of the organization have to be included in the investigation, but also from which sources data are collected. It is important to account for overlapping between different systems.
- *Temporal parameters*: The time frame for the specific information and the frequency of data collection within the given period have to be determined.
- *Technical parameters*: These parameters describe which information has to be included at which granularity.

These parameters should not be considered as rigid. One should rather rely on the dynamic adjustment of parameters reflecting the needs and capabilities of the organization's data acquisition.

For a sensible evaluation of collected data in the central environmental management information system, the data have to fulfill a number of conditions:

a) *Identification*: Every distinct material and energy flow has to correspond to a position in the ecological accounting frame. It must be possible to ascertain the ecological account number unambiguously from the name of the source system and a key of the material or energy flow data in this system. This translation could be accomplished by the aid of an allocation table.

b) *Completeness*: A sensible evaluation of corporate environmental influences necessitates the completeness of collected data within the given frame of investigation. Gaps have to be well documented and, if possible, be filled by approximations.

c) *Reliability*: Measuring data usually entails measurement errors that can propagate through ensuing calculations, possibly even amplified. This can result in false results, diminishing the value of collected data. The quality and reliability of data is mainly determined by the methods of acquisition and calculation used to obtain the final results. The methods therefore have to be documented including estimates of possible errors. This is also necessary for approximation methods and their accuracy.

d) *Reproducibility*: The documentation of data acquisition methods is also necessary for their reproducibility. In case of uncertainties, users should be able to inquire. Accordingly, names, phone numbers and email-addresses of responsible employees should be maintained alongside collected data.

e) *Consistency*: Evaluation of data can be hindered considerably by differences in accuracy, aggregation level, quality and other factors. A false sense of security can arise when inconsistent data are aggregated. To prevent this, the level of accuracy has to be well documented. It is also important to obtain data in the same physical unit, if necessary by conversion.

f) *Conciseness*: To reduce the costs for collecting and processing meta-information, only important additional data should be collected. They should nonetheless enable a good understanding of the context of the core data, fulfilling the aforementioned requirements. It might be useful to set up a database with acquisition and calculation methods and refer to it from the core data.

The EcoExplorer

The EcoExplorer is a Java-based search tool for the management of environmental metadata. It helps EMIS users in localizing and retrieving relevant environmental information. The underlying metadata is formatted in the Extensible Markup Language (XML). Using the meta-language XML instead of HTML offers the following benefits[7] :

- *Extensibility*: HTML provides a fixed tag-set which is not extensible. By "not extensible" we mean that users have no possibility to declare their own tags or attributes for special purposes.
- *Structure*: With HTML it is not possible to model data at any level of complexity, which is needed to represent database schemas or object-oriented hierarchies
- *Validity*: With HTML it is not possible to check data for structural correctness.

While the Java platform is a platform for distributing code securely and portably around networks, XML technology can do the same for data, offering a clean, platform-neutral way to represent content[8] . While XML is a suitable data format for heterogeneous networks, applications written in Java can be used to process this data.

There are a lot of XML processing applications written in Java. They can be classified in at least two groups of applications:

a) XML editors for the creation of any kind of XML document or any kind of "Document Type Definitions" (DTD).

b) Applications tailored to specific DTDs. These programs can only process particular applications of XML such as the newly developed "Chemical Markup Language" (CML).[9]

Our EcoExplorer program package follows a different strategy, which lies in between. Since we believe that different types of environmental metadata need different types of documents, users are free to create their own DTD by using our DTDEditor. The main program can process every document, as long as it refers to a DTD created with the DTDEditor. The DTDEditor can create any DTD as long as it describes a table-like data structure. Consequently, 2-dimensional data structures (such as relations) can be modeled easily. All the XML-based data as well as DTDs are managed by using a graphical user interface which looks like an off-the-shelf database product. Stylesheets for publishing the data in a user-readable way are generated automatically.

The package consists of:

- *The EcoExplorer main program*: The main program offers a desktop from which the user can either start other programs or browse through the existing XML-based data. XML-documents are presented and can be edited. New documents can be created.
- *DTDEditor*: Every document which is generated with the EcoExplorer is "valid" in the way that it refers to a DTD. DTDs are created with the DTDEditor.
- *IndexMaker*: This program is for publishing selected XML-based data in the Internet in a read-only form. IndexMaker automatically generates a directory of the XML-based data to be published. It creates all the needed HTML pages and the links to the needed data.

The EcoExplorer main program

Our goal was to develop an application, which resembles the user interface of commercial database products. The program features the look and feel and the most important functionality of a database product. However, instead of storing the data in a proprietary database-format it uses XML as a storage format. Users familiar with database products can manage the XML-based data more easily and acceptance problems are minimized. According to the database terminology we will use the terms "record" and "field" instead of "top-level-element" and "nested element".

The program uses the flexibility of XML in such a way that it is not limited to a single document type. It can display and manage all data created using the "DTDEditor".

Figure 1 shows the main window of the EcoExplorer after the user has chosen a document containing environmental metadata about products in the directory. Whenever the EcoExplorer is started, it scans the available data, which is already stored in the system, and it builds up a directory tree, consisting of a hierarchy of XML documents.

Figure 1: EcoExplorer main program

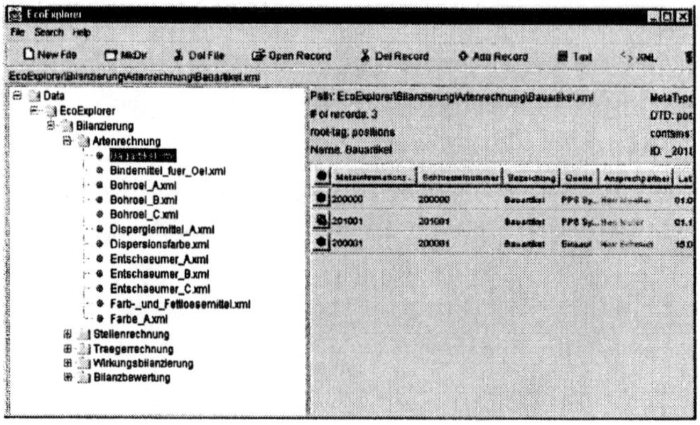

Figure 2: Editor for a record (EcoExplorer)

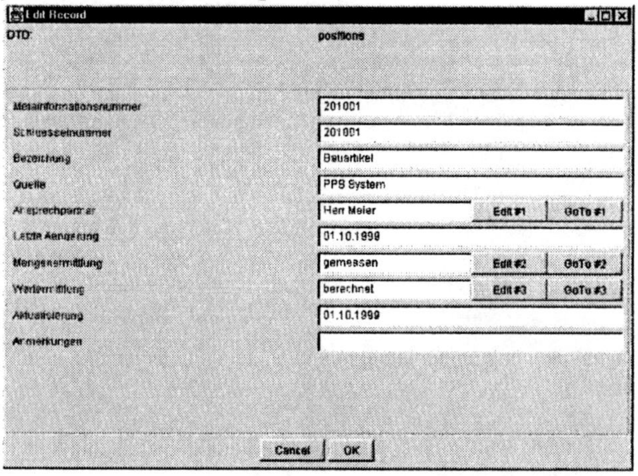

Figure 3: Window for convenient selection of target-records for a hyperlink (EcoExplorer)

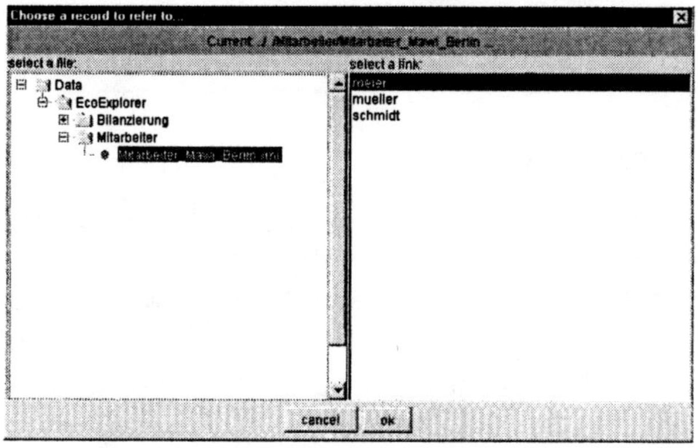

The user can either add documents to or delete documents from the directory tree. In addition, existing documents may be edited. The document to be displayed or edited will be parsed on the client side and its data is displayed as a table on the window's right hand. Figure 1 depicts the user's selection of the document "construction materials" ("Bauartikel") in our system for environmental metadata. As exemplified in the figure, the user wants to obtain information about the item with the metadata ID "201001".

The process of editing a record is depicted in Figure 2. The user can change the content of the fields of the record. In this example, a record for the item with the metadata ID "201001" is being edited. If a field was declared as "hyperlink", two additional buttons for editing the hyperlink or following the hyperlink appear. The user can also open an additional window for convenient selection of target documents and target records. By using this window, users can set links by a few mouse clicks (Figure 3). In this particular example, the user wants to create a link

Figure 4: DTDEditor

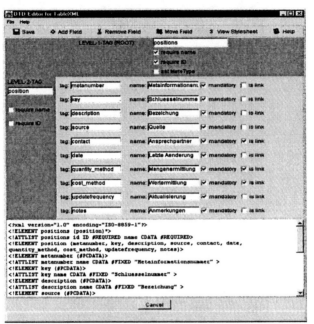

to the record of a person who is in charge of a particular item. He chooses to point to "Meier," who already has a record in the system. In general, hyperlinks can point to other documents or records in the system if they have an ID.

Whenever the user creates a new document, the selection of an underlying DTD from a list of available DTDs will be the first step. If none of the existing DTD fits the users' needs, they may create a new DTD by using the DTDEditor.

The DTDEditor

The DTDEditor is a tool for the convenient creation of DTDs and stylesheets. An existing DTD is a necessary precondition when the user wants to create new XML documents. One DTD may be shared by any number of XML documents.

Figure 4 depicts a DTD for environmental metadata under construction in the DTDEditor. The user can define all tags and attributes. Attributes are necessary to mark elements as hyperlinks, as mandatory fields, to set the names of elements or IDs. The system automatically generates a stylesheet which may serve to publish XML-based data in the Internet. Every change of the DTD is immediately shown in full text.

IndexMaker

The IndexMaker scans the existing XML-based data and builds a navigation tree consisting of hyperlinks to this data. The navigation tree is either a program

Figure 5: Automatically generated JavaScript code embedded in a HTML document (IndexMaker)

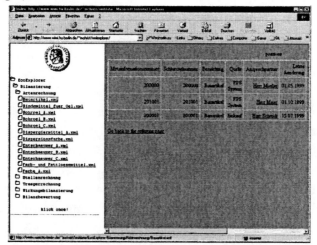

Figure 6: Automatically generated navigation tree (left) and chosen XML document (right) in a browser

automatically written in JavaScript by the IndexMaker, or an HTML file, which serves as a Table of Contents. The choice is up to the user. The resulting files are accessible by means of any web browser and serve as a portal to the XML-based data.

Figure 5 shows the main window of the program right after the user has started the automatic creation of an index file. Automatically created JavaScript code, which contains all the processing instructions for the navigation tree, is embedded in this index file.

Figure 6 shows the resulting navigation tree in a browser. The clickable navigation tree itself is depicted in the left part of the window. The chosen XML document containing environmental metadata about the material flow "construction materials" ("Bauartikel") is displayed on the right part of the window, using the stylesheet which was automatically generated by the DTDEditor.

EMS RECORDS AND INFORMATION MANAGEMENT: THE ACCOUNT SYSTEM

Eco-balancing and environmental accounting

According to ISO 14404, records are legal evidence of the operation of an EMS. They should cover[10] :
- legislative and regulatory requirements;
- permits;
- environmental aspects and their associated impacts;
- inspection, calibration and maintenance activity;
- monitoring data;
- details of non-compliance: incidents, complaints and follow-up action;
- product identification: composition and property data;
- supplier and contractor information;
- environmental audits and management reviews.

We will focus here on the environmental aspects and their associated impacts. A large part of the environmental impact of an organization can be tracked back to the material and energy exchange of the organization with its (natural) environment. The material and energy flow inventory of an EMIS and the common cost accounting are based on nearly the same data. Our structure of the material and energy flow inventory is therefore similar to the corresponding structures in cost accounting, consisting of (Arndt /Günther 1996, 123-125):

- *Cost/Environmental Accumulation (eco-balance sheet of the organization)*: collection of the material and energy flow information of a specified period, each material and energy flow contains information about its quantity (in physical mass or energy measuring unit) and costs. The cost/environmental accumulation is the basic component of this ecological balance sheet approach.
- *Cost/Environmental Department Accounting (eco-balance of production systems)*: calculation of the department's material and cost flows in an accounting spreadsheet.
- *Cost/Environmental Product Accounting (eco-balance of products)*: calculation of a product's material and cost flows per unit (Cost/Environmental Unit Product Accounting) or per period (Cost/Environmental Period Product Accounting).

The Software System ACCOUNT

ACCOUNT is an interactive software tool for an organization's eco-balance sheet and environmental accounting. The basic architecture of ACCOUNT is

Figure 7: Set of metadata IDs ("Metadaten-Nummer") with the associated metaclass ("Rechnungstyp") for the material flow position "Bauartikel"

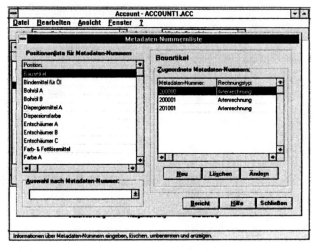

designed according to the common standards of Microsoft Windows 3.1. It is therefore relatively easy to integrate this 16-bit PC-based software system into the computer environment of even very small organizations. ACCOUNT is developed in ObjectPascal with Borland DELPHI 1.02.

The ACCOUNT system has six modules: material and energy flow inventory (input/output balancing), environmental impact assessment, valuation, and reporting. In ACCOUNT we support the association of economic and ecological information in an organization's ecological balance sheet. The reporting module of ACCOUNT processes only simple kinds of reports, such as input/output balance sheets. For extended reporting, the user of ACCOUNT has the opportunity to export the environmental data to a separate spreadsheet and presentation software tool.

In ACCOUNT every material and energy flow contains a metadata ID. Whenever there is a change in any field of the metadata for a specific material or energy flow, the EcoExplorer will generate a new metadata ID. For example, the material flow "construction materials" ("Bauartikel") has been modified in the attribute "contact person." The contact person for the metadata ID "200000" is "Mueller," for "200001" it is "Schmidt," and for "201001" it is "Meier" (see fig. 1). The set of metadata IDs for each material and energy flow position will be imported from the EcoExplorer into ACCOUNT. Moreover, every metadata ID is associated with a metaclass ("Rechnungstyp"). The metaclass describes the type of EMS element in which this specified metadata ID is used, e.g. metaclass = "accumulation" ("Artenrechnung") for the cost/environmental accumulation. Users of ACCOUNT can also edit manually the metadata ID and the metaclass of a material and energy flow position (Fig. 7).

Figure 8: The ACCOUNT user edit interface of the cost/environmental accumulation component with the focus on the metadata ID combobox

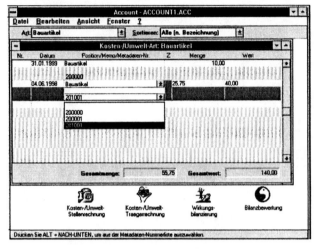

In ACCOUNT the identification of the material and energy flows is as in the organization's bookkeeping. The user can edit different entries (material and energy positions) for a material or energy flow in a certain period. Each material or energy position belongs to a material and energy class ("Art"), which is different from the metaclass. The material and energy class is a period aggregation of a set of material or energy positions that are physically or technically similar. To reduce the costs of collecting material and energy flow data, ACCOUNT supports the data import of the organization's cost accounting system because most of this data is useful for the cost/environment accumulation component. After that the user of ACCOUNT can edit manually the environmentally relevant data that the organization's cost accounting system does not contain, such as emission data or

Figure 9: Parametrized start of the ACCOUNT system

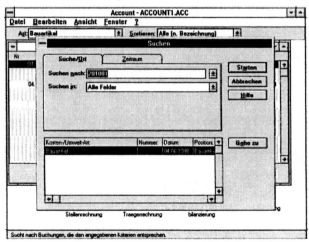

metadata IDs. According to the selected material or energy position, ACCOUNT assembles the set of corresponding metadata IDs in a combobox (Figure 8).

Links between EcoExplorer and ACCOUNT

The EcoExplorer is a search tool that helps users in localizing, retrieving and accessing relevant environmental information. If users want to access a material or energy flow they localized with the EcoExplorer, they can perform a parametrized call of the ACCOUNT system from the EcoExplorer. Therefore the EcoExplorer writes into the start script of the ACCOUNT system the user chosen metadata ID, the associated metaclass and the request to do a search in the ACCOUNT system with these two parameters. In ACCOUNT we use a special section of the account.ini file as the start script. After that the EcoExplorer starts the ACCOUNT system. During the start the ACCOUNT system runs his search function with the metadata and the metaclass parameter (here for example, the metadata ID "201001" and the metaclass "accumulation") and presents the results (figure 9). If there is more than one material or energy flow result, the user can choose one and go there directly using the goto-button ("Gehe zu").

CONCLUSION

The EcoExplorer program package is the core part of an EMIS. In order to cope with the problem of heterogeneous data and systems, the developers used Java and XML as the underlying technologies. Both technologies are platform-independent and particularly designed for heterogeneous networks. Automatically generated stylesheets are used to publish data on the Web. The EcoExplorer main program is for internal use only. It allows the actual management of environmental metadata. The IndexMaker serves to make XML data public. It builds up a navigation tree consisting of XML documents, which can be accessed from external users over the Internet.

The EcoExplorer serves not only as method database or as product database. New types of environmental data can be put into the system in a very flexible way by just adding new DTDs to the system. As the amount of data increases, convenient search functions help the user in finding the needed data.

In ACCOUNT we suggest an approach of registering material and energy flows with their corresponding costs, With this approach the system can easily manage the organization's cost and environmental data. ACCOUNT as a representative element of an environmental management (information) system can be linked the our EcoExplorer. Therefore the user can search, retrieve and access material and energy flows in ACCOUNT throughout the EcoExplorer.

REFERENCES

Arndt, H.-K. and Günther, O. (1996). ACCOUNT - a Software System for the Core Functionalities of an Environmental Management Information System, in Lessing, H. and Lipeck, U. W. (Eds.), *Informatik für den Umweltschutz*, 10. Symposium, Hannover, Marburg, pp. 118-127.

Bosak, J. (1996). XML, Java, and the Future of the Web, in *World Wide Web Journal: XML – Principles, Tools, and Techniques* (ed. Winter, 2:4), pp. 219-227.

Byous, J. (1999). Co-Stars in Networking – XML and Java Technologies, <Webpage: http//java.sun.com/features/1999/03/xml.html>, access at 27. of March.

Günther, O. (1998). *Environmental Information Systems*, Berlin/Heidelberg/ New York.

International Organization for Standardization (ISO) (1996). Environmental management systems, Specification with guidance for use (ISO 14001: 1996), Geneva (CH).

International Organization for Standardization (ISO) (1998). Environmental management systems - General guidelines on principles, systems and supporting techniques (ISO 14004: 1998), Geneva (CH).

Murray-Rust, P. and Rzepa, H.-S. (1999). Chemical Markup, XML, and the Worldwide Web. 1. Basic Principles, in *Journal of Chemical Information and Computer Sciences*, 39 / 06, pp. 928 – 942.

ENDNOTES

[1] ISO 14001 (1996), p. 6.
[2] ISO 14001 (1996), p. 8.
[3] Günther (1998), pp. 153-155.
[4] ISO 14004 (1998), p. 9
[5] ISO 14004 1998, p. 26.
[6] Arndt/Günther (1996), p. 120.
[7] Bosak (1996), pp. 219-227.
[8] Byous (1999).
[9] Murray-Rust/Rzepa (1999) pp. 928-942.
[10] ISO 14004 (1998), pp. 28-29.

Chapter 24

The Virtual Web-Based Supply Chain

Ashok Chandrashekar
IBM Corporation, USA

Philip Schary
Oregon State University, USA

The virtual Web-based supply chain is emerging as a new form of industrial organization. This paper discusses the concept as a juncture of three forces: the virtual organization, Web-based communication and the application service provider (ASP). The virtual organization is a familiar concept in many industries, even without electronic connections. Web-based communication provides access and networks with new institutions. The ASP makes rapid change and flexible connections feasible. Together they establish focus, flexibility and rapid response to change in demand and customer requirements. Casting it in a strategic framework of structure, process and organization provides a basis for projecting its future.

INTRODUCTION

The concept of the supply chain is now familiar territory (Houlihan, 1985). Successive stages of closely coordinated product and material flow become a process of long-linked technology (Thompson, 1967). Similarly the virtual organization, even without computer connections, is recognized in practice (Hedberg et al., 1994, Davidow and Malone, 1992). The new elements are the impact of the Internet with the World Wide Web, and the application service provider (ASP). Together they create a new form of business organization with implications for major sectors of the industrial world. This new form promises the ability to supply

Previously Published in *Managing Virtual Web Organizations in the 21st Century: Issues and Challenges* edited by Ulrich J. Franke, Copyright © 2002, Idea Group Publishing.

customer requirements more directly than ever before through focus, flexibility, adaptability and capacity.

The supply chain was enabled through electronic communication and transaction-oriented software, first to link functions within the enterprise, then to customers and suppliers, spanning a process from resources to final customers. The traditional supply chain involves long-term relationships, such as an underlying IT system with direction from a dominant organization. It is an inter-organizational process linking functional activities to serve a common customer (Hammer and Champey, 1993).

This view is now being modified by new developments. Software extends beyond corporate boundaries with faster, high capacity Internet connections, creating new directions for strategy through ease of access, speed, capacity, simplicity and low cost. It changes the rules so dramatically that it reorders business organization and the nature of competition.

Observers project business-to-business (B2B) electronic trading exchanges as the major thrust of the Internet economy, encompassing customers, suppliers, manufacturers and service providers (Radjou, 2000). It is driven by the efficiency and simplicity of electronic transactions, compared to older computer-based legacy systems and manual procedures. The reach of the virtual Web-based supply chain however goes farther. It enables focused systems of supply to appear for a specific need and then disappear until a similar need arises.

This chapter emphasizes organization of the virtual chain beyond the exchange process, managing a sequence of activities leading to delivery of products specifically configured for a customer. We begin with the concept of the Web-based supply chain. It is built on the underlying concepts of the virtual organization and the Web with other technologies to organize the process. We then turn to the implications for strategy. The final section projects a future that is almost upon us, with some unresolved issues. The focus is on organizational impacts of technology on management and strategy, not the technology per se.

THE CONCEPT OF THE VIRTUAL WEB-BASED SUPPLY CHAIN

The traditional supply chain emphasizes long-term fixed relationships, with close collaboration for both product creation and delivery. In one sense, relationships are already virtual, because all firms deal with external sources of supply and services to some degree. They rely on proprietary firm-resident software and communications with a limited number of partners. Partners should have visibility extending over the entire span of the chain, share plans and contribute innovation in product and process development. It presupposes an atmosphere of trust and management integration for joint planning, control and sharing data. Integration becomes the basis for specific investments both in IT and operations, and connections through software and EDI connections. This model remains valid for many industries, even allowing for change in information technology (IT).

The Design

The virtual Web-based supply chain (denoted in the this discussion as the virtual chain) departs from this traditional form. It begins as less a linear sequence of activities than a network of possible partners for selection. Essentially, it is a generalizable process without necessarily permanent partners. The Web serves as a communication and coordination system, to coordinate operations and potentially a means to collaborate. The potential scope ranges from the simple to the complex, depending on whether standard components (possibly purchased through B2B business-to-business exchanges) or proprietary designs involving collaboration with supplier and customer are used.

Figure 1 depicts a typical virtual chain with three different exchange sites. A customer negotiates with a lead firm who then initiates the supply chain in the first exchange. The firm and its web of potential providers then form the chain through other exchanges. The network therefore emphasizes flexibility. The information flow may take a different path than the physical flow. The virtual chain is thus completely flexible and does not necessarily involve long-term relationships. The lead firm decides whether to perform operations in-house or to subcontract them to outside vendors. A third-party logistics provider could coordinate inventory and product movement, even absolving the lead firm from operational control

Figure 1: The Web-based supply chain

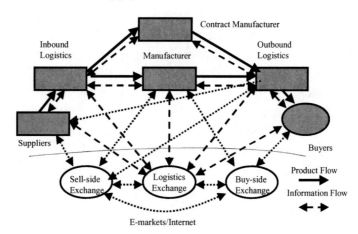

A single organization could utilize both traditional and virtual chains as parallel operations. Traditional supply chains would serve the market for standardized proprietary products and services; virtual chains would supplement it in different situations such as: 1) providing commodity items for the market, 2) additional temporary production or logistics capacity to meet peak demands, or 3) customized items to meet special customer product requirements. The virtual chain thus can either stand alone or provide flexibility to supplement existing arrangements.

The characteristics of the emerging virtual chain are:

- Orientation to customer requirements
- Operation in response to real-time customer orders
- Flexible response to changes in market requirements
- Organization around tasks rather than organizations
- A process orientation around complementary competencies

THE NEW ELEMENTS

The combination of new developments enables the virtual chain: the virtual organization, the configuration of computers and Web-based communications and the ASP. We discuss each in turn.

Virtual Organizations

The many definitions of virtual organizations include elements in common separate geographically distributed functionally diverse organizational units collaborating as a network in a common purpose, managed by teams in a process orientation (e.g., De Sanctis and Monge, 1999; Moshowitz, 1994, 1997; Pihkala et al., 1999). Their relationships are determined by their complementary activities. Selection depends on a specific need at a particular time. Tenure can be short. Davidow and Malone (1992) describe the network relations as an "ever-varying cluster of common activities in the midst of a vast fabric of relationships" (p. 7).

For some authors, the virtual organization is a single enterprise, for others a series of connected enterprises with task specialization, contractual relations and permeable boundaries, as a supply chain. In this mode, the virtual organization is a dynamic organization structure to be reconfigured to match changing conditions. Pihkala et al., 1999) emphasize that "...the virtual organization breaks the rigid assumptions of organizations and their stability in time."

The essential characteristics are dispersed actors, resources and activities serving a global objective. In the resource-based business strategy, the virtual organization (and by implication, the virtual chain) combines resources and capabilities to create unique, complementary competencies, providing flexibility, fast response and adaptation to supply products and services to meet the needs of the market (Wernerfeldt, 1984; Peteraf, 1993).

Moshowitz (1994) abstracts a theoretical base of enabling factors: simplification, combinatorial freedom and switching. Simplification subdivides tasks to allocate among organizational units. Combinatorial freedom assigns tasks and units to meet new requirements. Switching changes connections and resources as needs arise. The ability to change interorganizational structure rapidly becomes the hallmark of the virtual chain.

Management acts as entrepreneur, bringing organizations together for a common goal, serving in the role of both broker and manager (Miles and Snow 1992). Moshowitz divides the virtual organization into a supervising metamanagement and the fulfilling "satisfiers." Management establishes market connections, defines tasks and selects the specific "satisfiers." The selection process can even be automated using pre-selection to establish qualified partners (Hoogewegen, 1999). In later discussion, it will be identified as a Web community" (Franke, 1998).

The critical management role is to provide the "glue" that holds the virtual organization together (Pihkala et al., 1999). Trust between manager and members is essential. Motivation is difficult to maintain. Bonding and loyalty are weak, with potential conflict and a high risk of failure. The importance of a shared vision should not be underrated, related not only to immediate products or customers, but also to potential operations reflecting the collective competencies of members. The critical competence for the manager as broker is a network competence, the ability to organize and supply the guiding vision.

Computers and Communications

By universal recognition, computers and electronic communication have enabled the virtual organization and the virtual chain. Coordination required over transactions can only come through the communication network. This includes software, the Web, standardization of data, and the physical capacity of the network itself.

Software makes the virtual chain possible. The role of software has progressed from functionally-oriented programs such as warehouse management, production scheduling and transportation management functions to firm-oriented enterprise resource planning (ERP) systems with internal transaction management. The functional walls and organizational boundaries are now breached by supply chain management software that connects the lead firm with customers and suppliers. At present, problems of compatibility among software packages from different vendors, act as a further barrier to coordination. Their development is limited in both scope or capabilities such as scheduling production in real-time, but progress makes the goal of interorganizational data visibility and coordination more attainable.

Web-Based Communication

Electronic communication becomes the centerpiece for both transactions and building inter-unit relationships. Transactions can be routinized and automated. Relations however develop from informal communication. Together, they free the organization from both geographic and structural constraints (Ahuja and Carley, 1999). Moshowitz describes the "pillars of virtual organization:" 1) standardizing interactions, 2) treating knowledge separately from the individual, as in programming machine operations, and 3) abstracting information from operations, as in the use of real options, financial instruments, to hedge against operational risks. Together they form a central core of information.

Communication in traditional supply chains relies on a variety of modes, from written documents to telephone and fax. EDI was a major step forward for direct computer-to-computer connections but is limited to prescribed data, messages and file formats. Its advantage lies in the high level of security as a separate communication system. It is costly, with limited access and is inflexible in switching among multiple customers and partners. Installation and training add to this cost and created a lucrative business for EDI service providers.

In contrast, the Internet and the Web have ease of access, low training requirements and low direct costs of installation. Access becomes pivotal in determining the success of the virtual chain (Noumens and Bouwman, 1995) The ease of access provides an advantage in the ease of connecting new suppliers and customers, although the problems of user computer system and software remain. The Web portal becomes the gateway and entry point for suppliers and customers and a marketing tool for the customer to make inquiries, place orders and specify product options.

Web communications can include standard EDI messages using EDIFACT and ANSI X.12, but the real contribution lies in its content flexibility. Both data and personal messages can be transmitted in a variety of forms. Groupware promotes collaboration. CAD and other visual images can be exchanged. The Web provides a rich potential for communication

The Web also has disadvantages: the current lack of high-speed service, potential disruption, incompatibility of Web products, and inadequate Web infrastructure. Inadequate capacity and disruption may be partially solved through redundant networks. Security problems are more overshadowing. The ability to penetrate networks makes the entire chain vulnerable to disruption or theft of data. Solutions include establishing firewalls around intranets and extranets to prevent unauthorized entry. Another is to require authentication of transactions through certifying current users and documents.

Standardization of data and product descriptions presents further difficulties. Product codes can be proprietary, promoted for internal efficiency, or oriented to specific industries. Data mapping to identify codes and languages is critical for coordination. The data gap will ultimately be reduced through XML, a meta language to identify and tag data files, with additional code indicators for specific industries, assisted by translation dictionaries such as Rosetta.net.

Bandwidth is the governing constraint on communication. The current shift to fiber-optic cable networks promises a major expansion in capacity (Gilder, 2000). The change opens up new possibilities for collaborative software, complex model images, training modules and personal visual dialog and conferencing. Growth depends less on technology than on organizational context.

Exchanges and Trading Networks

Business-to business (B2B) exchanges are the most publicized element of the virtual chain. They have been the source of both optimism and disappointment. Their essential structure consists of buyers and sellers connected through an e-hub as an electronic marketplace. Most transactions are concerned with prices for clearly described, comparable products sold on specifications in a catalog. This description fits business purchase items, but not with ongoing commitment by both buyers and sellers. Kaplan and Sawhney (2000) note "exchanges are not designed to support systematic or contractual purchasing" (p.101).

Kaplan and Sawhney also distinguish between spot and systematic sourcing on one hand and operations versus manufacturing inputs on the other. Maintenance, repair and operating supplies are sold through catalogs. Manufacturing items are usually purchased under contract except where unanticipated requirements appear, where supplementary transactions can involve exchanges. In the end, however, exchanges have limited capabilities compared to other business transactions.

Horizontal exchange offers wide product ranges across an industry. Vertical exchanges specialize by industry. Competition pushes more exchanges into a vertical focus on narrower product scope.

Exchanges work best when they are equally balanced between buyers and sellers. Too few sellers leads to monopolistic pricing; too many sellers or too few buyers to unprofitable pricing. The result is that both buyers and sellers move to other means of conducting transactions.

Future exchanges however may differ. Using the financial services industry as a prototype, they (Kaplan and Sawhney, 2000) project five different solutions:
- Mega exchanges–the currently conventional model.
- Specialist originators–intermediaries that will assist buyers and sellers to define the product objects to assist them in the transaction.

- E-speculators–risk takers who would take positions in the products they sell in search of profit.
- Solution providers–exchanges with analysis support to aid in purchasing decisions.
- Asset swaps–exchanges that avoid the formal exchange process by exchanging commodities, future positions and production capacity.

The B2B trading network exchange began as auctions, matching price bids and offers, searching only for the lowest price with little role in either pre- or post-matching activities. This role has now expanded beyond price discovery to multiple criteria such as delivery schedules, adding supporting activities. Some exchanges such as Covisint (covisint.com, 2001; Weiss, 2000) offer added services or links to other exchange sites for logistics and other services necessary to complete the transaction as end-to-end services. Three supplementary features to support transactions are: supply chain inventory management, product development and procurement administration. In addition, B2B exchanges now provide transaction control, order tracking, order fulfillment and accounting modules.

Exchanges add unique capabilities to the virtual chain. Suppliers are added or dropped in a dynamic process with changing players for each transaction. A variety of matching mechanisms can be used, including reverse auctions, direct price and delivery quotations. Exchanges become an arena for pricing, scheduling, delivery and financial terms. Future additions may include self-financing, warehousing and brokerage.

Automation can enhance the use of exchanges. When a buyer seeks specific product components, the order message triggers a series of automated actions: searching an electronic product catalog with prespecified supplier selection criteria. The exchange sends RFQs to suppliers and then collates and forwards them to the buyer for automated selection. It then initiates supporting logistics activities: analysis, delivery, transport planning and documentation. These messages, place-holders for action, await responses from other parts of the system. One action has the capability to trigger a chain of automated actions.

Application Service Providers (ASPs)

The application service provider (ASP) enhance the ability to switch partners (Paul 2001; *Fortune*, 2001; Harrington, 2000; *Infoworld*, 2000). ASPs host software for users, in lieu of their own networks. The ASP can take over the client's information system to be available on user demand, investing, installing, managing and upgrading software, and technical problems. Responsibility for software shifts to the ASP, while the user integrates applications and data, makes organizational adjustments and provides training. One potential disadvantage is a loss of competitive advantage with common ASP hosting (Davenport, 1998).

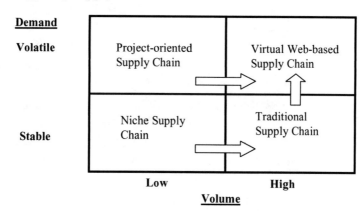

The roles of user and system manager must be well defined. The ASP can become the central node in the supply chain information system, providing access and communication for customers, suppliers and the managing organization. Users access software and receive and supply data for customers and suppliers through predefined extranets. Users are responsible for decisions with their own data. The ASP usually determines the software architecture and dictates the speed of response, flexibility for new requirements and scalability. They also become responsible for system capacity, software upgrading, monitoring, data mapping standards and security.

The structure of ASPs is only emerging now. Some software application remains with the customer and other software with the ASP, requiring compatibility. Three different role models for ASPs are 1) "the pure play," using best-of-breed software, 2) the integrated software provider presenting a single unified product, and 3) a convergence of the ASP and the trading exchange. Some ASPs now specialize. ERP software often requires its own server. Logistics software generates its own set of providers. The ASP can be independent, or hosted internally. As control shifts toward the ASP, the chain manager may also become the host of the ASP.

Some companies with ASPs have gone back to their own systems, largely because of cost, data and software compatibility capacity and security problems. Further they are subject to failing providers and networks, losing their ability to operate.

STRATEGY

The virtual supply chain changes business organization (Moshowitz, 1994, 1997; Tapscott et al., 2000). It starts not like a traditional supply chain with stable relationships, but as a clean slate with new connections. The foundation

Figure 2: Types of supply chains

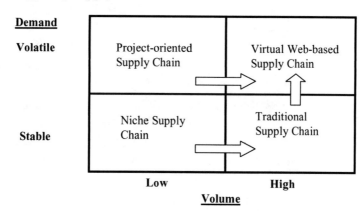

is the core and outsourcing paradigm (Hamel & Prahalad, 1994; Quinn, 1993). A lead firm organizes a process with other firms to perform activities to deliver a product in response to an identifiable market need. The lead firm maintains control over a strategic core, but contracts for other activities that do not provide unique superiority. It results in two interdependent, complementary networks: information and operations, both supporting the delivery of finished products to match specific customer requirements. In this section we consider the essential elements of strategy for the virtual chain: structure, management and decisions. They are interdependent in that structure sets the management tasks, both leading to strategic choices.

Structure

The virtual chain fits a particular set of conditions. Figure 2 describes supply chains in two dimensions: demand stability and volume. Stable demands involve staple products with predictable forecasts. Volatile demands involve both changes in products and volumes.

With low volume and stable demands, the niche supply chain can be handled with minimal coordination. Traditional supply chains have stable demands with high volume. Low volume operations, as in construction, suggest project management, but volatile demands matched to high volume could become virtual chains. Project-type supply chains can become virtual but may be economically undesirable. These last two also have a common dimension; they only last for the life of the project. In effect, the virtual chain must apply the decision context of project management to a process with higher volume.

Highly turbulent industries adopt the virtual organization model because of flexible production, real-time order fulfillment, rapid response and short development cycles. Their markets change rapidly, losing stability of product lines and the ability to predict revenues. Small-scale pilot projects become large-scale operations. Stable industries renovate themselves as virtual chains. This points toward a convergence. While all business arrangements are not conducive to virtual chains, the general direction is inescapable.

The most significant element is the ability to switch connections. This flexibility comes at a price. The cost of switching involves enterprise and supply chain software for control over transactions, data, training and connections with partner organizations. Software investment alone may run to several million dollars. Adding the costs of data collection, coding, editing and mapping for compatibility both between software programs and organizations, and the combined costs of coordination and IT management, the total limits the number of competitors.

Costs can be shifted. ASPs can assume the cost and responsibility for software installation, maintenance and upgrading in return for higher monthly or transaction charges. The net effect is to increase the costs of managing volatility. Virtual chains then become not general applications, but relevant to industries such as high technology with high volume and volatility where the payoff from flexibility is high.

Switching partners becomes more common in B2B market exchanges. As an auction, a single seller confronts multiple buyers, or more recognizably as a reverse auction, where a single buyer meets several potential suppliers. The common use lies in price-searching mechanisms. However, exchanges such as Covisint offer other services and links to other exchanges to complete the fulfillment process.

Some lead firms use private B2B exchanges. Prequalified suppliers quote bids on particular standardized items in an electronic catalog, reducing many procurement items and their profit margins to the status of commodities. Vendors are selected by price, delivery dates, or available production capacity. Exchanges simplify transactions and administration, reducing both time and costs.

Short-term relationships do not always prevail. The virtual supply chain also adds value at each stage of the process. Value is embodied in information incorporated within the product and its associated services. The strategic issue is how to capture value for competitive advantage. This may require coordination with suppliers over extended time periods, stabilizing the relationships during the development phase, and possibly into production.

Management

Directing the virtual chain is evolving with a management role not clearly established. At the most basic level, it must balance potential customers and prospective suppliers, matching specific customer requirements with the defining technologies for competitive advantage. The most salient issues for managers include sensing the market, managing relations with the Web community and managing the information system.

The virtual chain alternates between two types of leadership. The organizational structure of virtual chains appears to take two divergent paths, depending on the path of interaction. Ahuja and Carley (1999, p.751-52), note that "overall, we expect that when routine tasks are performed in a highly structured network, and non-routine tasks are performed in a less structured (loose) network, superior performance will result." Supply management tends to be hierarchical, although operating decisions are made where actions are performed. Coordination necessitates joint planning and execution. Routinized boundary-spanning transactions utilize lateral communication but are centralized and hierarchical for control, coordinated by supervisory lead organizations. Communication is largely unidirectional, and negotiation deals with structured problems such as production scheduling and capacity planning.

Collaborative systems for product and process development require freedom for interaction among participants for creativity and innovation with participative decisions. Communication is informal and bidirectional, as in joint product development. Some observers (Franke, 1999) note not permanence, but rotation in response to particular expertise. Leadership becomes decentralized, although the lead firm may coordinate the communication network hierarchically.

Sensing the Market

Sensing the market becomes the primary task, setting direction for the chain. However, the process is not simple. In many cases, the market evolves with the technology. One immediate source of information on product preferences and options comes from direct customer orders entering into the production system. Another is customer collaboration in product design, forecasting and sales planning. Other sources test the market through experimentation (Brown and Eisenhardt, 1998), placing basic products with customers to incorporate their experiences into further development (Moore, 1996). Technologies and markets together define the strategic direction.

Managing the Web Community

The second major task is to forge the organization, managing suppliers, both currently active and latent. Moore (1996) describes the task: "The function of ecosystem (virtual chain) leadership is valued by the community because it enables members to move toward shared visions, to align their investments, and to find mutually supportive roles" (p.26). This requires a sense of present and future direction of the technologies and recruiting firms with relevant expertise. It establishes strategic vision for motivation and profitability.

Relationships take the form of coordination, cooperation or collaboration (Bressler and Grantham, 2000). One objective of leadership is to extend collaboration. The taxonomy of potential partnerships includes:

- Standardized commodity suppliers in market relationships but who must coordinate operations.
- Integrated suppliers sharing process knowledge and participating in joint planning.
- Collaborative suppliers involved in both product and process development.
- Latent collaborators available for future development activities.

They reflect varying degrees of both complexity and creativity (Bressler and Grantham, 2000). Routine procurement is low in both dimensions. Project management and production involves complexity without necessarily creativity. Full collaboration involves both complexity and creativity.

The Web Community itself is a collection of organizations with potential concern with the economic outcome of the virtual chain, including customers and current and potential (latent) suppliers (Franke, 1999). Membership includes pre-qualified members with a potential connection to the virtual chain. Criteria include standardization of operations, computer systems and data for rapid response, trust and a common identification with the overall vision of the virtual chain.

Membership is fluid, depending on orientation of the virtual chain and the projects in which it engages. Suppliers are often encouraged to participate in other chains to develop their own competencies, and reduce their dependence on a single project or virtual chain (Miles & Snow, 1992). The task here is to maintain a fine balance between the needs of the chain and preserving the vigor of its members.

Trust is critical in partner relations. Establishing it is difficult when tenure is short and partners have incomplete assurance of follow-on business. The penalties for failure however are high. Motivation through a common vision becomes the strongest foundation, supplemented by personal contact, reputation and the accumulation of experience. The danger of losing control over exposure of corporate data is central to the trust issue.

Managing Information

The third task of management revolves around the information system. In some cases, the specific responsibility for managing the information system falls to a technical leader, creating a second source of direction. Information requirements place the IT manager in a crucial position, able to define the operating characteristics of the virtual chain (Moshowitz, 2001).

Supply chain operations are data-rich. Their information systems must have standardized formats for coordination between computer systems and organizations. The chain must also be transparent to suppliers, management and customers if possible. They should have access to actual and forecast demand as the data become available.

Collaborative systems are less structured and more open to diverse forms of communication, including voice and visual modes. Collaboration requires the ability to transmit complex imagery and data. It also requires maintaining the community through casual connection. The advent of broadband communication enables proliferation of communication technologies such as video streaming for conferencing and informal contact across time and space.

Strategic Choices

The long-term nature of the virtual chain permits only general targeting: a set of competencies searching for a specific niche within a broader market. The task is to determine what characteristics should match requirements that may be only emerging but not yet fully defined. There is no single strategy, but one that is continually in flux, searching for different partners for new roles or using established partners in new roles.

Supply operations require tight coordination. Forecast demand, actual orders and production schedules should be made selectively available to suppliers on the basis of need. The short tenure of the virtual chain makes the problem of sharing sensitive data difficult because of the need to establish trust between partners. Establishing trust in advance becomes important in building the Web community.

Products and service determine long-term competitive advantage. Product design enters the virtual chain through software such as collaborative product commerce, a set of coordination and design tools for new products (Hutt & Ross, 2000). Modularity in product design is also important (Baldwin & Clark, 1997). Modular products assembled at the last possible moment reduce response time in online order fulfillment, while also reducing finished product inventory. They also create the flexibility to supply a full range of products and product options. Finally product modularity defines the boundaries of supplier component production.

The tenure of the virtual chain is determined by the project. The chain however may be reconstituted with new partners for other projects, drawing on the community as a pool of suppliers. This provides it with the virtues of agility and avoids retention of activities without a role in a given project configuration.

The agility of the virtual chain is determined in part by the ease and speed of response. Virtual supply chains respond to changes in volume or product by the choice of suppliers (Chandrashekar & Schary, 1999). Agility may always not provide lasting advantage over competitors, although management skills may provide short-term advantage. Lasting advantage comes from unique knowledge-intensive products and services, usually involving partner collaboration. Collaboration involves time. The result is a trade-off in flexibility, determined by the role of the virtual chain in the marketplace–unique products versus shorter time-to-market cycles. The first stresses use of proprietary product development; the second, off-the-shelf components. The first potentially provides a potential barrier against competition; the second depends directly on agility.

Strategy in the end is shaped by competition. The virtual chain is oriented to serve short-term demands and niche markets too small for major competitors (Porter, 1980). Short tenure leads to "hit-and-run" actions that recognize and respond to market needs quickly. Issues of market share do not apply, as virtual chains try to stay ahead of competition. Virtual chains may utilize high levels of competency in product development, but they must be nimble to stay ahead of competition. Ultimately they become vulnerable because of their high transaction costs to competition from later lower cost rivals. Timing of market entry and exit become competitive tools.

THE FUTURE

In one sense, the future has already arrived. Dell Computers and Cisco have demonstrated the ability to operate with minimal production facilities, relying on their suppliers. Automobile companies such as General Motors will soon introduce Web-based customer order systems leading directly into production planning. Taiwan Semiconductor Manufacturing Company now uses a system where customers design their own chips for production.

The future virtual chain will include:

- Close collaboration with customers
- Multiple paths from suppliers to customer
- Management freedom to change both organization and partners
- Flexible networks as a critical element in competition
- Common standards for product components and communication
- Use of automated processes wherever feasible.

Virtual chains will not completely replace traditional supply chains, but their agility will satisfy increasing demands for product variety. At the same time, this flexibility comes through costly software and communication systems, defining their role in medium-sized markets. Small enterprises become virtual without formal supply chain connections. Larger firms only become agile by creating smaller scale units.

Market exchanges would standardize product components, reducing the power to differentiate. Differentiation places pressures to collaborate with suppliers. This will be favored by the developing capabilities of IT, expanding capacity in broadband communications and further development of collaborative software. The trade-off between rapid response and collaborative product development will become an opportunity to differentiate virtual supply chains according to purpose.

The ability to organize and manage virtual chains can become a skill in its own right, a source of advantage that under some conditions may be difficult to counter. The example has already appeared in the Hong Kong-based company (Magretta, 1998). The firm that began as a trading company now creates and manages short-term supply chains for garment retailers, using computer-based planning and communication.

CONCLUSION

The virtual chain developed as the conjunction of the virtual organization, IT and electronic communication. It is both a new paradigm and an extension of an older form of organization. It takes on an expanding role through its ability to connect organizations as an integrated short-term system to supply markets. It brings agility, the power to select markets and match their requirements through high-level competencies. We cannot predict its future evolution except within broad parameters. How far collaborative processes penetrate the virtual chain will be specific to the situation and technology. The virtual chain itself appears to be emerging as an independent vehicle, with its own advantages from organizational skills. The convergence between IT and supply chains will require a combination of management skills that may be difficult to find.

REFERENCES

At Your Service. (2000). *InfoWorld*, October, 36-37.

Baldwin, C. Y., and Clark, K. B. (1997, September-October). Managing in an age of modularity. *Harvard Business Review, 75,* 84-93.

Bressler, S. E. and Grantham, C. E. (2000). *Communities of Commerce.* New York: McGraw-Hill.

Brown, S. L. and Eisenhardt, K. M.(1998). *Competing On The Edge: Strategy As Structured Chaos.* Boston: Harvard Business School Press.

Chandrashekar, A. (2000, November). *Research issues in supplier network management—Future trends.* Paper presented at Decision Sciences Institute Annual Meeting, Orlando, FL.

Chandrashekar, A. and Schary, P. (1999). Toward the virtual supply chain: The convergence of IT and organization. *International Journal of Logistics Management, 10*(2) 27-39.

Covisint. (2001). Retrieved January 22, 2001 from the World Wide Web: http://www.covisint.com/.

Davenport, T. (1998). Putting the enterprise into the enterprise system. *Harvard Business Review,* July-August, 76, 121-29.

Davidow, W. H. and Malone, M. S. (1992). *The Virtual Corporation.* New York: Harper Business.

De Sanctis, G. and Monge P. (1999). Introduction to the special issue: Communication processes for virtual organizations. *Organizational Science,* 10(6), 603-703.

Evans, P. and Wurster, T. S. (year). *Blown to Bits Boston.* Boston: Harvard Business School Press.

Fortune (2001). *Apps on Tap (Winter Tech Guide),* 142, 217-220.

Franke, U. (1999). The virtual Web as a new entrepreneurial approach to network organizations. *Entrepreneurship and Regional Development,* 11, 203-229.

Hamel, G. and Prahalad, C. K. (1994). *Competing for the Future.* Boston: Harvard Business School Press.

Hammer, M. and Champy, J. (1993) *Reengineering the Corporation*. New York: HarperBusiness.

Harrington, L. (2000). The ABCs of ASPs. *Dot.Com*, November, 15-18.

Hedberg, B., Dahlgren, G., Hansson, J. and Olve, N. G. (1994). *Virtual Organizations and Beyond*. Chichester, England: Wiley.

Hoogeweegen, M. R., Teunissen, W. J., Vervest, P. H. M. and Wagenaar, R. (1999). Modular network design. *Decision Sciences*, 20(4), 1073-1103.

Houlihan, J. B. (1985). International supply chain management. *International Journal of Physical Distribution and Materials Management*, 15(1), 22-38.

Hutt, K. and Ross, G. (2000). *Collaborative Product Commerce Manufacturing Systems*, December, 18, 64.

Kaplan, S. and Sawhney, M. (2000). E-hubs: The new B2B marketplaces. *Harvard Business Review*, May-June, 78, 97-103.

Magretta, J. (1998). Fast, global and entrepreneurial: Supply chain management, Hong Kong style. *Harvard Business Review*, September-October, 76, 103-114.

Miles, R. E. and Snow, C. (1992). Causes of failure in network organizations. *California Management Review*, Summer, 24, 53-72.

Moore, J. F. (1996). *The Death of Competition*. New York: HarperBusiness.

Mowshowitz, A. (1994). Virtual organization: A vision of management in the information age. *The Information Society*, 10, 267-288.

Mowshowitz, A. (1997). Virtual organization. *Communications of the ACM*, 40(9), 30-37.

Mowshowitz, A. (2001). *Virtual Organization: The New Feudalism Computer*, April, 112-111.

Nouwens, J. and Bouwman, H. (1995). Living apart together in electronic commerce: The use of information and communication technology to create network organizations. *Journal of Computer-Mediated Communication*, 1(3). Retrieved M D, Y from the World Wide Web: http://jcmc.huji.ac.il/vol1/issue3/nouwens.html.

Paul, L. G. (2001). The ASP dilemma. *Electronic Business*, January, 99-102.

Peteraf, M. (1993). The cornerstone of competitive advantage: A resource-based view. *Strategic Management Journal*, 14, 179-191.

Pihkala, T., Varamaki, E. and Vesalainen, J. (1999). Virtual organization and the SMEs: A review and model development. *Entrepreneurship and Regional Development*, 11, 335-349.

Porter, M. E. (1980). *Competitive Strategy*. New York: The Free Press.

Porter, M. E. (2001). Strategy and the Internet. *Harvard Business Review*, March, 79, 63-77.

Quinn, J. (1993). *Intelligent Enterprise*. New York: The Free Press.

Radjou, N. (2000). Deconstruction of the supply chain. *Supply Chain Management Review*, November-December, 30.

Schary, P. B. and Skjoett-Larsen, T. (2001). *Managing the Global Supply Chain* (2nd ed.). Copenhagen Business School Press forthcoming.

Schrage, M. E. (1995). *No More Teams!* New York: Currency Doubleday.

Shuga, M. J. and Carley, K. M. (1999). Network structure in virtual organizations. *Decision Science*, 10(6), 741-757.

Tapscott, D., Nicol, D. and Lowy, A. (2000). *Digital Capital*. Boston: Harvard Business School Press.

Thompson, J. D. (1967). *Organizations in Action*. New York: McGraw-Hill.

Weiss, P. (2000). Covisint–Implications for logistics. *Automotive Logistics*, 3(2) 18-23.

Wernerfeldt, B. (1984). A resource-based view of the firm. *Strategic Management Journal*, 5, 171-180.

Wise, R. and Morrison, D. (2000). Beyond the exchange: The future of B2B. *Harvard Business Review*, November-December, 78, 86-96.

About the Editor

Jerzy Kisielnicki received a Ph.D. at the Warsaw School of Economics (S.G.P.i.S.) in 1969, and received a doctorate of Habilation in 1876 at the Warsaw University, Poland. He became a professor of economics in 1986, and he's been a full professor since 1992. Dr. Kisielnicki has been the head of the Department of Information Systems in Management and Faculty of Management at Warsaw University since 1972, and has been the head of the Department of Organisation and Management at the School of Economics (WSHiP) since 1995. His interests are organisation and management, systems analysis, management information systems, process innovation (reengineering), strategic management, and transition systems organisation and management in market economy. He is a member of the Information Resources Management Association and the Institute for Operations Research and the Management Science TIMS-ORSA. Dr. Kisielnicki is a member of the Board of Organisation and Management in Polish Academy of Science and is the head of the Scientific Council of Polish Society of Systems Information. He has had about 220 publications, some of the major books being: *Programming Development for Branch Industry* in 1972, *Computer Systems of Programming the Development of Industry* in 1976, *Economic Problems in Computer Systems* in 1981, *Computer Methods - Design and Application* in 1981, *Methods of Systems Analysis* in 1986, *Systems Information for Economic Restructuring* in 1987, *Management Information Systems* in 1988, *Information Infrastructure of Management* in 1993, *Encyclopaedia of Business* (12 entries) in 1995, *Information Systems in Business* in 2001 and *Organisation and Management* in 2001. Dr. Kisielnicki was an assistant and head of the department at the Institute of Food Technology from 1960-1971, and he was the head of the department at the Research Computer Centre - OBRI from 1971-1975. He was the head of the Department of Management Systems Modelling at the Systems Research Institute of the Polish Academy of Science from 1975-1979. He was the Deputy Director of Design at the Centre for Design & Application of Computer Science from 1979-1981. Dr. Kisielnicki was a scientific worker and visiting professor for the Central Economics and Mathematics Institute of the Soviet Academy of Science from 1988-1990. He was the Vice President of the Private Independent College of Business and Administration from 1990-1995. He was the co-ordinator of the TEMPUS-CUBIS programme in Poland from 1990-1994 and the co-ordinator of the TEMPUS-FIGURA programme in Poland in 1995-1998.

Index

A

B

C